SOLANO COMMUNITY COLLEGE
3 7045 00020 4117

D1017035

Howells: *A Century of Criticism*

Howells

A Century of Criticism

Edited by
KENNETH E. EBLE

SOUTHERN METHODIST UNIVERSITY PRESS
DALLAS, TEXAS

Library of Congress Catalog Card Number: 62-13275

SECOND PRINTING 1970

Printed in the United States of America

For Peggy

Preface

THIS VOLUME attempts to bring together those critical articles which will give the reader a sense of William Dean Howells' growth as a writer as well as a sense of the position he occupied in the literary scene from 1860 to his death. It also includes a sampling of critical articles from 1920 to the present, which show the decline and rise of Howells' reputation and some of the matters which are of special interest to Howells scholars today. I have chosen articles from periodicals rather than from books because periodical pieces are less readily available and because they reflect more immediately attitudes and changes in attitudes toward Howells and his work.

Part I is a chronology from 1860, when Howells' first book of poems was reviewed, to 1920, the date of his death. I have tried to select the articles written during this period which disclose the many aspects of Howells as a literary man and which bring out various responses to the literary principles which Howells championed in his novels and essays. Part II is a collection of studies written since his death which disclose changing attitudes toward Howells as he has become an object of modern literary scholarship. Though I have indicated in the introductory notes the direction of modern criticism, I have chosen to group the selections under various topics which are of special interest to Howells readers and scholars.

In both sections, I have reproduced the articles as first printed, though I have taken the editorial liberty of correcting obvious typographical errors and in a few selections of reducing documentation and deleting irrelevant or too specifically detailed material. The deletions have been pointed out in the citation of the original source and are indicated in the article by the conventional marks of ellipsis.

It has not been possible to print more than a small portion of the writing Howells' life and work have provoked. Though the collection includes many articles which, in my judgment, are among the best criticisms of Howells, it has had to leave out many excellent pieces. Because my aim was to represent a wide variety of critical opinions over the years and to provide the reader with an introduction to Howells and his place in American literature, excellence was not the sole criterion for selection of articles. To the writers of articles I have used, specific thanks is given below. To the many writers I have had to pass over, my sincere regrets.

To those writers, editors, and publishers who have granted permission to reprint copyrighted material, my thanks—Harper & Brothers and the trustees of the Estate of Samuel L. Clemens (Mark Twain) for Mark Twain's "William Dean Howells"; Alfred A. Knopf, Inc. for H. L. Mencken's "The Dean"; C. Hartley Grattan for his "Howells: Ten Years After"; the Duke University Press and the individual authors for Herbert Edwards' "Howells and the Controversy over Realism in American Fiction," Edwin Cady's "A Note on Howells and 'the Smiling Aspects of Life,'" W. F. Taylor's "William Dean Howells and the Economic Novel," James B. Stronks's "William Dean Howells, Ed Howe, and *The Story of a Country Town*" and "Howells's Opinions on the Religious Conflicts of His Age . . . ," by H. G. Belcher (Blackstock); the *New Republic* and Newton Arvin for his "The Usableness of Howells"; *Publications of the Modern Language Association* and Edwin Cady for "The Neuroticism of William Dean Howells"; the National Council of Teachers of English and Everett Carter for "The Palpitating Divan"; the *Modern Language Quarterly* and Arnold Fox for "Howells' Doctrine of Complicity"; the *American Scholar* and Nannine Joseph, literary executor of the estate of Lloyd Morris, for "Conscience in the Parlor"; the Purdue Research Foundation for "Howells or James?—an Essay by Henry Blake Fuller"; Henry Steele Commager and the *New York Times Book Review* for "For Fifty Years a Literary Dynamo"; James L. Woodress and the University of Texas *Studies in Literature and Language* for "The Dean's Comeback: Four Decades of Howells Scholarship"; to the *American Quarterly* for my "Howells' Kisses"; and to the *Saturday Review* and the

Public Trustee as Executor of the Estate of George Bernard Shaw and the Society of Authors for "Told You So: A Review of *The Garroters.*"

I wish also to acknowledge my general indebtedness to George Arms and William Gibson, whose bibliographical and critical work has helped all Howells scholars, to Clara and Rudolf Kirk, whose introduction to the American Writers Series *Howells* is still the best short biography, and to Lewis Leary, Columbia University, under whom I completed a doctoral dissertation on Howells.

Finally, my thanks to my colleagues in the English Department at the University of Utah; to Dean Jack Adamson; to Don Walker, to whom I have constantly turned for advice; to Mrs. Sally Allen, secretary; to my typists, Mrs. Helen Winn and Barbara Wright; and, once again, to my wife.

KENNETH E. EBLE

Salt Lake City, Utah
March 27, 1962

Contents

Howells: *A Century of Criticism*

Introduction

Few American writers have been so central to literature in so many ways and for so many years as William Dean Howells. Yet, as with many authors who are historically important, Howells' works are more read about than read. Even when they are read, the reader is not likely to become at once aware of Howells' high position among American writers of the late nineteenth century.

A great change in temper has taken place from his time to our own. Compared with either popular or serious novels of today, Howells' fiction is not so much dated as dull. And yet, despite the quietness of the commonplace, a number of Howells' novels have won a following. *The Rise of Silas Lapham, A Hazard of New Fortunes, A Modern Instance,* and *Indian Summer* are now in paperbacks, and if not widely read by the general public, are becoming staples of college literature courses. Howells wrote no book as widely accepted as *Huckleberry Finn,* no body of fiction as attractive to the critic as Henry James's. But being third to Mark Twain and Henry James is no small distinction, and Howells is clearly that.

More, Howells was the American man of letters in ways that neither Mark Twain nor James could claim. The journalism of which he often tired exercised a continuing influence on the practice of American fiction from the 1870's on. So great did this influence become that the writers growing up in the early twentieth century had to break from Howells' kind of realism to establish their own literary manner. In a somewhat similar way, Howells himself had broken from the tradition of the sentimental novel, the vogue of the romance, in the 1870's and 1880's.

The ups and downs of Howells' reputation are easy to chart. Howells' first appearance among the New England men of letters turned out to be, as Holmes said to Lowell, "the laying on of hands." From Lowell through James T. Fields, Howells was passed on the power and prestige that went with being the editor of the *Atlantic.*

His position there may partially account for the favorable response to most of his early work. It was not until he turned from the novels of innocent girls and good young men to more serious and demanding subjects that he began to arouse more than conventional praise or polite disaffection.

English critics took exception to his work as soon as his career was sufficiently advanced to engage their attention. Two kinds of American readers made adverse criticisms: those who felt he had betrayed them by turning away from the idylls of courting and marriage, and those who felt his direction was right but his execution faulty. Controversy over realism versus romance served to make Howells more widely known, and to make "realism" a commonplace of literary conversation. From 1890 to 1910, he was the "dean" of American letters. His works were sought after; his editorial voice, chiefly from *Harper's,* was listened to; his critical principles were widely advocated.

Then, the decline. With the death of Mark Twain in 1910 and of Henry James in 1916, Howells' closest literary friends were gone. By that time, his literary audience was fast disappearing. In Ambrose Bierce's opinion, his chief appreciators had always been "fibrous virgins, fat matrons, and oleaginous clergymen." After his death and throughout the twenties, Howells was as far from the modern literary temper as Niagara Falls was from Pamplona, Lydia Blood from Lady Brett.

The thirties restored him. The revival of interest was not primarily literary. It was social and economic. The Howells who was so sharply critical of the American economic system in the 1890's now seemed surprisingly modern. The revival of interest was also helped along by the development of American literature into a fit subject for graduate study in the universities. Though the first American dissertation on Howells was written in 1917, the second did not appear until George Arms's "The Social Criticism of William Dean Howells," in 1939. Since then, there have been dozens of academic studies on various aspects of Howells' life and works.

At the present time, Howells' place, if not precisely among the first rank of American authors, is secure among those literary men of primary importance to the development of American literature and thought. The critical intelligence, which Henry James claimed had not rendered Howells its tribute by 1912, has certainly given him his due in the past twenty years. If this is all James had in mind, then Howells' "really beautiful time" has come. Not only has much been written about him, much has been written well.

Howells' critical principles and these principles put into practice have stimulated later scholars to face some basic matters of literary theory in dealing with Howells' work. Howells' humanitarian sympathies, his self-taught command of European literature, his scrupulous conscience, his reticence, his long life extending from American pastoral innocence to industrial insecurity have provoked writers of many kinds—scholars, historians, journalists, novelists—to confront his work. Part of the results can be found in these pages.

Part I

Howells as a Literary Man
1860-1920

1860

This year was young William Dean Howells' annus mirabilis. *He published his first book of poems just before Christmas, 1859; James Russell Lowell reviewed it favorably in the* Atlantic Monthly *in April; and four of his poems had appeared in the* Atlantic *by that time. Later in the year he published a campaign life of Lincoln, and in July made his pilgrimage to New England to meet Lowell, James T. Fields, Hawthorne, Emerson, and Holmes. When he returned to Columbus, he met Elinor Mead, his future wife. With the election of Lincoln in November, he was not far away from the post of consul in Venice, which he was to assume the next year. Five years later he became assistant editor of the* Atlantic, *and five years after that, editor.*

Howells' collaborator, John J. Piatt, published many volumes of verse from 1866 to 1897. His wife was also a poet. Howells wrote a graceful tribute to him after his death (Harper's, *July, 1917), calling his poetry "the first volume of expression of the Western life in the love of the Western earth and sky."*

JAMES RUSSELL LOWELL

Poems by Two Friends

A Review

THE TWO FRIENDS are Messrs. John J. Piatt and W. D. Howells. The readers of the "Atlantic" have already had a taste of the quality of both, and, we hope, will often have the same pleasure again. The volume is a very agreeable one, with little of the crudeness so generally characteristic of first ventures,—not more than enough to

From the *Atlantic Monthly,* V (April, 1860), 510-11. The book's exact title is *Poems of Two Friends.*

augur richer maturity hereafter. Dead-ripeness in a first book is a fatal symptom, sure sign that the writer is doomed forever to that pale limbo of faultlessness from which there is no escape upwards or downwards.

We can scarce find it in our hearts to make any distinctions in so happy a partnership; but while we see something more than promise in both writers, we have a feeling that Mr. Piatt shows greater originality in the choice of subjects, and Mr. Howells more instinctive felicity of phrase in the treatment of them. Both of them seem to us to have escaped remarkably from the prevailing conventionalisms of verse, and to write in metre because they have a genuine call thereto. We are pleased with a thorough Western flavor in some of the poems, especially in such pieces as "The Pioneer Chimney" and "The Movers." We welcome cordially a volume in which we recognize a fresh and authentic power, and expect confidently of the writers a yet higher achievement ere long. The poems give more than glimpses of a faculty not so common that the world can afford to do without it.

1872

Among the reviewers of Howells' early books were Henry James, Henry Adams, Brooks Adams, James Russell Lowell, G. W. Curtis, and Charles Eliot Norton. Their Wedding Journey, *reviewed below by Henry Adams, was Howells' first novel. It was preceded by two books on his Italian years and a collection of sketches from his first years in Cambridge. By 1872, through his essays and his position on the* Atlantic, *Howells had become a well-known man of letters.*

Henry Adams was teaching history at Harvard and editing the North American Review *at the time this was written. In 1880, he published his first novel,* Democracy, *and in 1884, a second,* Esther.

HENRY ADAMS

Their Wedding Journey

A Review

AN INTERESTING QUESTION presents itself to the cautious critic who reads this little book, and who does not care to commit himself and his reputation for sound judgment irretrievably to the strength of such a gossamer-like web: it is whether the book will live. Why should it not live? If extreme and almost photographic truth to nature, and remarkable delicacy and lightness of touch, can give permanent life to a story, why should this one not be read with curiosity and enjoyment a hundred or two hundred years hence? Our descendants will find nowhere so faithful and so pleasing a picture of our American existence, and no writer is likely to rival Mr. Howells in this idealization of the commonplace. The vein which Mr. Howells has struck is hardly a deep one. His dexterity in follow-

From the *North American Review,* CXIV (April, 1872), 444-45.

ing it, and in drawing out its slightest resources, seems at times almost marvellous, a perpetual succession of feats of sleight-of-hand, all the more remarkable because the critical reader alone will understand how difficult such feats are, and how much tact and wit is needed to escape a mortifying failure. Mr. Howells has a delicacy of touch which does not belong to man. One can scarcely resist the impression that he has had feminine aid and counsel, and that the traitor to her sex has taken delight in revealing the secret of her own attractions, so far at least as she knows it; for Mr. Howells, like the rest of mankind, after all his care and study, can only acknowledge his masculine incompetence to comprehend the female character. The book is essentially a lovers' book. It deserves to be among the first of the gifts which follow or precede the marriage offer. It has, we believe, had a marked success in this way, as a sort of lovers' Murray or Appleton; and if it can throw over the average bridal couple some reflection of its own refinement and taste, it will prove itself a valuable assistant to American civilization.

1879

Thomas Wentworth Higginson was one of the first to assess Howells' general position in American letters. His remarks about Howells' influential position on the Atlantic *and his comments upon the limited scope of Howells' early work are particularly discerning.*

Higginson grew up in Cambridge, Massachusetts, the son of the steward of Harvard College. He was a prolific writer, an interesting man, whose long life (1823-1911) coincided with the development of American literature from its first flowering to its early maturity. It was to Higginson that Emily Dickinson sent her first poems in 1862. The essay below was one of a number of short studies of American authors. Other essays surveyed Henry James's early career, pointed out the eminence of Hawthorne, found Poe's genius essentially flawed, and concluded that Thoreau would outlast both Emerson and Carlyle.

THOMAS WENTWORTH HIGGINSON

Howells

IT HAS perhaps been a misfortune to Mr. Howells, that in his position of editor of "The Atlantic Monthly" he has inevitably been shielded from much of that healthful discussion which is usually needed for the making of a good author. Sir Arthur Helps says, that, if ordinary criticism gives us little, it is still worth having: if it is not marked by common sense, it still brings to us the common nonsense, which is quite as important. But the conductor of the leading literary magazine of a nation is very apt to escape this wholesome ordeal. Delicacy of course forbids his admitting any mention of himself,

From the *Literary World,* X (August 2, 1879), 249-50. Reprinted in *Short Studies of American Authors* (Boston, 1880), pp. 32-39.

whether for praise or blame, within his own pages. Moreover, his leading literary contemporaries are also his contributors; and for them to discuss him freely, even elsewhere, is like publicly debating the character of one's habitual host. Compare the position, in this respect, of Mr. Howells and Mr. Henry James, Jr. Their writings are equally conspicuous before the community; their merits are equally marked, and so also are their demerits, real or attributed; yet what a difference in the amount of criticism awarded to each! Each new book by Mr. Howells is received with an almost monotonous praise, as if it had no individuality, no salient points; while each story by Mr. James is debated through and through the newspapers, as if it were a fresh Waverley novel. I see no reason for this difference, except that Mr. Howells edits "The Atlantic Monthly," and that all other American writers are, as it were, sitting at his table, or wishing themselves there. He must himself regret this result, for he is too essentially an artist not to prize honest and faithful criticism; and it is almost needless to say that his career as an author has been thoroughly modest and free from all the arts of self-praise.

The peculiar charm of his prose style has also, doubtless, had its effect in disarming criticism. He rarely fails to give pleasure by the mere process of writing, and this is much, to begin with; just as, when we are listening to conversation, a musical voice gratifies us almost more than wit or wisdom. Mr. Howells is without an equal in America—and therefore without an equal among his English-speaking contemporaries—as to some of the most attractive literary graces. He has no rival in half-tints, in modulations, in subtile phrases that touch the edge of an assertion and yet stop short of it. He is like a skater who executes a hundred graceful curves within the limits of a pool a few yards square. Miss Austen, the novelist, once described her art as a little bit of ivory, on which she produced small effect after much labor. She underrated her own skill, as the comparison in some respects underrates that of Howells; but his field is—or has until lately seemed to be—a little bit of ivory.

This is attributing to him only what he has been careful to claim for himself. He tells his methods very frankly, and his first literary principle has been to look away from great passions, and rather to elevate the commonplace by minute touches. Not only does he prefer this, but he does not hesitate to tell us sometimes, half jestingly, that it is the only thing to do. "As in literature the true artist will shun the use even of real events if they are of an improbable character, so the sincere observer of man will not desire to look upon his heroic or occasional phases, but will seek him in his habitual moods of vacancy and tiresomeness." He may not mean to lay this down as a canon of universal authority, but he accepts it himself; and he accepts with it the risk involved of a too-limited and microscopic range. That he has finally escaped this peril, is due to the fact that his method went, after all, deeper than he admitted: he was not merely a good-natured observer, like Geoffrey Crayon, Gentleman, but he had thoughts and purposes, something to protest against, and something to say.

He is often classed with Mr. James as representing the international school of novelists, yet in reality they belong to widely different subdivisions. After all, Mr. James has permanently set up his easel in Europe, Mr. Howells in America; and the latter has been, from the beginning, far less anxious to compare Americans with Europeans than with one another. He is international only if we adopt Mr. Emerson's saying, that Europe stretches to the Alleghanies. As a native of Ohio, transplanted to Massachusetts, he never can forego the interest implied in this double point of view. The Europeanized American, and, if we may so say, the Americanized American, are the typical figures that re-appear in his books. Even in "The Lady of the Aroostook," although the voyagers reach the other side at last, the real contrast is found on board ship; and, although his heroine was reared in a New-England village, he cannot forego the satisfaction of having given her California for a birthplace. Mr. James writes "international episodes;" Mr. Howells writes inter-oceanic episodes: his best scenes imply a dialogue between the Atlantic and Pacific slopes.

It was long expected that there would appear some sequel to his "Chance Acquaintance." Bostonians especially wished to hear more of Miles Arbuton: they said, "It is impossible to leave a man so well-dressed in a situation so humiliating." But the sequel has, in reality, come again and again; the same theme re-appears in "Out of the Question," in "The Lady of the Aroostook;" it will re-appear while Mr. Howells lives. He is really contributing important studies to the future organization of our society. How is it to be stratified? How much weight is to be given to intellect, to character, to wealth, to antecedents, to inheritance? Not only must a republican nation meet and solve these problems, but the solution is more assisted by the writers of romances than by the compilers of statistics. Fourth of July orators cannot even state the problem: it almost baffles the finest touch. As, in England, you may read every thing ever written about the Established Church, and yet, after all, if you wish to know what a bishop or a curate is, you must go to Trollope's novels, so, to trace American "society" in its formative process, you must go to Howells; he alone shows you the essential forces in action. He can philosophize well enough on the subject, as where he points out that hereditary wealth in America as yet represents "nothing in the world, no great culture, no political influence, no civic aspiration, not even a pecuniary force, nothing but a social set, an alien club life, a tradition of dining." But he is not at heart a philosopher; he is a novelist, which is better, and his dramatic situations recur again and again to the essential point.

It is this constant purpose which gives dignity and weight to his American delineations, even where he almost wantonly checks himself and disappoints us. Were he merely, as some suppose, a skilful miniature-painter of young girls at watering-places, his sphere would be very circumscribed. At times he seems tempted to yield to this limitation—during his brief foray into the path of short dramatic sketches, for instance. These sketches provoked comparison with innumerable French trifles, which they could not rival in execution. "Private Theatricals" offers the same thing on a larger scale, and under still greater disadvantages. Mrs. Farrell reveals herself, at the first glance, as a coquette too shallow and vulgar to be really interesting; and she never rises above that level until she disappears from the scene, flinging her last net for the cow-boy in the pasture. Her habit of flirting is a garment deliberately put on, an armor that creaks in the wearing. But if you wish to see how a Frenchman draws a coquette, read "Le Fiancé de Mlle. St. Maur," by Cherbuliez. The coquetry of Mme. d'Arolles is always round her as an atmosphere, intangible, all-embracing, fold within fold; she coquets even with a rudimentary organ in herself that might be called her conscience; and then, besides this enveloping atmosphere, she wears always a thin garment of social refinement that seems to shield her even when the last shred of decorum is about to drop. She is a thoroughly artistic creation; in watching her never so closely, you cannot see the wires pulled; but in "Private Theatricals" we seem constantly to have notice given, "Please observe, Mrs. Farrell is about to attitudinize!"

The moral of all this is, that Mr. Howells cannot be, if he would, an artist *per se,* like Droz, in reading whose brilliant trifles we are in a world where the execution is all, the thought nothing, and the moral less than nothing. Nor does he succeed, like Thackeray, in making a novel attractive without putting a single agreeable character into it: Thackeray barely accomplished this in "Vanity Fair;" Mr. Howells was far less successful in the most powerful and least satisfactory of all his books, "A Foregone Conclusion." The greatest step he has ever taken, both in popularity and in artistic success, has been won by trusting himself to a generous impulse, and painting in "The Lady of the Aroostook" a character worth the pains of describing. The book is not, to my thinking, free from faults: the hero poses and proses, and the drunken man is so realistic as to be out of place and overdone; but the character of the heroine seems to me the high-water mark of Mr. Howells. It has been feared that he would always remain the charming delineator of people who were, after all, undersized,—heroes and heroines like the little *figurines* from Tanagra, or the admirable miniature groups of John Rogers. He has now allowed himself a bolder sweep of arm, a more generous handling of full-sized humanity; and with this work begins, we may fain believe, the maturity of his genius.

1883

"In England," Henry James wrote of Howells' novels in 1886, "...it is a marked feature of the growing curiosity felt about American life that they are constantly referred to for information and verification." This essay in Blackwood's *is the first extended discussion of Howells' fiction in a British periodical. Though the long-standing literary quarrel between England and America frequently becomes the subject of the essay, the writer has a sharp eye for falseness in Howells' realistic treatment of character and incident in his latest novels. The length of the article and the sharpness of the analysis testify to the dominant position of Howells and Henry James in American fiction at this date. A portion of the introduction and the lengthy recounting of the plots of the novels have been deleted.*

ANONYMOUS

American Literature in England

...WE MAY ADD, before we go on, Mr. Howells's opinion on a similar subject of literary art, to that treated by Mr. Warner. He does not tell us that he cannot understand English, nor we American; but he says that our old canons are worn out at least in fiction, of which craft he assures us Mr. James is at present the head.

"The art of fiction has in fact become a finer art in our day than it was with Dickens and Thackeray. We could not suffer the confidential attitude of the latter now, nor the mannerism of the former, any more than we could endure the prolixity of Richardson or the coarseness of Fielding. These great men are of the past, they and their methods and interests; even Trollope and Reade are not of the present."

From *Blackwood's Magazine,* CXXXIII (January, 1883), 136-61.

There is one great advantage which the artist who looks fondly back upon the past has over the worshipper of the present—his position is one of humility at least, and gracious decorum. He does not challenge a comparison between the old glories of his fathers and his own brand-new and dazzling achievement. When a writer of fiction commits himself so terribly as to allege that the art of which he is a professor is finer than the art of Thackeray, the punishment which he prepares for himself is so prodigious that it becomes ridiculous. But no one we believe will be cruel enough to make the suggested comparison, and measure Mr. Howells against Thackeray. He is so far safe in the inferiority of his stature. A little while ago it was Scott whom all our young cockerels had outgrown. For that matter, Shakespeare has been outgrown a number of times in the chronicles of the ages, both upon the stage and in the closet, but somehow has come back again, and still holds his own—though Pope and Voltaire were very sure that the dramatic art had improved immeasurably in the interval between his barbarous age and theirs. So we don't doubt that, even in America, the old gods will outlive the temporary dazzling of Mr. Henry James's fine style, and delicate power of analysis, and even the setting down given to them by the critics. Mr. Howells proceeds to add that the fine, nay finer, finest art of fiction in America is largely influenced by French fiction, especially by Daudet. Now M. Daudet is so largely influenced by Dickens, that we might, without extravagance, call him the literary son and heir of that great novelist; so it is evident that all this brave talk about that mannerism which cannot now be suffered, means only that the American likes a literary influence better when he gets it diluted by way of France, and through a strange land, than when it comes to him direct from his ancestral shores.

These two magnificent professions of faith, or of revolt, are both contained in the November number of the Century.' We shall in consequence look to that magazine for the fiction of the future—with hope, for Mr. Howells says it is a finer art than any we have as yet known; yet with some alarm, for Mr. Warner advertises us that we shall be utterly unable to understand it. This is sad, but it is an excitement to look forward to; and though it may be somewhat humiliating, it will be a fine lesson to see the critics of England gathered round the American periodical, endeavouring devoutly to spell out, through the intricacies of the American language, the last and greatest development of the novel—not as it was in the vulgar days of story-telling, but perfected with all the recent improvements, and adapted to the latest necessities of the time.

We cannot—space forbidding us—enter into any discussion now of Mr. Howells's description of this superlative production of art—how it has abandoned moving incident, and avoids all manner of dire catastrophe; and how, indeed, it is "an analytic study rather than a story." It will be better for the reader that we should come direct to the row of charming little books with which we began. Mr. Howells, as we have seen, takes to himself the credit of having discovered, and not having yet lived long enough to regret that he discovered, Mr. Henry James. The English public has taken a much longer time to discover Mr. Howells; and it is, we think, chiefly owing to the agency of the 'Century' that he has stepped into the region of visibility between the two worlds on which we have finally made his acquaintance. He is a better type of the American novelist than Mr. James, by right of being less accomplished, and moving within a more contracted circle of observation. An artist, when he possesses the conditions of greatness—a writer, when he has in any degree that indescribable addition to all gifts which we call genius—is thereby disqualified from being a type of any class or country. He becomes himself a recognisable power, but he is not a specimen any longer. Mr. Howells, however, is not too great to be a specimen. For all we know he is the very best example of the American novelist *pur sang* that we are likely to attain to. He has not the simplicity of the former generation. Hawthorne, so far as we remember, was never on tiptoe to hear what other people were thinking of America, but told his weird and wonderful tale with the composure of a man in his own country, with an abundant audience to whom it had not occurred to forestall foreign criticism by any alarmed defence of national peculiarities. Mrs. Stowe, if we may be permitted to mention her in the same breath, had an equal freedom from belligerency, and so had the first simple exponents of New England who made that primitive country familiar to us, perhaps, before the lofty critic who concludes us incapable of understanding it was born. Mr. Howells is far more distinctively American than any of these writers. He is the champion of America, terribly conscious of everything that can be said to her discredit, and ready to defy and annihilate, for misconception of her, the innocent and startled European who had no thought of the kind. The stray members of other countries who flit across our author's path are regarded by him, not in the light of their own national characteristics, but of this all-pervading patriotism. An Austrian officer, an Italian priest, appear to him only in the guise of a victim of the American Girl—an Englishman is nothing else than a critic or enemy of his beloved country. In this way he is national to the very finger-tips. But in other respects he is not quite shaped according to his own canons. His books are stories—and often very pleasant ones—not analytic studies; he condescends to complete them, which is a thing Mr. James never does; and after his lovely hereoine has done as much damage among susceptible hearts as he thinks proper for her, he takes the trouble to show us how things come right for her in the end, and how she marries the man of her heart, and lives happy ever after, as we are always glad to have our heroines do. His tales are not exciting, but they are tales with a gentle current of interest in them—a beginning and an end. We may add also for the encouragement of the reader, whose imagination may have been alarmed by the report that the 'Saturday Review' considers Mr. Howells to write American, and the 'Century' pronounces American to be incomprehensible to the English critic—that he will have no difficulty whatever in understanding these stories. There is no such bewildering difference of manners as Mr. Dudley Warner hopes, nothing unintelligible in the language, no mystery of any kind which a small amount of ingenuity will not be competent to fathom. We are not half-surprised enough indeed (we feel), nor is our delicacy shocked, as Mr. Howells defiantly intends it to be, with incidents which he flatters himself only American innocence and purity could render harmless, but which it requires a strain of politeness on our part to see any harm in at all. The chief point indeed in these books which will astonish the reader, is the aspect under which we ourselves appear in them. Recent English fiction since the days of Dickens has been complimentary to the American. Mr. Reade gets a great deal of fun out of Joshua Fullalove, but the appearance of that delightful salt-water philosopher is always hailed with satisfaction. Mr. Besant's Californian, in the 'Golden Butterfly,' is a rough diamond of the first water. Mr. Trollope's "American Senator" is a benevolent philosopher, whose wisdom is equal to every call upon it. But the American novelist is by no means so kind. Even Mr. James is very condescending to his Englishman when he introduces him, and he leaves the Englishwoman alone, as something not to be ventured upon. But Mr. Howells goes further; he has no patience at all with us. Our conduct during the war, when so many of us sympathised with the wrong side, was disgraceful and revolting: however that is over and past, and he allows that it is perhaps better to forget it, if possible. But there is an innate folly and stupidity in us, which he can neither forget nor forgive. And, bad as we are, our ladies are worse: for them there is not a word to be said. Indeed we fear that the character of English women is in a bad way on the other side of the Atlantic. This is a very curious and novel exhibition of sentiment, and, being without precedent, we do not know how to deal with it. When we were at war with France in the old days, and the combatants on both sides were by way of detesting each other, the Frenchman who swore everlasting hatred to John Bull made an exception in favour of *les Anglaises.* But whether it is that everything in American sentiment is coloured by the reign of the Young Girl, and her champion is so deeply sworn to her service that he can look upon no competitor with patience, or whether it is that there is something in the Englishwoman which exercises an inexplainable repulsion upon the American, we cannot tell. But the phenomenon is extraordinary. It comes out generally, in an allusion by the way, as if the writer were afraid to trust himself to treat the subject openly. Lord Skye, in 'Democracy,' when asked something about his countrymen, declines the subject, as if he too felt that it was hopeless, and that there was not a word to say for them. "Lydia's aunt," says Mr. Howells, "affected the English style, but some instinctive elegance betrayed her, and every Englishwoman there knew and hated her as an American." Even Hawthorne, if we remember rightly, notwithstanding the natural *finesse* of his genius, was betrayed into a sort of brutal coarseness when he touched upon this subject. Here is Mr. Howells's opinion of the nation in general. He is discussing a highly disagreeable English painter in Venice, who is introduced in at least two of his stories, and very likely is intended for a portrait.

"I have been wondering if, in his phenomenal way, he is not a typical expression of the national genius—the stupid contempt for the rights of others; the tacit denial of the rights of any people who are at English mercy; the assumption that the courtesies and the decencies of life are for use exclusively towards Englishmen. This was in that embittered old wartime; we have since learned how forbearing, and generous, and amiable Englishmen are; how they never take advantage of any one they believe stronger than themselves or fail in consideration for those they imagine their superiors; how you have but to show yourself successful in order to win their respect, and even affection."

We promise the innocent reader, who is perhaps totally unaware of having given any offence to Mr. Howells, that this is the thing most difficult to understand in the book. We are astounded by so sudden a slap in the face when we are reading on tranquilly, in the utmost peacefulness, with no conscious envy or hatred in our hearts. We are afraid we neither believe America to be stronger than ourselves, nor imagine her to be our superior; but (always barring the sore subject of copyright) we are conscious of not the smallest offensive feeling towards America. We think indeed that Napoleon's famous tactic of hanging a bookseller—an operation no longer within the scope of our desires in England—might perhaps be tried with advantage in New York; but that is a matter of detail, and does not affect the general question. By the way, supposing that English sympathies were largely enlisted for the South, were not the rebel States also Americans? The American speculates very freely, and so indeed do all our neighbours, as to the possibilities about our colonies, and the likelihood that they will break off from us when they please. We do not take offence at this, and why should it not be permitted to us to believe that huge America might have been none the worse off being two instead of one? But we do not live with our eyes fixed upon America, as our novelist thinks. Mr. Howells speaks bitterly of the "three lines of exquisite slight" with which the 'Saturday Review' dismisses the book of one of his heroes; but who among us knows or inquires in how many lines we are dealt with by the—Boston journal, whatever it is; which holds the position in America of the 'Saturday Review'? And to return to a smaller but still bitterer grievance, we think it highly unlikely, though our information on this point is necessarily defective, that Englishwomen, becoming conscious by some instinctive elegance that there is an American woman on the spot, recognise her for such, and hate her. This perhaps is to credit the average Englishwoman with greater discrimination than she possesses. Probably instinctive elegance would suggest a Frenchwoman to her, whom she would not hate, but examine furtively to see how her gown was made, and to wonder if that was the last Paris fashion; for France is a nearer neighbor, to whom we can run in when we like, and she is the recognised guide in these matters. These are mistakes; and unfortunately they are very like the sort of mistakes which persons of humble origin are apt to make when sudden wealth lands them unexpectedly in a different position to that in which they were born, and it is very difficult for them not to think that the unknown people around them are on the watch to find out any little blunder they may make. America is old enough and sufficiently accustomed to her importance to have entirely got over this petty sentiment, and it is a pity to find it so marked and evident in the latest development of her literary powers.

Mr. Howells's tales may be divided into two classes—those in which the scene is laid exclusively in America, and those in which Europe, or rather Venice, is partially the background. To the former belong the latest work of the author, 'A Modern Instance,' and the shorter and slighter tales entitled, 'A Chance Acquaintance,' 'A Counterfeit Presentment,' 'Out of the Question,' and a curious romance of spiritualism called 'An Undiscovered Country.' The others transplant their personages to the canals and palaces of Venice, in which place Mr. Howells was for some time consul, according to a habit our Transatlantic relations have of rewarding merit. Our author seems a little doubtful about the appropriateness of the reward. He speaks of one holder of the office who "knew as much about a consul's business as any of the authors or artists with whom it is the tradition to fill these offices in Venice;" but he has at least made ample use of his own term of office. Of these stories there are three—one of which at least is among the most interesting of Mr. Howells's productions, 'The Lady of the Aroostook.' They are very simple in construction, dealing with no passions or intricate complications of the mind, such as delight some contemporary novelists, but almost exclusively with the troubles that cross a young woman's path, and, by implication, a young man's, in the way of getting married, with a little admixture of the natural, and sometimes amusing, cares of the parents and guardians connected with the affair. The *dramatis personae* are—first and foremost, the heroine, who, everybody tells us, occupies so very large a space in American society and ideas—the "young girl" whose presence and sway everywhere, as Mr. Henry James informs us, purifies conversation, and keeps every *propos risqué* and disagreeable suggestion out of social intercourse. She is a very distinct type of the perennial heroine of romance, but individually there is not much variety in her. She appears in Mr. Howells's pages under different names, being at one time Lydia, at another Lily, Leslie, Florida, &c. She does not bear much resemblance to Daisy Miller, that audacious picture which has found so little favour in American eyes, being much more lady-like and self-restrained, and submissive to ordinary decorums, though not without many an indignant protest against them. She is indeed generally of higher social standing than Miss Miller, and, therefore, with perceptions more easily awakened. It is needless to add that she is beautiful beyond description, that she goes nowhere without producing an immediate impression—the railway carriage and the *table d'hôte,* in the absence of more extended fields, being sufficient to secure her a succession of triumphs. Beyond this it would be difficult to say very much about her. Mr. Howells would scorn himself if he did not analyse; but there is indeed very little to be analysed in so simple a symbol. The heroine is supported by one hero more or less worthy of her, and constructed from the beginning to become her mate, but who is far more instructed than she is, generally fidgety about breaches of decorum, and almost invariably belonging to the highly cultivated and sophisticated class, which knows its Europe on its finger-ends, and has nothing more particular to do than to roam about the haunts of antiquity and cross and recross the patient Ocean—and by a great many aspirants and confidants. She has a surrounding of anxious but helpless people, who sometimes, when they are not her parents, do interfere a little to keep her straight, with an overwhelming sense of the responsibility and alarm at their own boldness, but who, when they have the natural charge of her, look on with anxiety but impotence, and a sense that, to thrust themselves into her confidence, would be ill-bred in the extreme. These social elements are novel—or, at least, the atmosphere which surrounds them is novel;—but when we have had one group, we have had all. The circumstances vary a little, though not even these so much as we could wish; and to tell the truth, there are very few circumstances. But the characters scarcely vary at all. The young lady is the same throughout, with different names. Sometimes she has been brought up in great homeliness and simplicity, sometimes she is the child of luxury; but so strong is the "instinctive elegance" in the American girl, that the little schoolma'am from Massachusetts is quite as well bred and actually as well dressed, though her country aunt makes her gowns, as the fine young women who are dressed by Worth and have had every advantage of travel; and the young men are as nearly the same as possible, with the slight difference that some of them have a profession, which, however, sits upon them very lightly. They are not poor; they have none of the struggles that our young men go through. They are all in a position to marry when they think proper, and, in the meantime, to cross the Atlantic as often as seems to them good, and to live an easy life about Italian towns.

[A long recounting of the plot of The Lady of the Aroostook *has been omitted.]*

The really "American thing" in it is, we think, quite undiscovered either by the author or his heroes, and that is the curious confusion of classes which attributes to a girl brought up on the humblest level, all the prejudices and necessities of the highest society. . . . We are all accustomed to the wonderful capabilities of young ladies in novels to assimilate themselves to an elevated station; but this is a little more than that inalienable gift. And if it is an Americanism, it is one of the best we have heard of as yet. It carries out the stories we used to be told in what must have been an elementary chapter of American life—of the ladies who had to perform all their own household work, without any damage to their gentility, and who kept up their reading and their music, and even their white hands, all the same—stories which, if apocryphal, were pleasing. All these familiar fables have disappeared from the highly artificial and conventional world of *nouveaux riches* to which we are introduced by Mr. James. But if Mr. Howells be right, here is our democratic ideal again.

The picture in 'Foregone Conclusion' of the poor young inventor-priest, whom another American consul introduces to another beautiful young lady (with her mother), to teach her Italian, is extremely pathetic, and even tragical. Priests who fall passionately in love with pretty young women, are by common consent almost banished from the higher class of fiction. The tragedy in such a case is too easy, the circumstances too painful.... Don Ippolito is by far the highest effort Mr. Howells has made. It is a little theatrical and conventional, but at the same time there is a touching realization of the simplicity of the stainless and inexperienced life in the poor fellow's wild, futile hopes, his impossible inventions, and still more impossible love; and the contrast between his tragic reality and the impertinent superficialism of the young man of the world, the commonplace and trifling printer, who patronises and does not understand him, is sketched with much effect. The impassioned scene in the garden, when he betrays his love and is met with the horrified exclamation of "You—a priest!" from the girl who has been urging him to throw off the priestly office, and whose penitence and pity only suffice to soften the death-blow her soft hand has given him, reaches the verge of tragic power. The process of his self-deception all through is worked out with understanding and sympathy: and though Don Ippolito's certain negation of belief adds a double horror to his imprisoned existence, and makes it almost too painful for the use of romance, yet the conception shows a knowledge of human nature under its special Italian conditions which far surpasses anything else Mr. Howells has attained. The trifling little duets for tenor and soprano which fill the other volumes of this series belong to an altogether inferior world, and are not to be mentioned in the same breath. In this character, once, and once only, our author touches upon something higher than the mere drawing-room, or—we beg his pardon—parlour comedy of superficial life.

Among the books which treat of the lives of Americans at home, the most remarkable is the 'Modern Instance,' which has appeared during this year in the 'Century.' It is not a pleasant book, nor one we should recommend to the reader who is either sick or sorry; but perhaps, from this very fact, it is more powerful than any of Mr. Howells's previous works. It is the story of two headstrong and indisciplined young people, and of their marriage and misery. It is impossible to imagine that it was designed from the beginning to illustrate in one way or other the facility of divorce in America, which begins to frighten the philosopher and statesman; probably this design has been adopted at the end, and a purpose and moral suddenly tacked on to a work which was intended only to trace the gradual declension and degradation of one of those amiable-mannered and not bad-hearted reprobates, who are the favourite warnings and subjects of fiction. For our own part, we should be disposed to imagine that the conclusion was not that which the author had originally intended, and that he has been beguiled from the straight way of art in order to enforce a principle. However this may be, the work is full of glimpses of American life of the most instructive kind, all the more so that the book is written in simplicity and good faith for its natural audience, and with none of that uncomfortable defensive attitude and defiant braggadocio which disfigure the others. . . .

[A portion of the plot summary of A Modern Instance *has been omitted.]*

Our space does not suffice us to trace the cleverness of Bartley, or the manner in which he makes his way in journalism—first quite legitimately and with great success, but at last with a gradual deterioration and overreaching of himself, which lands him in misery and shame. He is a sort of vulgar Tito, without any of the tragic elements involved in George Eliot's great and terrible conception,—dropping from dishonesty to dishonesty, from indulgence to indulgence, with no more heroic result than that of getting fat and slightly dissipated, and losing character even with the not too scrupulous journalists with whom he is surrounded. We fail indeed to see his motive for risking his settled position by the stolen account of a rough adventurer's wanderings which he contributes to another newspaper while himself editor of the 'Events,' thus involving a brother editor in a cheat, and offending his own proprietor for the most trifling profit. It seems rather too like doing wrong for the sake of doing wrong—an unprofitable occupation. His other sins do not strike us as very heavy. He drinks a great deal of beer, which makes him fat, and this is, no doubt, a mistake. But he has his trials. Marcia, when seized with a fit of often utterly unreasonable jealousy, has a way of marching up-stairs and locking herself into her own room, which could not have been pleasant; and when on one of these occasions Bartley goes out, and, after much wandering about in the night, gets so many glasses of "hot-Scotch" that he becomes inarticulate, and has to be taken home in the middle of the night by the intolerable prince of virtue Ben Halleck, who is Mr. Howells's good hero, we cannot but feel that there is a certain amount of justification for the escapade. The way, however, in which every divergence from the path of sobriety is dealt with in these books, is very remarkable. We have already referred to the young inebriate of the Aroostook. An almost shrillness of passionate indignation is in every reference to this sin. The old classification of those sins of the flesh as much more venial than the sins of the intellect, which makes Dante keep his gluttons and sensualists in the milder circles of hell, and plunge his liars and traitors into the profoundest depth, is reversed in the New World. Our sympathies are greatly with the older treatment of the subject, and justice requires us to ask whether the identification of it as the one thing intolerable is altogether just. We doubt still more whether it is wise: and it is not merciful at all.

The conclusion of this book, is, we think, a mistake. The foolish couple, married in haste, on the insecure footing of a foolish girl's violent passion, part at last in an equally violent outburst of her jealousy, for which we suppose Mr. Howells intends us to believe there is no reason. Bartley, who by this time finds his life generally impracticable, leaves her, and for two years there is nothing heard of him. Marcia's passion, as is usual, ends in violent penitence, and as wild a longing for the man she never ceases to love, as that which first precipitated her into his arms,—and she waits during these two years in an agony of anxiety for his return. At the end of this period, chance throws into the hands of the insupportable Halleck an

Indiana newspaper, in which she is summoned to appear to answer the demand of Bartley for a divorce. Immediately the whole party is swept away on a gust of wrath, led by the implacable and vindictive Squire, and half against Marcia's will, to the far-distant corner in which the case is to be decided. The 'Century' magazine declares that Mr. Howells has influenced public opinion in a powerful manner against divorce by this picture. We confess we cannot see how it should be so. Had it been a plea for divorce, we should have comprehended it better. For indeed there would seem to be no human advantage, apart from the most sacred view of the matter, in keeping together by force two people so utterly unadapted to harmonise, and to whom clearly life has become impossible in any pretence at union. The scene, however, is not without power; though we are quite taken by surprise by the elevated diction and correct language in which Squire Gaylord, inspired at once by love and hatred, addressed the Court at Tecumseh on his daughter's behalf, falling prostrate at the conclusion in a fit of paralysis. (By the way, is paralysis understood to be brought on by excessive emotion? We wonder what the 'Lancet' has to say on this subject? It is so invariably in novels.) Even here, in all the whirl of indignant rage and passion, with the really tragic figure of the old father rising against the strange background, we confess to a certain indulgent sentiment towards Bartley, though he is a cheat and a liar. The virtuous and genteel people in the book are, without exception, odious. The vindictive old Squire and the passionate Marcia are always a little high-flown, and require of the easy, unprincipled, good-natured rascal a hundred virtues quite unknown to him; yet the fact that he is always on the point of being good when his wife flies in his face, or some particularly discouraging accident happens, shows that Mr. Howells has relentings over Bartley, who is the only really sweet-tempered individual in a painful but powerful book. It is altogether the strongest face which the author has put before us; and if he will forget the foreign reviews, and the stupidity and hostility of the English, and illustrate frankly, without any polemical intention, the society he knows, there is no telling how far he may go. A 'Modern Instance' is better than 'Washington Square,' Mr. James's appalling contribution to the internal history of American domestic life: but if Mr. Howells will accept a suggestion from an English critic, let him take a little more pains with his gentlemen. We allow in his favour the proverbial difficulty of forming a hero who shall not be more or less a lay-figure; but we hope the impertinent fineness, which is very different from refinement, of his Stanifords and Ferrises, is not the best America can do. We take an interest in Bartley Hubbard, notwithstanding his sins and meannesses and dishonesties. We are sorry for him, and almost think him not irreclaimable. But Ben Halleck is utterly irreclaimable: a desire to kick him is the warm impulse in our mind at his every appearance. Why should so limp and boneless a being stand as the representative of the best kind of American? Give us, then, the worst, we cry with effusion—the miner in all his savagery, the wild logger in the woods, even the smart editor. We have enough of the nerveless moral *dilettante* in our own obsolete society. To see him cropping up in America as the representative of all that is best and purest, is the last and most painful exemplification of the fact that there is nothing new under the sun.

The question faced here, "Howells or James?" is an interesting third-person comment upon the growing differences between James's and Howells' brands of realism. Howells had made his own comments in his piece, "Henry James, Jr.," in the Century, *November, 1882. James's comment upon Howells is the next essay in this collection.*

Henry Blake Fuller was a Chicago writer whose career as a novelist began in 1890. In an essay in 1899, Howells cited Fuller's Chicago books, The Cliff Dwellers *and* With the Procession, *as two of a number of American novels which could handle "the wolfish problems of existence... without staggering around or stuttering." Fuller regarded Howells as the writer who had shown him the right direction to take.*

HENRY BLAKE FULLER
Edited by DARREL ABEL

Howells or James?

THIS PAPER by Henry Blake Fuller was apparently completed in 1885. By this date William Dean Howells, who at the outset of his fictional career had been classified as an "idyllist" and romancer, was now explicitly committed to realism, and had acknowledged Henry James to be the leader of a new American school of realistic novelists. Howells called realism "almost the only literary movement of our time that has vitality in it," and praised James as the leader of the new movement in the United States:

The art of fiction has in fact become a finer art in our day than it was with Dickens and Thackeray.... The new school derives from Hawthorne and George Eliot rather than any others; but it studies

From *Modern Fiction Studies,* III (Summer, 1957), 159-64. Reprint permission granted by Purdue Research Foundation.

human nature much more in its wonted aspect, and finds its ethical and dramatic examples in the operation of lighter but not really less vital motives. . . . This school, which is so largely of the future as well as the present, finds its chief exemplar in Mr. James; it is he who is shaping and directing American fiction, at least.[1]

While Howells was thus praising James as the chief exemplar of the new realism, who was shaping and directing American fiction, Fuller was venturing to doubt both James's realism and his Americanism. Fuller cannot have failed to understand what Howells was saying about James, but he thought Howells' praise was too generous. He thought Howells' realism was more realistic than James's, and his Americanism more American; and thought Howells himself ought to be acknowledged as the shaper and director of American fiction.

HOWELLS OR JAMES?

The literary gossip of the last ten years, whether of tongue or type, has perhaps employed no phrase with more assiduity or gusto than that of "Howells and James." The language, in its printed form, at least, has even been enriched with a doubly hyphenated adjective which seems to express more fully and exactly than any less modern phrase a certain sort of hero and heroine, a certain sort of plot, and a certain set of ideas with regard to the methods and ends of fiction. Such being the case, one may well justify himself in the intimation that this particular expression has perhaps been a trifle overworked, and allow himself the suggestion that so well worn a collocation of words now give way to the related but dissimilar one of "Howells *or* James?" Substituting, then, for the complacent period the restless mark of interrogation, let us now consider points of difference instead of points of similarity,—asking ourselves which of these two representative writers is to be pronounced most instrumental in the shaping of American fiction, and which of them will ultimately come to be recognized as most firmly and completely a factor in an historical American literature. Mr. Howells, it is true, generously conceded, a year or so ago, the first place to Mr. James. But the vigorous and dextrous opening of his own new serial in the November *Century [The Rise of Silas Lapham]* clearly indicates that his hand has lost none of its mastery, and his prompt and authoritative welcome lately extended to certain newcomers in the ranks of Realism,[2] unmistakably shows that he does not consider his own position that of a subordinate; so he will perhaps tolerate the hint that to him and not to his friend is entrusted the direction of our contemporary novel-writing, and that he, rather than any one else, may be allowed by the opinion of another generation, the place of undisputed chief. It is worthwhile, on this point, to note the attitude of each toward life and society in general, and toward American life and society in particular.

We may say, in general, and for the purpose of a direct comparison, that Howells is a realist, and James an idealist. Few, perhaps, who have in mind Mr. James' first and most famous "international" effort will regard the creator of Daisy Miller—least of all, the perpetrator of Daisy Miller's little brother—as an idealizer. But a man has a right to ask that we judge him by his highest and best, by the nature of that whose representation is to him most congenial and self-satisfying. If, then, Mr. James' most finished and elaborate portraits of persons are marked with exceptional attributes of wit, polish, beauty, culture, wealth, intellect,—and if his most careful and ambitious portraits of places (the phrase is his own) result, after his own peculiar process of selection, rejection, and combination, in a whole of unblemished picturesqueness and unbroken harmony, his claim to the title of idealist seems placed beyond dispute. That he deals, ultimately, in realities, is true enough; but a realism made up of select actualities is pretty apt to come out idealistically in the end.

Now we, in these days of democracy, take a very frank and undisguised interest in ourselves; we are a good deal concerned with our own day and generation—in our art as well as elsewhere, Literature, monopolized for a great many long centuries by fortune, beauty, splendor, and general heroics, has at length descended to the common level of general humanity, and has consented to take an interest in plain every day people and plain every day happiness. Flora, goddess of flowers, is no longer the airy, radiant, lily-crowned nymph of the Renaissance; a clever young Parisian has shown her to be simply a plain old peasant woman in sabots and frilled cap with a big basket of astors and geraniums at her side. We are not ashamed to confess that at the present time we take but a limited interest in, for example, an Achilles or a Beatrice, while we vehemently discuss, *con amore,* the character of a Bartley Hubbard or the doings of a Lydia Blood. It may be safely said that this state of things has come to stay; such an interest in ourselves, once aroused, is pretty apt to be permanent. We shall not so greatly care to hear about other things when we can hear so much and so minutely about ourselves. Realism seems coincident with modern democracy, and the advance of the one will doubtless be accompanied by the spread of the other. Realism as Mr. Howells himself has lately said, is but a phase of humanity; and the writer who is most thoroughly permeated with the realistic spirit may confidently expect the widest hearing and the securest place.

Again: Mr. Howells' attitude toward life is sympathetic; Mr. James' is rather the reverse. James has, of course, his own peculiar sympathies and predilections, but they are of a very exclusive and circumscribed character. He regards life as a superficies; Howells looks at it as a substance. James makes a survey of it; Howells gives us a cross-section of it. The one is satisfied with the cultivation of the mere top-dressing; the other has a healthy liking for the honest clay and gravel of the great middle stratum. James has, of course, his due liking for virtue, truth, justice, and the rest, but he does not always appear to appreciate them at their full value when unlinked with fortunate circumstances and the culture of a refined society. Howells, on the other hand, can interest himself sympathetically in all the qualities—not the good, merely; but the doubtful and the bad as well—which may present themselves to him in his actual contact with society in any of its forms. He himself declares that the study of human life, if close, is sure to be kindly. And a hearty sympathy with the general life of the community has never met with a readier recognition and response than it meets with today.

The present attitude of these two authors, respectively, with regard to our own particular life and society, assuredly need not be made matter for formal exposition. But it is interesting to note that within the last few years the attitude of the one has materially changed, while that of the other has become, if anything, more statuesquely immovable. The time is not far back when both Howells and James were stationed at the far end of that transatlantic bridge which it is the chief boast and distinction of the latter to have constructed between the Old World and the New. Howells, with a clear perception of the direction in which the cat—to use the common phrase—was about to jump, crossed over a few years back (pausing in the middle for the "Foregone Conclusion" and the "Lady of the Aroostook") and has steadfastly remained with us ever since. James, with a perception less clear, or from preferences not easily to be overcome, has held to the same remote standpoint that he occupied when his striking figure was first discerned by the modern novel-reader. A year back, indeed, he sent Lady Barberina over to us; but she didn't stay long. That each is now permanently established on his own ground, and fully fixed as to his own point of view, the fall announcements of the publishers made yet more sure. Mr. Howells, in the "Rise of Silas Lapham" will still farther extend the field of sympathetic realism which he first entered in the "Modern Instance." Mr. James, in the "Princess Casamassima" (in whom we may confidently recognize the striking figure of an old acquaintance) will bring to a still higher degree of perfection his own particular little garden of exotic culture which has already blossomed with "Roderick Hudson" and the "Portrait of a Lady."

A common complaint against the novels of both Howells and James—how easily the phrase runs off!—has been that most of them have been unduly taken up with various small and insignificant questions of social manners and usages that ruffle the mere surface of society without by any means stirring its depths. But there are now indications that the depths are to be stirred, after all. The stratification of our society has undeniably begun, and symptoms of the movement are coming to appear in print. Now the novel in our day has become the great universal medium. New theories in philosophy, new ideas in art, new phases in religion, politics, and what not, now hasten to enclose themselves within the covers of a "fiction." And if all these, why not sociology, as well? May we not reasonably look for the formulation of American society in the pages of the *Atlantic* or the *Century?* And such a process—to whom would we most willingly entrust it, to Howells or to James? Who would do it most kindly, most sympathetically—he who deals with the normal earning of money at home, or he who prefers to deal with the exceptional and privileged spending of money abroad? He who lives amongst us and knows us intimately and treats us all with the fullest measure of good will; or he who alienates himself from us, knows us, in general, none too perfectly, and doesn't feel sure but that we are a big mistake, after all? With the strong intimation that Mr. Howells has just given of his design to bring order out of our social chaos, I am glad to remember that he is an "Ohio man," and it was toward Ohio, let us recollect, that Mr. Matthew Arnold directed his gaze when searching for the "average American."

Mr. James, no doubt, would be glad to like us, if he could; perhaps he has even conscientiously endeavored to do so. But an undue insistence upon agreeable externals has worked to prevent his becoming acquainted with us as we really are. He leaves us in no doubt that he prefers, for instance, weather-stained stucco to freshly-painted clapboarding; and a pair of sabots strikes in him a responsive chord that a pair of plain cowhide boots quite fails to affect. The boots and the clapboarding repel him; so he stays over there with his sabots and his stucco. Mr. Howells' organs of aesthetic digestion are much more healthy and vigorous. He approaches boldly all the various externals of American life—grotesque though they may be, and ugly, and irritating, and distressing—which so often cause us to quail before the gaze of our European censors, and subdues them instead of letting them subdue him. He can print the word "buggy" without the help of quotation marks, and writes "guess" with an unconscious freedom that Mr. James has never attained.

Howells, in fine, has come to the mountain: James seems to expect that he can bring the mountain to him. A few loose stones and boulders, it is true, have rolled his way; but the general form and outline of the mountain have not been materially changed, and its firm base is probably quite as immovable as it ever was. There is a strong probability that Mr. James, notwithstanding his very exceptional gifts and his score of delightful qualities, will sometime come to find himself a "thing apart" in a sense and to an extent that he does not now foresee. From his isolated position he may come to regard, with a feeling approximating envy, the comfortable position of a competitor who, believing that there's no place like home, has made himself the leader and centre of a school whose members, working in fields however scattered, have an aim and a method that should render them worthy of an appreciative hearing and the objects of an affectionate pride.

1. "Henry James, Jr.," Century, XXV (Nov., 1882), 28. The English quarterlies were incensed at Howells' opinion that the future of the novel lay with continental realism rather than with the discursive subjectivism of Dickens and Thackeray, and also by his suggestion that American novelists, especially James, were making more significant advances than British writers. For an account of the ensuing hubbub, see Edwin H. Cady's *The Road to Realism* (Syracuse University Press, 1956), pp. 218-221.

2. See Howells' "Two Notable Novels," *Century,* XXVIII (August, 1884), 632-634. In this review of Howe's *Story of a Country Town* and Bellamy's *Miss Ludington's Sister,* Howells wrote: "Not the least interesting thing about them was the witness they bore of the prevalence of realism in the artistic atmosphere to such degree that two very differently gifted writers, having really something to say in the way of fiction, could not help giving it the realistic character."

1886

Henry James reviewed many of Howells' works, beginning with Italian Journeys *in 1868. Their close friendship began about this time and in its first years was probably helpful in shaping both men's literary aspirations. This long essay is not only the most thorough and penetrating of James's criticisms of Howells, but one of the most discerning articles on Howells in the nineteenth century. It examines Howells' work at a crucial point in his career. From this time on, Howells' novels were to become more explicitly novels of social criticism and much less likely to be found "a ground for national complacency."*

HENRY JAMES

William Dean Howells

AS THE EXISTENCE of a man of letters (so far as the public is concerned with it) may be said to begin with his first appearance in literature, that of Mr. Howells, who was born at Martinsville, Ohio, in 1837, and spent his entire youth in his native state, dates properly from the publication of his delightful volume on *Venetian Life*—than which he has produced nothing since of a literary quality more pure—which he put forth in 1865, after his return from the consular post in the city of St. Mark which he had filled for four years. He had, indeed, before going to live in Venice, and during the autumn of 1860, published, in conjunction with his friend Mr. Piatt, a so-called "campaign" biography of Abraham Lincoln; but as this composition, which I have never seen, emanated probably more from a good Republican than from a suitor of the Muse, I mention it simply for the sake of exactitude, adding, however, that I have never heard of the Muse having taken it ill. When

From *Harper's Weekly*, XXX (June 19, 1886), 394-95.

a man is a born artist, everything that happens to him confirms his perverse tendency; and it may be considered that the happiest thing that could have been invented on Mr. Howells's behalf was his residence in Venice at the most sensitive and responsive period of life; for Venice, bewritten and bepainted as she has ever been, does nothing to you unless to persuade you that you also can paint, that you also can write. Her only fault is that she sometimes too flatteringly—for she is shameless in the exercise of such arts—addresses the remark to those who cannot. Mr. Howells could, fortunately, for his writing was painting as well in those days. The papers on Venice prove it, equally with the artistic whimsical chapters of the Italian Journeys, made up in 1867 from his notes and memories (the latter as tender as most glances shot eastward in working hours across the Atlantic) of the holidays and excursions which carried him occasionally away from his consulate.

The mingled freshness and irony of these things gave them an originality which has not been superseded, to my knowledge, by any impressions of European life from an American standpoint. At Venice Mr. Howells married a lady of artistic accomplishment and association, passed through the sharp alternations of anxiety and hope to which those who spent the long years of the Civil War in foreign lands were inevitably condemned, and of which the effect was not rendered less wearing by the perusal of the London *Times* and the conversation of the British tourist. The irritation so far as it proceeded from the latter source, may even yet be perceived in Mr. Howells's pages. He wrote poetry at Venice, as he had done of old in Ohio, and his poems were subsequently collected into two thin volumes, the fruit, evidently, of a rigorous selection. They have left more traces in the mind of many persons who read and enjoyed them than they appear to have done in the author's own. It is not nowadays as a cultivator of rhythmic periods that Mr. Howells most willingly presents himself. Everything in the evolution, as we must all learn to call it today, of a talent of this order is interesting, but one of the things that are most so is the separation that has taken place, in Mr. Howells's case, between its early and its later manner. There is nothing in *Silas Lapham,* or in *Doctor Breen's Practice,* or in *A Modern Instance,* or in *The Undiscovered Country,* to suggest that its author had at one time either wooed the lyric Muse or surrendered himself to those Italian initiations without which we of other countries remain always, after all, more or less barbarians. It is often a good, as it is sometimes an evil, that one cannot dis-establish one's past, and Mr. Howells cannot help having rhymed and romanced in deluded hours, nor would he, no doubt, if he could. The repudiation of the weakness which leads to such aberrations is more apparent than real, and the spirit which made him care a little for the poor factitious Old World and the superstition of "form" is only latent in pages which express a marked preference for the novelties of civilization and a perceptible mistrust of the purist. I hasten to add that Mr. Howells has had moments of reappreciation of Italy in later years, and has even taken the trouble to write a book (the magnificent volume on *Tuscan Cities*) to show it. Moreover, the exquisite tale *A Foregone Conclusion,* and many touches in the recent novel of *Indian Summer* (both this and the *Cities* the fruit of a second visit to Italy), sound the note of a charming inconsistency.

On his return from Venice he settled in the vicinity of Boston, and began to edit the *Atlantic Monthly,* accommodating himself to this grave complication with infinite tact and industry. He conferred further distinction upon the magazine; he wrote the fine series of "Suburban Sketches," one of the least known of his productions, but one of the most perfect, and on Sunday afternoons he took a suburban walk—perfect also, no doubt, in its way. I know not exactly how long this phase of his career lasted, but I imagine that if he were asked, he would reply: "Oh, a hundred years." He was meant for better things than this—things better, I mean, than superintending the private life of even the most eminent periodical—but I am not sure that I would speak of this experience as a series of wasted years. They were years rather of economized talent, of observation and accumulation. They had the foundation of what is most remarkable, or most, at least, the peculiar sign, in his effort as a novelist—his unerring sentiment of the American character. Mr. Howells knows more about it than anyone, and it was during this period of what we may suppose to have been rather perfunctory administration that he must have gathered many of his impressions of it. An editor is in the nature of the case much exposed, so exposed as not to be protected even by the seclusion (the security to a superficial eye so complete) of a Boston suburb. His manner of contact with the world is almost violent, and whatever bruises he may confer, those he receives are the most telling, inasmuch as the former are distributed among many, and the latter all to be endured by one. Mr. Howells's accessibilities and sufferings were destined to fructify. Other persons have considered and discoursed upon American life, but no one, surely, has *felt* it so completely as he. I will not say that Mr. Howells feels it all equally, for are we not perpetually conscious how vast and deep it is?—but he is an authority upon many of those parts of it which are most representative.

He was still under the shadow of his editorship when, in the intervals of his letter-writing and reviewing, he made his first cautious attempts in the walk of fiction. I say cautious, for in looking back nothing is more clear than that he had determined to advance only step by step. In his first story, *Their Wedding Journey,* there are only two persons, and in his next, *A Chance Acquaintance,* which contains one of his very happiest studies of a girl's character, the number is not lavishly increased. In *A Foregone Conclusion,* where the girl again is admirable, as well as the young Italian priest, also a kind of maidenly figure, the actors are but four. Today Mr. Howells doesn't count, and confers life with a generous and unerring hand. If the profusion of forms in which it presents itself to him is remarkable, this is perhaps partly because he had the good fortune of not approaching the novel until he had lived considerably, until his inclination for it had ripened. His attitude was as little as possible that of the gifted young person who, at twenty, puts forth a work of imagination of which the merit is mainly in its establishing the presumption that the next one will be better. It is my impression that long after he was twenty he still cultivated the belief that the faculty of the novelist was not in him, and was even capable of producing certain unfinished chapters (in the candor of his good faith he would sometimes communicate them to a listener) in triumphant support of this contention. He believed, in particular, that he could not make people talk, and such have been the revenges of time that a cynical critic might almost say of him today that he cannot make them keep silent. It was life itself that finally dissipated his doubts, life that reasoned with him and persuaded him. The feeling of life is strong in all his tales, and any one of them has this rare (always rarer) and indispensable sign of a happy origin, that it is an impression at first hand. Mr. Howells is literary, on certain sides exquisitely so, though with a singular and not unamiable perversity he sometimes endeavors not to be; but his vision of the human scene is never a literary reminiscence, a reflection of books and pictures, of tradition and fashion and hearsay. I know of no English novelist of our hour whose work is so exclusively a matter of painting what he sees and who is so sure of what he sees. People are always wanting a writer of Mr. Howells's temperament to see certain things that he doesn't (that he doesn't sometimes even want to), but I must content myself with congratulating the author of *A Modern Instance* and *Silas Lapham* on the admirable quality of his vision. The American life which he for the most part depicts is certainly neither very rich nor very fair, but it is tremendously positive, and as his manner of presenting it is as little as possible conventional, the reader can have no doubt about it. This is an immense luxury; the ingenuous character of the witness (I can give it no higher praise) deepens the value of the report.

Mr. Howells has gone from one success to another, has taken possession of the field, and has become copious without detriment to his freshness. I need not enumerate his works in their order, for, both in America and in England (where it is a marked feature of the growing curiosity felt about American life that they are constantly referred to for information and verification), they have long been in everybody's hands. Quietly and steadily they have become better and better; one may like some of them more than others, but it is noticeable that from effort to effort the author has constantly enlarged his scope. His work is of a kind of which it is good that there should be much today—work of observation, of patient and definite notation. Neither in theory nor in practice is Mr. Howells a romancer; but the romancers can spare him; there will always be plenty of people to do their work. He has definite and downright convictions on the subject of the work that calls out to be done in opposition to theirs, and this fact is a source of much of the interest that he excites.

It is a singular circumstance that to know what one wishes to do should be, in the field of art, a rare distinction; but it is incontestable that, as one looks about in our English and American fiction, one does not perceive any very striking examples of a vivifying faith. There is no discussion of the great question of how best to write, no exchange of ideas, no vivacity nor variety of experiment. A vivifying faith Mr. Howells may distinctly be said to possess, and he conceals it so little as to afford every facility to those people who are anxious to prove that it is the wrong one. He is animated by a love of the common, the immediate, the familiar and vulgar elements of life, and holds that in proportion as we move into the rare and strange we become vague and arbitrary; that truth of representation, in a word, can be achieved only so long as it is in our power to test and measure it. He thinks scarcely anything too paltry to be interesting, that the small and the vulgar have been terribly neglected, and would rather see an exact account of a sentiment or a character he stumbles against every day than a brilliant evocation of a passion or a type he has never seen and does not even particularly believe in. He adores the real, the natural, the colloquial, the moderate, the optimistic, the domestic, and the democratic; looking askance at exceptions and perversities and superiorities, at surprising and incongruous phenomena in general. One must have seen a great deal before one concludes; the world is very large, and life is a mixture of many things; she by no means eschews the strange, and often risks combinations and effects that make one rub one's eyes. Nevertheless, Mr. Howells's standpoint is an excellent one for seeing a large part of the truth, and even if it were less advantageous, there would be a great deal to admire in the firmness with which he has planted himself. He hates a "story," and (this private feat is not impossible) has probably made up his mind very definitely as to what the pestilent thing consists of. In this respect he is more logical than M. Émile Zola, who partakes of the same aversion, but has greater lapses as well as greater audacities. Mr. Howells hates an artificial fable and a *dénouement* that is pressed into the service; he likes things to occur as they occur in life, where the manner of a great many of them is not to occur at all. (He has observed that heroic emotion and brilliant opportunity are not particularly interwoven with our days, and indeed, in the way of omission, he *has* often practiced in his pages a very considerable boldness. It has not, however, made what we find there any less interesting and less human.)

The picture of American life on Mr. Howells's canvas is not of a dazzling brightness, and many readers have probably wondered why it is that (among a sensitive people) he has so successfully escaped the imputation of a want of patriotism. The manners he describes—the desolation of the whole social prospect in *A Modern Instance* is perhaps the strongest expression of those influences—are eminently of a nature to discourage the intending visitor, and yet the westward pilgrim continues to arrive, in spite of the Bartley Hubbards and the Laphams, and the terrible practices at the country hotel in *Doctor Breen,* and at the Boston boarding-house in *A Woman's Reason.* This tolerance of depressing revelations is explained partly, no doubt, by the fact that Mr. Howells's truthfulness imposes itself—the representation is so vivid that the reader accepts it as he accepts, in his own affairs, the mystery of fate—and partly by a very different consideration, which is simply that if many of his characters are disagreeable, almost all of them are extraordinarily good, and with a goodness which is a ground for national complacency. If American life is on the whole, as I make no doubt whatever, more innocent than that of any other country, nowhere is the fact more patent than in Mr. Howells's novels, which exhibit so constant a study of the actual and so small a perception of evil. His women, in particular, are of the best—except, indeed, in the sense of being the best to live with. Purity of life, fineness of conscience, benevolence of motive, decency of speech, good nature, kindness, charity, tolerance (though indeed, there is little but each other's manners for the people to tolerate), govern all the scene; the only immoralities are aberrations of thought, like that of Silas Lapham, or excesses of beer, like that of Bartley Hubbard. In the gallery of Mr. Howells's portraits there are none more living than the admirable, humorous images of those two ineffectual sinners. Lapham, in particular, is magnificent, understood down to the ground, inside and out—a creation which does Mr. Howells the highest honor. I do not say that the figure of his wife is as good as his own, only because I wish to say that it is as good as that of the minister's wife in the history of *Lemuel Barker,* which is unfolding itself from month to month at the moment I write. These two ladies are exhaustive renderings of the type of virtue that worries. But everything in *Silas Lapham* is superior—nothing more so than the whole picture of casual female youth and contemporaneous "engaging" one's self, in the daughters of the proprietor of the mineral paint.

This production had struck me as the author's high-water mark, until I opened the monthly sheets of *Lemuel Barker,* in which the art of imparting a palpitating interest to common things and unheroic lives is pursued (or is destined, apparently, to be pursued) to an even higher point. The four (or is it eight?) repeated "good-mornings" between the liberated Lemuel and the shop-girl who has crudely been the cause of his being locked up by the police all night are a poem, an idyl, a trait of genius, and a compendium of American good nature. The whole episode is inimitable, and I know fellow novelists of Mr. Howells's who would have given their eyes to produce that interchange of salutations, which only an American reader, I think, can understand. Indeed, the only limitation, in general, to his extreme truthfulness is, I will not say his constant sense of the comedy of life, for that is irresistible, but the verbal drollery of many of his people. It is extreme and perpetual, but I fear the reader will find it a venial sin. Theodore Colville, in *Indian Summer,* is so irrepressibly and happily facetious as to make one wonder whether the author is not prompting him a little, and whether he could be quite so amusing without help from outside. This criticism, however, is the only one I find it urgent to make, and Mr. Howells doubtless will not suffer from my saying that, being a humorist himself, he is strong in the representation of humorists. There are other reflections that I might indulge in if I had more space. I should like, for instance, to allude in passing, for purposes of respectful remonstrance, to a phrase that he suffered the other day to fall from his pen (in a periodical, but not in a novel), to the effect that the style of a work of fiction is a thing that matters less and less all the while. Why less and less? It seems to me as great a mistake to say so as it would be to say that it matters more and more. It is difficult to see how it can matter either less or more. The style of a novel is a part of the execution of a work of art; the execution of a work of art is part of its very essence, and that, it seems to me, must have mattered in all ages in exactly the same degree, and be destined always to do so. I can conceive of no state of civilization in which it shall not be deemed important, though of course there are states in which executants are clumsy. I should also venture to express a certain regret that Mr. Howells (whose style, in practice, after all, as I have intimated, treats itself to felicities which his theory perhaps would condemn) should appear increasingly to hold composition too cheap—by which I mean, should neglect the effect that comes from alternation, distribution, relief. He has an increasing tendency to tell his story altogether in conversations, so that a critical reader sometimes wishes, not that the dialogue might be suppressed (it is too good for that), but that it might be distributed, interspaced with narrative and pictorial matter. The author forgets sometimes to paint, to evoke the conditions and appearances, to build in the subject. He is doubtless afraid of doing these things in excess, having seen in other hands what disastrous effects that error may have; but all the same I cannot help thinking that the divinest thing in a valid novel is the compendious, descriptive, pictorial touch, *à la Daudet.*

It would be absurd to speak of Mr. Howells today in the encouraging tone that one would apply to a young writer who had given fine pledges, and one feels half guilty of that mistake if one makes a cheerful remark about his future. And yet we cannot pretend not to take a still more lively interest in his future than we have done in his past. It is hard to see how it can help being more and more fruitful, for his face is turned in the right direction, and his work is fed from sources which play us no tricks.

1888

Howells' growing popularity and the notoriety of his "realistic" method provoked this parody of The Rise of Silas Lapham. *The parody is not very funny, chiefly because the parodist, John Kendrick Bangs, was not a very funny writer. Such a parody, however, demonstrates one more way in which Howells' critical principles were brought to the attention of the general reader.*

John Kendrick Bangs was well known as a humorist in the eighties and nineties. He wrote many books and traveled widely as a humorous lecturer. He was on the editorial staff of Harper's *during a part of the time that Howells was associated with that magazine. Only the first part of the parody is included here.*

JOHN KENDRICK BANGS

The Rise of Hop O' My Thumb

A Parody

WHEN Barclay Williams went to interview Hop O' My Thumb for the "Solid Men of Fairy-land" series which he undertook to finish up for the "Decade" after he had paid the debts of that newspaper and acquired its ownership, My Thumb received him in his private office by previous appointment.

Barclay hesitated, as he entered the door, whether he should wipe his feet on the mat or not. To be sure there was a sign requesting him to do so pinned upon the upper left-hand panel of the door, but a large sea-green inscription, WELCOME, upon the mat itself seemed to forbid any such familiarity. Unfortunately his embarrassment was considerably augmented by Hop O' My Thumb himself,

---

From *New Waggings of Old Tales* (Boston, 1888), pp. 18-46.

who, upon hearing a footstep without, cleared his throat and pushing his chair backward about two feet from his desk began to wonder whose footstep it was. He thought he recognized the squeak of the shoes as belonging to Barclay, but he was not certain enough on the point to come to any definite conclusion; so turning half way round he arose from his chair and started to walk toward the door, glancing furtively at the transom as he did so.

"Come in," he said.

Barclay still hesitated. There was something in Hop O' My Thumb's tone that contributed further to his uncertainty on the question of the door-mat. If he wiped his feet on My Thumb's WELCOME, My Thumb might be angry; on the other hand, if he disregarded the warning on the door-panel he still might give offence. A hurried glance at his shoes decided him. They were not at all muddy, and then he remembered that he had come from his house in a cab and that the shoes were new. He smiled quietly to himself, and remembering his early athletic successes at college he jumped easily over the mat and found himself confronted by his host, whose misgivings as to whether or not Barclay was a creditor had led him to put on his seven-league boots in the interval between his invitation to enter and the entrance of his guest.

"Oh, it's you, is it?" said Hop O' somewhat absently, spurning a three-legged stool across the room to where Barclay stood and motioning him to be seated.

"How did you guess?" asked Barclay, surprised at this sudden recognition.

"I don't know," replied Hop O' My Thumb with charming *naiveté*. "Because you look so like yourself, perhaps, or because you—" then he stopped and fondled his watch-chain nervously. It was evident that he could not think of any other reason. Barclay felt his embarrassment coming over him again, and inadvertently broke the end of his lead-pencil.

"What do you want, young man?" continued My Thumb, recovering his composure with some apparent effort.

"Your life," said Barclay. "We want the lives of all the great men of Fairy-land for the 'Decade.' "

Hop O' My Thumb was somewhat startled at Barclay's first words, and a nervous movement of the legs placed him some distance from the interviewer. He had forgotten to remove the seven-league boots. Another nervous twitch, however, brought him back to Barclay's side in time to hear his last words. Barclay wondered at this sudden disappearance and equally sudden reappearance of his host, but he was too well bred to express any surprise. He merely made a mental note of it for the treatise on the Eccentricities of Genius, which he was preparing for a future number of the "Pacific Monthly."

"We want to hear about this Ogre business, you know—and—" here Barclay faltered ever so slightly. He was a Bostonian, and he was proud of it, but he did not want to appear too proud. With much effort he finished his sentence, however. "And how you were befriended by the—the beans." Barclay blushed.

Hop O' My Thumb looked at him silently and then laughed. He was amused at the Interviewer's embarrassment, and made no effort to conceal it.

"All right," he said; "where do you want me to begin?"

"Might begin with your poor but honest parents," suggested Barclay, elevating his eyebrows....

1890

Hamlin Garland probably met Howells in 1886, shortly after he had come to Boston from the Middle West as Howells himself had done twenty-five years before. This essay, written when Garland was thirty, shows how ardent a disciple he had become. The first part of the essay, not reprinted here, surveys Howells' career as a novelist, emphasizing his growth from a novelist who "amused the public" to one whose "convictions are begotten and sustained by a spirit of a great social movement." The last part of the essay, a discussion of Howells and realism, is included here as the response of a young writer who found in realism his own literary creed and as a representative document in the controversy over realism in which Howells was the central figure.

Hamlin Garland was one of many young writers who received Howells' encouragement. Main-Travelled Roads, *published in 1891, was called to the public's attention by Howells in the "Editor's Study," which he was then writing in* Harper's. *Garland's collection of critical essays,* Crumbling Idols, *appeared in 1894.*

HAMLIN GARLAND

Mr. Howells's Latest Novels

. . . Criticism of Mr. Howells, with previous writers or living writers as criteria, has no value. He can be criticised properly in but one way —by comparison with life. Is he true? is the question to be asked. If he is false to his subject or to himself, then objections are valid. But to say that he is not Scott, or Dickens, or Hugo, or Dumas is certainly true, but it is not criticism. That he is different is a merit and a distinction, not, surely, because Scott and Dickens were not great,

From the *New England Magazine,* II (May, 1890), 243-50.

but because they no longer represent us. Art, in its progress, refuses to be held accountable to the past. It claims for itself the right to depict in its own way, its own time, just as its predecessors did.

As a critic Mr. Howells may be said to represent the idea of progress in ideals. He stands over against the idea of the statical in art and literature; he is on this point in complete harmony with Ibsen, Valdés, Posnett, and Taine. He emphasizes and exemplifies the sayings of Emerson and Whitman, that "there is more wool and flax in the field"; that there are no bounds to art, that each age should be accountable only to itself, and that the only criterion of the novelist and painter is life and its magnificent reality. This philosophy does not attempt to lessen the true power and beauty of Scott, Dickens, Hugo, Raphael, Velásquez, or Corot, but it declines to take them as models. It gives them due honor for the great work they did in their place and time, and believes that in this day and land they would have been among the radicals. They were all "the radicals" in their day. In short, realism, as voiced by Valdés and Howells, has but one law: "the artist must be true to himself." He should write or paint of that which he knows the most about and cares the most about. He should write and paint as nearly as possible as though no other man ever painted or wrote in the world. If this is done, nothing that he paints or writes will be trivial or vulgar, for it is impossible to love a trivial thing. "The greatest poet hardly knows littleness or triviality. If he breathes into anything that was before thought small, it dilates with the grandeur and life of the universe," says Whitman. Valdés, in perhaps the best essay on realism ever published, repeats the thought.

Realism, in truth, is not a theory but a condition of mind upon which a law is founded. The condition is a *genuine love for reality.* Some people seem to have great difficulty in understanding this. The realist does not write of common things so much because he hates romantic things as because he loves actualities,—present, near at hand. Realism has been dragged in the mire, has been taken to mean tanks and fire-engines on the stage, and filth and fury in the novel;

but the feeling that underlies the realism of Tolstoi, Valdés, and Howells has nothing in common with this sensationalism. It aims at embodying in art the common landscapes, common figures, and common hopes and loves and ambitions of our common life. It loves normal people, unarranged landscapes, and colors that are not "harmonized." It believes in the physiological rather than the pathological, in the sane and sunny rather than in the abnormal and monstrous; and the justification and the proof of this growing condition of mind are seen in the increasing number of artists of the truth, whose works find favor and reward.

All this Mr. Howells has stood for amid assaults that would have driven another man from the field. Serene and self-poised he has gone on his way, with but a few companions apparently, but in reality with a host at his back. Personal assaults upon him, assaults often from those who cannot and dare not grant to the realist the same privilege the realist grants the conservative, are of no value. The radical, the realist, has no objection to the conservative's adoration of the past, of the heroic, of Scott, of Shakespeare. All he asks is the chance of going on in a humble way of liking modern things, and believing in the present and the future. And he has a suspicion that the case of the conservative is weak in proportion to his vehemence in denouncing the opinions which he persists in calling too baseless and absurd to be worth notice.

If realism is only a passing shadow cast by Mr. Howells and others, its enemies are wasting a deal of valuable time,—it will pass of itself, and the glorious sun of romance will soon illumine the land, and we shall all prefer blue roses to red.

Personally one of the most genial and lovable of men, Mr. Howells is the last person to be taken as a controversialist. His ready laugh and inexhaustible fund of humor make the casual acquaintance wonder if this can be the author of *A Hazard of New Fortunes* and the target of all the conservative criticisms. But there come moments when the head droops and the strength of the face comes out, and the eyes deepen and darken, till the visitor sees before him one of the greatest personalities in America,—a personality so great that it is content to become the humble percipient and recorder of realities, and so sure of itself as to bow to no criterion but truth.

Mr. Howells carries the sturdy figure and the direct and simple bearing of the man whose boyhood held many a hardship, and who has fought his way to where he is against poverty and discouragement. No man could be more democratic, more approachable, more sympathetic. He has the poet's love for nature, for color, but above all, love for humanity. As one writer has well put it, Mr. Howells "knows how it is himself." This is the quality which makes the author of *Annie Kilburn* and *A Hazard of New Fortunes.* It is a quality that is endearing him daily to new circles of readers, who feel that he is stating their case, is voicing their hopes and defeats and longings. The *dilettante* reader may reject Mr. Howells, but earnest, thinking, suffering men and women find him greater and deeper and truer every day.

As the art which Mr. Howells represents declines to be held accountable to any age, or land, or individual, so it discourages discipleship. It says to the young writer: "Look to nature and to actuality for your model—not to any book, or man, or number of men. Be true to yourself. Write of that of which you know the most and feel the most, and follow faithfully the changes in your feeling. Put yourself down before common realities, common hopes, common men, till their pathos and mystery and significance flood you like a sea, and when the life that is all about you is so rich with drama and poetry, and the vista of human thought and passion so infinite that you are in despair of ever expressing a thousandth part of what you feel, then all idea of discipleship will be at an end. Your whole aim will be to be true to yourself and your infinite teacher, nature, and you will no longer strive to delineate beauty, but truth, and at last truth will be beauty."

The realist of the stamp of Valdés and Howells, so far from being "materialistic," is really a mystic. He reaches at last the mysticism of the philosopher, to whom matter is as mysterious as spirit;

of Whitman, who says that "every cubic inch of space is a miracle." "In nature," says Valdés, "there is nothing great or small; nothing is trivial absolutely. All depends upon the mind perceiving; and values are relative in art as in all else." So that to call the work of these realists vulgar or material is to beg the question. To whom are they vulgar or trivial? To say that the modern novel deals largely with the particular is true; that is its distinction. This has been superbly stated by Véron: "We care no longer for gods or heroes, we care for men." And Grant Allen in a recent article has stated the same point, recognizing for the first time the difference between the aims of the real American novelist and all previous fiction.

"The modern American novel is built upon principles all its own, which entirely preclude the possibility of introducing those abrupt changes, sensational episodes, improbable coincidences, which to our contemporary English romance are indispensable ingredients. *It is the real realism, the natural naturalism;* it depends for its effects upon the faithful, almost photographic, delineation of actual life, with its motives, its impulses, its springs of action laid bare to the eye; but with no unnatural straining after the intenser and coarser emotions of blood and fire, no intentional effort to drag in murder, crime, or fierce interludes of passion, without adequate reason. If these things belong by nature to the particular drama as it rises spontaneous in the author's brain, fall into their places they will and may; but the drama certainly won't go out of its own fixed path on purpose to look for them. One has only to glance at the whole past history of literary evolution in order to see that this new conception marks a step in advance—a step along precisely the same lines as all previous advances in the development of the story-telling faculty in humanity at large. For the story starts with the miraculous and the mythical. Gradually, however, as time goes on, the story becomes more human, more definite, more conceivable, more terrestrial. It descends to earth, it condescends to particulars. But still adequacy of motive, consistency of character, accuracy of delineation, are little insisted upon. The critical faculty, as yet but vaguely aroused, can hardly be shocked at all by the sudden spectacle of the good man becoming bad, or the bad man good, at a stroke of the pen, by impossible conversions and impossible coincidences, by motiveless crimes or unexpected dénouements."

Only when the development of literature and art, the incessant change of ideals from age to age, is recognized, as the comparative critic sees it, can full justice be done to the group of young writers now rising in America, who represent this new tendency, and of whom Mr. Howells is the champion and the unquestioned leader.

1895

Howells did a great deal of writing for the stage. From 1876 until 1911, he wrote over thirty plays, farces, dramatic sketches, and comic operas. He wrote dramatic versions of three of his own novels and collaborated with Mark Twain on Colonel Sellers as a Scientist. *Yet his plays are of minor interest and add little to his reputation. "They will do," Howells wrote, "to amuse the idleness and the intolerable leisure of young people of good society...."*

George Bernard Shaw was drama critic of the Saturday Review *when this was written. His own dramatic career was beginning about this time. Perhaps his admiration for Howells was related to both men's sympathy toward socialism. Shaw helped found the Fabian Society in 1884. Howells dated his own leaning toward socialism (see the next essay in this collection) from 1888.*

GEORGE BERNARD SHAW

Told You So

A Review of *The Garroters*

...BY THE WAY, I have discovered, quite by accident, an amusing farcical comedy. Somebody told me that there was a farce by Mr. W. D. Howells at the Avenue Theatre. I looked in the daily papers, but could find no mention of the name of Mr. Howells. However, it was evidently quite possible that the management had never heard of Mr. Howells, just as they had apparently never heard of me. So I went, and duly found the name "Howels" on the programme. The little piece showed, as might be expected, that with three weeks' practice the American novelist could write the heads off the bunglers to whom our managers vainly appeal when they want a small bit of

From the *Saturday Review*, LXXX (December 7, 1895), 761-62.

work to amuse the people who come at eight. But no doubt it is pleasanter to be a novelist, to have an intelligent circle of readers comfortably seated by their firesides or swinging sunnily in hammocks in their gardens, to be pleasantly diffuse, to play with your work, to be independent of time and space, than to conform to the stern condition of the stage and fight with stupidity before and behind the curtain....

1898

At the time this notice was written, Howells had been actively creating novels of social protest for ten years. A Hazard of New Fortunes, *his most impressive protest novel, was begun in 1887, soon after the conviction and sentencing of the anarchists involved in the Haymarket riot. Howells was one of the few men of letters to challenge the justice of the trials. He wrote a strong letter on the subject to the New York* Tribune *(November 6, 1887), and an even stronger one which he did not mail. He continued to protest against economic injustice until death.*

Howells' economic beliefs have been extensively studied. One of the earliest studies, Walter F. Taylor's "William Dean Howells and the Economic Novel," is included in Part II of this book.

ANONYMOUS

Howells as a Socialist

WILLIAM DEAN HOWELLS is warmly hailed as a brother Socialist by the editor of *The American Fabian* (New York, February), who has this to say of the services that Mr. Howells has rendered to the Socialist movement:

"He has made his art the instrument of a great purpose. His 'Annie Kilburn'; his 'A Hazard of New Fortunes'; his 'The World of Chance' wherein the alleged 'laws of business' are considered to be merely accidental and undeterminable sequences; his 'A Traveler from Altruria,' the most definite and comprehensive expression of his social ideals; and his 'Letters of an Altrurian Traveler,' describing from the view-point of a Socialist the characteristics of the plutocratic city of New York, have set many thousands of minds forward on the right path.

From the *Literary Digest,* XVI (March 19, 1898), 340-41.

"A realist in fiction, he has not, like one branch of the school of realism, descended to the depicting of the darker and more vicious attributes of certain abnormal types of humankind, nor, like another branch of that school, painted merely the superficial emotions and activities of better types; he has pictured for us our own time, the struggle of mankind one against another and against all others, in the fierce battle for bread; he has urged the obligation of brotherhood upon all of us, and has shown us the goal of a practicable, attainable Utopia. At the head of American *litterateurs,* he has not temporized with, nor glossed over, nor praised the false sentiments and beliefs which pass current for wisdom and morality among the selfish and unthinking, tho he well may have known that acquiescence therein would be to his material advantage; he has, on the contrary, used his tremendous power toward the shattering of these entrenched falsities, and has striven to awaken in his readers the spirit of the new ideals. Particular abuses were sought to be corrected by Dickens, Thackeray, and George Eliot. But the social purpose of these writers is far below the splendid aim of Howells, who attacks the whole economic framework of modern society."

Concerning Mr. Howells's conversion to Socialistic views and the degree to which he how holds them, the editor of *The Fabian* gives the following account:

" 'It was ten years ago,' said Mr. Howells the other day, 'that I first became interested in the creed of Socialism. I was in Buffalo when Laurence Gronlund lectured there before the Fortnightly Club. Through this address I was led to read his book, "The Cooperative Commonwealth," and Kirkup's article in the Encyclopedia Britannica. Afterward I read the "Fabian Essays"; I was greatly influenced also by a number of William Morris's tracts. The greatest influence, however, came to me through reading Tolstoi. Both as an artist and as a moralist I must acknowledge my deep indebtedness to him."

" 'But you do not recognize a close affinity between Tolstoi's doctrine and that of modern Socialism?' was asked. 'For instance, in "A Traveler from Altruria," you deny the right of a man to do wrong to others with what is his own, and would use repression to prevent it.'

" 'Tolstoi's influence is on the moral side,' he replied. 'I recognize the impractibility of much of his ethics. Yet he has the logic of the situation. As has been said of another, "he is logical, but not reasonable." The idea of force is repellent to me. I would not use it when it can be avoided. The extreme to which Tolstoi would carry non-resistance to violence, I cannot, of course, share in. Yet there have been, and are, cases of those who, either as individuals or sects, have held to non-resistance and have not been exterminated. Think of the persecution of the Quakers. Yet, despite it, they have thrived.'

" 'True, but should not one recognize that, temporary persecutions in the earlier days excepted, the Quakers have always been protected by force? The individual Quaker living in England or America is protected from invasion of his rights by the whole force, civil and military, of the government under which he lives. Supposing a community of Quakers were placed in a neutral strip of ground between three powerful nations hungry for their expropriation. What would become of them?'

" 'Oh, yes, their case would be different. They would doubtless lose their independence (which they might not mind), and probably also they would be cruelly exploited. As I said, the idea of force and compulsory obedience is repellent to me; still, the weak must be protected and justice to all be assured. It may be said that with so much existent use of force—cruel, extra-legal, and ill-regulated—it becomes necessary to oppose it with a beneficent, altruistic, corrective force.'

" 'What are the prospects for Socialism in America?' was asked.

" 'As to that, who can say? One sees the movement advancing all about him, and yet it may be years before its ascendency. On the other hand, it may be but a short time. A slight episode may change history. A turn here or a turn there, and we may find our nation headlong on the road to the ideal commonwealth.' "

1902

The majority of articles about Howells in the twentieth century are written by academic scholars. This essay by Brander Matthews is one of the first. It is also one of the earliest to focus upon Howells as a critic.

Brander Matthews was graduated from Columbia University in 1871. His appointment to a chair of dramatic literature at Columbia in 1900 was the first of its kind in America. He remained there until 1924, five years before his death. During a life devoted to literature, he published, in addition to many critical essays, short fiction, plays, and novels.

BRANDER MATTHEWS

Mr. Howells as a Critic

"IN THESE latter days there is no artist who is not also a critic," so Turgenef once wrote to Flaubert; "in you the artist is very great, and you know how much I admire him, and love him; but I have also a high idea of the critic, and I am very happy to have his approval." It was in a private letter that the French novelist thus expressed his favorable opinion of the Russian, for neither of them was ever an open practitioner of the art of criticism. That they both kept for their friends their final convictions as to the true aim of the modern novel and as to the degree of success with which this ideal had been attained by one or another of their contemporaries and predecessors, and that they both refused resolutely to discuss in public the principles which underlie the fascinating craft of the story-teller—this reserve was very likely advantageous to the reception of their own works, since each of these was taken for what it was, and it was not required to be an exemplification of any theory which its author

From the *Forum,* XXXII (January, 1902), 629-38.

might have set forth in analyzing the narratives of some other novelist. This reticence from criticism had the further advantage for Flaubert and for Turgenef that they avoided arousing against their own books the noisy animosity of the ardent admirers of every dead and gone novelist, whose fading pages they might, perhaps, have failed to laud as loudly as ignorant partisanship would demand.

This voluntary self-exclusion from the arena of literary debate may have been for the immediate advantage of the two novelists themselves; but it was indisputably to the disadvantage of the rest of us, who wanted to be as fully enlightened as to Turgenef's theory of fiction, as we had been, or were to be, informed about M. Zola's and Mr. Henry James's and Robert Louis Stevenson's. We should have been glad to know Flaubert's opinion about the art which he found so despairingly difficult and to which he devoted himself with so Benedictine a determination. To those of us who are keenly interested in any art, there is never any criticism so suggestive and so interpretative as that of the artist himself. Where is there any inquiry into the principles of painting so penetrative and so subtle as Fromentin's—unless perhaps it is Mr. John La Farge's? Where is there any discussion of the elusive art of acting so acute and so stimulating as Cibber's—unless it is Mr. Joseph Jefferson's? Of a truth the critics are not "those who have failed in literature and art"; rather are they those who have succeeded; and when accomplished craftsmen are willing to talk freely about their calling, the rest of us had best keep silent and profit by what we can pick up.

It is well that we should be reminded now and again why it is that the artist always has precedence over the critic. Indeed, the artist must come first, or else the critic would have no subject-matter. All that the critic can be expected to do is to study the masterpieces in a vain search for the secret of their lasting beauty. And for this task, so difficult and so delicate, none are so fit as those fellow-craftsmen who happen also to have the faculty of articulate expression. Not every artist's opinion is worth having; for he may lack philosophy to understand not only his own processes, but even his own aims. It is not easy even for the intelligent artist—and how few artists, pictorial or literary, are really intelligent!—to disentangle the principles which, when he is at work, he is forever applying consciously or unconsciously or subconsciously. But even from those who have only a limited insight into their own methods and who have no firm grasp of the vital principles of their art, there is sometimes something to be gleaned by which the cautious enquirer can benefit. The contribution of any single artist may be narrow; and more often than not his theory will be found to be only an attempt to expound his own practice: it will discover itself only as the result of his own way of doing things, and not as the cause. The criticism of a fellow-craftsman is rarely without the color of a fellow-feeling; and we cannot fairly expect it to be achromatic. But none the less ought we to be able to profit by it.

Of all the American authors at the opening of the new century, Mr. Howells is easily the most multifarious. It is as a novelist that he has presented himself most frequently; but he has also attempted the stage, although no one of his original dramas has had the good fortune to establish itself in the theatre. He has revealed himself as a poet of sombre imaginations, not made visible elsewhere in his works. He has given us a series of charming books of travel. He is one of the most delightful of our essayists, with an exquisite felicity of phrase, akin to Heine's. He is one of the most delicate of our humorists, with a reserve that recalls Hawthorne's. And he is a constant critic of contemporary literature, gracious of manner and courteous of phrase, except when expressing his scorn of what seems to him unworthy, mean, and base.

Such of his critical writing as he has selected for the brief immortality of a book is contained in half a dozen volumes. The first of these, published in 1887, was given up to sympathetic appreciations of the "Modern Italian Poets"; and it is perhaps the closest approach he has ever made to criticism of the more formal and academic type. Acceptable as the volume was to readers of cosmopolitan culture, it was necessarily without the personal note which has made his later opinions more interesting to the average American, who has only a languid liking for the literature of other languages. This personal note was struck firmly in the tiny tome called "Criticism and Fiction," which was published in 1891. In this little book, made up out of earlier articles then first set in order, Mr. Howells said boldly what he thought about certain idols of the market-place; and probably no one was more surprised than he at the turmoil he created. To many placid creatures of habit, the publication of this little book was very like the explosion of a bomb in a reading-room; and the reverberation has not yet died out.

Most of us like to move through life along the line of least resistance; and we are inclined to resent any sudden call to think out the reasons for our opinions. Mr. Howell's declaration of the faith that was in him could not fail to shock many a prevalent prejudice; and at times his manner was not so persuasive as it might be—if, indeed, it was not fairly to be described as frankly aggressive. Himself free from the vulgar superstition of admiration for things once admired but no longer admirable, Mr. Howells wasted no perfunctory praise on what he had described as "those classics common to all languages —dead corpses which retain their forms perfectly in the coffin, but crumble to dust as soon as exposed to the air." He did not foresee that his plain speech about these unwholesome inheritances from our fathers would savor of impiety; that it would seem to some almost like a violation of the sanctity of the tomb.

As so often happens in cases of like character, when we go back to see what it was that caused all this commotion half a score of years ago, we have some difficulty in discovering just where the dynamite was concealed. We see that the little book is plainly too insistent in its tone, too intolerant of the dullards, too impatient with those who persist in liking the things they ought not to like and in disliking the things they ought not to dislike, and who have no health in them. But it is not so very iconoclastic after all, even if we do detect a desire to "speak disrespectfully of the equator." At bottom all that Mr. Howells had done was to voice once again the demand that art, and more especially the art of fiction, should deal with life simply, naturally, and honestly. This has ever been the watch-cry of the younger generation in every century. It is what the more open-minded of mankind have been striving for ever since the earliest of critics was able to compare the second artist with the first to the disadvantage of the second. A protest against sham and shoddy, a plea for sincerity, it could not help being very like the hundreds of other pleas and protests, apologies and prefaces, with which the histories of literature are filled.

Mr. Howells's plea and protest was straightforward and plain spoken. The novelist should deal truthfully with his material, which is human life in all its breadth and in all its depth. He should not sophisticate it, nor should he in any wise attempt to idealize it. He is to be a witness sworn to tell the truth, the whole truth, and nothing but the truth. "The object of a novel should be to charm through a faithful representation of human actions and human passions, and to create by this fidelity to nature a beautiful work"—according to the pertinent dictum which Mr. Howells translated from Señor Valera. The novelist should deal with the mean of human life, and not with the exceptional, the abnormal, the monstrous, or else he will surely violate just proportion and present but a distorted vision of the world as it really is.

Above all, he will set up no false ideals of self-sacrifice, of heroism, of strength, of passion; for who is the novelist that he shall presume to improve upon human nature as it is? It was Emerson who said with his pithy shrewdness that "the foolish man wonders at the unusual, but the wise man at the usual"; and Carlyle it was who declared that for grown persons reality was the only genuine romance. The novelist must not falsify the simpler and saner ideals. He must refrain from the wild, the visionary, the exaggerated, the freakish. He must deal with the man as he sees him and with woman as he sees her; observing carefully, with whatever insight and imagination he may have, and then recording faithfully the things of good report and the things of evil report. He must keep his pages free from the hectic flush, which follows when passion is exalted above principle. Though he must needs show sin and sorrow and suffering, he can never palter with the everlasting standards of right and wrong.

Before any work of the imagination there is one imperative question: "Is it true—true to the motives, the impulses, the principles that shape the life of actual men and women?" And "this truth," Mr. Howells declares, "which necessarily includes the highest morality and the highest artistry—this truth given, the book cannot be wicked and cannot be weak; and without it all graces of style and feats of invention and cunning of construction are so many superfluities of naughtiness." Although this is more pungently put, there is nothing so new in this, nothing that many earlier writers had not striven to say as best they could; and, had Mr. Howells confined himself to preaching again the eternal verities, it may be that this sermon of his would have aroused as few of his auditors from their slumbers as other sermons are wont to do.

But Mr. Howells waked up the congregation by making a direct personal application of his principles—by naming names, by pointing out how Scott and Dickens and Thackeray had strayed from the path of truth. Then the British journalists, always supersensitive to American criticism, rose in their rage and emptied the vials of their wrath on the head of the American novelist, as they had years before cried out shrilly at a chance remark of an American romancer. Mr. Howells had instant proof of the pertinence of his own remark that "whatever is established is sacred for those who do not think." Not only did the rash American writer bring out the defects of the sacredly established Scott and Dickens and Thackeray, but he dared to express his own preference for Jane Austen and for Anthony Trollope. He even went farther, and said boldly that certain Russians and Spaniards and Italians set a better example than any then to be had in the English language.

The same beliefs inspired the next volume of criticism, a book far less polemic in tone, or at least less militant, but quite as individual and as sturdy. "My Literary Passions," published in 1895, was pleasantly novel in form; it was a discursive record of the fleeting impressions made on Mr. Howells as he had discovered for himself one after another of the authors the world has agreed to accept as great. It was frankly an attempt to set down the personal equation. All criticism must be more or less autobiographic, even when the writer is most confident that he has succeeded in stepping off his own shadow. Nowadays it savors of conceit for any critic to maintain that he has been able to take himself out of the way, and that he is merely the medium through which the final judgment of mankind is expressing itself. "The adventures of one's soul in contact with masterpieces"—this is one of M. Anatole France's definitions of criticism; and it is good that a critic should have a soul, and better that he should keep it in contact with masterpieces as constantly as may be. In "My Literary Passions" Mr. Howells was as little academic as M. France himself; and he was also as sympathetic and as honest. He was aiming not so much to warn us against what he held to be noxious as to help us to enjoy what he found most refreshing and most nourishing.

Autobiographic also was the volume called "Literary Friends and Acquaintance," which was issued in 1900. In this personal retrospect Mr. Howells began by chronicling his first visit to New England and his earlier impressions of New York and Boston. Then he set down conversations, and a summary of their characteristics likely still further to increase the affection in which they are held. No other appreciations have been lightened by a more graceful vivacity. To the young man from the West these were the giants of the East, to be approached as Heine approached Goethe. That they were his countrymen made them only the more worthy of devotion, for the years of residence abroad had not denaturalized Mr. Howells. Even now he is not cosmopolitan, except in his artistic equipment, in his aesthetic inspiration; he is intensely American, irresistibly American; and he is never conceivably anything else.

"Heroines of Fiction" is the title of Mr. Howells's latest series of essays in criticism, and there is ingenious novelty in its scheme. It is an attempt to sketch the development of the fiction of our language in the nineteenth century by centring the attention of the reader upon the heroines, upon the fair creatures whom the heroes love and who by them are beloved again. It is a study of the evolution of the modern novel in which the stages of advance are marked by the increase in the insight, the sympathy, and the skill with which the successive masters have been able to body forth the ever-womanly. Mr. Howells holds that "a novel is great or not, as its women are important or unimportant." He holds also that truth is the one thing needful, and he is therefore not surprised to discover in his wanderings down the history of fiction that "apparently the ever-womanly refuses herself to the novelist who proposes anything but truth to nature; apparently she cannot trust him. She may not always be so very sincere herself, but she requires sincerity in the artist who would take her likeness, and it is only in the fiction of one who faithfully reports his knowledge of things seen that she will deign to show her face, to let her divine presence be felt. That is the highest and best fiction, and her presence is the supreme evidence of its truth to the whole of life."

"Heroines of Fiction" is as candid and as uncompromising as "Criticism and Fiction;" but it is far mellower in tone and its touch is almost caressing, as is becoming in a book pervaded by the presence of the ever-womanly. It is insinuating often, and it is rarely so rasping as was the earlier declaration of the same doctrine. It is more likely to win readers to think for themselves—and perhaps even to think scorn of themselves for their former relish for the quasi-romantic and the pseudo-heroic. Of course, it would be easy enough to detach judgments certain to evoke shrill protests from amiable readers too indolent to do their own thinking. It will be a shock to some to see George Eliot and Anthony Trollope set up as more representative British novelists than Dickens and Thackeray, as it will surprise others to note that Fielding portrays characters of a certain kind with "blackguardly sympathy." It must be confessed that this last phrase is doubtfully felicitous; and, even when we understand why it was uttered, we may still wonder whether it was not too one-sided, not to call it unfair. Apparently what Mr. Howells resents is the hearty animality of "Tom Jones," the rank coarseness of its masculinity.

On the other hand, Mr. Howells is tolerant toward Richardson, who seems on the whole sickly, whereas Fielding was on the whole healthy, as the barnyard is after all more wholesome than the hothouse. Fielding drew men as he saw them, clearly and honestly, while Richardson was above all a master of feminine psychology. Perhaps this accounts for the odd preference of Mr. Howells, who, although he has drawn men of a convincing veracity like Silas Lapham and Bartley Hubbard, has delighted especially in an analysis and a synthesis of woman. So also we may deem him unduly harsh in his condemnation of Thackeray for the confidential attitude which was perfectly natural to the author of "Vanity Fair," while he shows himself strangely tolerant toward Trollope, in whose works this confidential attitude is a borrowed artifice which some readers find perpetually exasperating. Trollope, again, whatever his merits, which were many and various, had one irredeemable vice—he was forever confessing carelessly that it was only a fiction he was telling. For a novelist this is the unpardonable sin.

Mr. Howells stands on less debatable ground when he is exposing the slovenliness of Scott's style and structure, and when he is calling attention to the thin theatricalism of Dickens in those scenes of empty effectiveness in which the author of the "Tale of Two Cities" revelled with an enjoyment that seemed almost sensuous. Mr. Howells has the firm earth beneath his feet, he is standing on the everlasting rock, when he protests against the "idiotic and detestable self-sacrifice" which "is preached in fiction," and when he points out that Lady Castlewood, already conscious that she does not love Esmond any longer as a son, is falsely made to promote his passion for her daughter. "This is a little too repulsive for belief"; just as in Dickens's tale we now reject what we once accepted, "the atrocious and abominable notion of Sidney Carton seeking to be guillotined in place of the husband of the woman he loves." And, as Mr. Howells says in another part of the book, it is well for the author to force his readers to think, which they do unwillingly, but which is often the best thing they can do; "to feel is comparatively cheap and easy."

The limitations of Mr. Howells's criticism are not merely the limits of his likings. He is no drifting impressionist with never an anchor to windward. He has a solid body of doctrine; he has a creed of his own to serve as a test. But his criticism, like that of most other critics, is at its best when it is affirmative rather than negative. It is most useful and significant when it is constructive, and its utility is least when it is most destructive; and here again it is like that of most other critics. It is profitable for us to be reminded that it was Maria Edgeworth and Jane Austen, estimable maids with a delicious sense of humor, transcending the ordinary portion of woman, that first "imagined the heroine who was above all a Nice Girl"—the Nice Girl "who still remains the ideal of our fiction" and "to whom it returns, with final constancy, after whatever aberration." It is advantageous to have it clearly stated that "in fiction women exist in the past, present, or future tense, the infinitive, indicative, potential, or imperative mood of love-making"; or "otherwise they do not exist at all, and no phantom of delight, masquerading in their clothes, suffices."

It is valuable to have our attention called to the fact that it was Charles Reade who first "perceived that there is something feline in every woman," and that "he also divined that in many and perhaps in most cases she wishes to use the arts of the cat for no worse purpose than getting a soft place in a man's soul and sweetly purring there." It is instructive to be told that "novelists ought not to have their favorites among their creations; as parents ought not to have their favorites among their children"; and there is no denying that "George Eliot has her preferences most distinctly" and that "she pursues some of her women with a rancor as perceptible as her fondness for others." And it is very suggestive to have it made plain that Trollope "has not shown the subtlest sense of womanhood; his portraits do not impart the last, the most exquisite joy; it is not the very soul of the sex that shows itself in them; but it is the mind, the heart, the conscience, the manner; and this is for one painter enough. Let Jane Austen catch their ultimate charm, and George Eliot their ultimate truth, and Hawthorne their farthermost meaning and intimations; Trollope has shown them as we mostly see them when we meet them in society and as we know them at home."

These quotations serve to show that Mr. Howells's criticism is often technical, not of structure only—although his technical criticism of form is abundant and acute—but more often of the handling of character; and after all it is by the handling of character that a novelist stands or falls. His form may be faulty and his manner may be careless—and here are two of the defects of the earliest very great novel, "Don Quixote." But if he can handle character so as to give the reader the full impression of life, then has he a chance of immortality. Other things he needs also, but this one is essential. It is because Cervantes could handle character with a large certainty and with searching imagination that "Don Quixote" survives, and even the slovenly conduct of the story cannot prevent. Scott, Dickens, and Thackeray could also handle character, each in his several way; and this is why they have been enrolled among the masters of fiction, even though no one of them had said the final word of his art, any more than Cervantes had said it.

However great Scott was, and Dickens, and Thackeray, they were none of them perfect artists; they were great in spite of gross derelictions from the highest standard. This is what Mr. Howells has tried to make plain even to careless readers; and it is for making this plain that careless readers are not willing to forgive him. Nothing is more certain to arrest progress than a smug satisfaction with the past—unless it is a slavish copying of the inferior models bequeathed to us by our more primitive predecessors. Nothing is more helpful than a clear understanding of the merits and of the demerits of the early masters. The merits are obvious enough, but the demerits need to be discovered and declared before they can serve as warnings. It is not a paradox but a truism that the art of fiction is a finer art to-day than it was when Thackeray was writing—just as it was a finer art in Thackeray's time than it was when Cervantes was writing. As Mr. Howells puts it pithily, it was the misfortune of Balzac that he "lived too soon to profit by Balzac"; and so Cervantes had lived too soon to profit by Cervantes. Those who refuse blindly to see any blemishes in the art of Balzac or of Cervantes, those who persist in upholding Scott and Dickens and Thackeray as impeccable artists, need to be reminded that ancestor-worship is no longer esteemed the highest form of religion.

It may be said that Mr. Howells has sometimes seemed somewhat over-strenuous in dwelling upon the errors and the mistakes of the earlier masters; and this charge may be admitted without hesitation. He has had to combat accepted opinions, and the combative mood tempts us to an over-statement of our own case and an under-statement of that of our opponents; and quite possibly Mr. Howells has yielded to this temptation oftener than needful. It has been urged also that Mr. Howells has shown himself careless of proportion, in that he has over-praised certain of his contemporaries while over-dispraising certain of his predecessors; and it may be admitted that this charge has now and then some slight evidence in its favor. Just as he drew attention to the defects of certain novelists of the past, so also he drew attention to the beauty and the truth which he saw in the work of certain writers of the present, and which the duller senses of the public had not recognized adequately. But they are very careless readers indeed who have asserted that Mr. Howells really sets up Mr. J. W. DeForest as the rival of Thackeray and that he holds Mr. H. B. Fuller as an equal of Balzac. They are not only careless, but perhaps a little stupid also, and even a trifle malevolent.

Yet, as the majority of readers, even of criticism, are always more or less careless, it may be that Mr. Howells himself has not been careful enough in the use of his scale. If by his inadvertence he has aroused animosity, where by a greater caution he might have won adherence, it is greatly to be regretted, not so much for his sake as for the sake of the readers themselves, who may allow prejudice to prevent their acceptance of the doctrines which Mr. Howells is setting forth. These doctrines may seem new in some of their applications, but they are old and eternal; they are rooted in the truth, and the truth will surely prevail.

Mr. Howells does not declare his theories merely to celebrate himself, as M. Zola has been accused of doing. He declares them rather because his character is forever forcing him to bear witness to the truth as he sees it. In criticism as in fiction character counts for as much as talent—in fact, character is an element of talent. It matters little whether Mr. Howells is dealing with the art and mystery of novel-writing or whether he is himself applying the secrets of the craft; we get the same impression of the man—a man of a large nature and of a transparent sincerity, liberal in his appreciations, loyal to his convictions, and little hampered by mere academic restrictions.

1906

Howells had no closer friend than Mark Twain. From the time of their first meeting in 1869, shortly after Howells had favorably reviewed Innocents Abroad, *until Mark Twain's death in 1910, they were frequently together, either in person or through correspondence. Howells' close friendship with both Mark Twain and Henry James discloses the breadth of his personal sympathies. Similar breadth in his literary sympathies helped make him central to literature from the Civil War until the turn of the century. This essay is the longest published comment by Mark Twain on Howells. The criticism is not incisive, and its turn to a close examination of style may suggest to some that Mark Twain, failing to be deeply stirred by Howells' work in other respects, found it convenient to turn to that which he and most of the literary world could admire without reservation. Such a surmise would not be justified.* The Mark Twain-Howells Letters *(ed. by Henry Nash Smith and William Gibson, 1960) show Mark Twain keenly responsive to Howells' work over the years. A letter from Mark Twain in 1885 began, "You are really my only author..." Shortly after the essay reprinted below first appeared, Howells wrote F. A. Duneka: "What magnificent praise Clemens has given me! Since I came a man nothing has touched me more."*

S. L. CLEMENS

William Dean Howells

IS IT TRUE that the sun of a man's mentality touches noon at forty and then begins to wane toward setting? Doctor Osler is charged with saying so. Maybe he said it, maybe he didn't; I don't know which it is. But if he said it, I can point him to a case which proves his rule. Proves it by being an exception to it. To this place I nominate Mr. Howells.

I read his *Venetian Days* about forty years ago. I compare it with his paper on Machiavelli in a late number of *Harper,* and I cannot find that his English has suffered any impairment. For forty years his English has been to me a continual delight and astonishment. In the sustained exhibition of certain great qualities—clearness, compression, verbal exactness, and unforced and seemingly unconscious felicity of phrasing—he is, in my belief, without his peer in the English-writing world. *Sustained.* I intrench myself behind that protecting word. There are others who exhibit those great qualities as greatly as does he, but only by intervaled distributions of rich moonlight, with stretches of veiled and dimmer landscape between; whereas Howells' moon sails cloudless skies all night and all the nights.

In the matter of verbal exactness Mr. Howells has no superior, I suppose. He seems to be almost always able to find that elusive and shifty grain of gold, the *right word.* Others have to put up with approximations, more or less frequently; he has better luck. To me, the others are miners working with the gold-pan—of necessity some of the gold washes over and escapes; whereas, in my fancy, he is quicksilver raiding down a riffle—no grain of the metal stands much chance of eluding him. A powerful agent is the right word: it lights the reader's way and makes it plain; a close approximation to it will answer, and much traveling is done in a well-enough fashion by its help, but we do not welcome it and applaud it and rejoice in it as we do when *the* right one blazes out on us. Whenever we come upon one of those intensely right words in a book or a newspaper the resulting effect is physical as well as spiritual, and electrically prompt; it tingles exquisitely around through the walls of the mouth and tastes as tart and crisp and good as the autumn-butter that creams the sumacberry. One has no time to examine the word and vote upon its rank and standing, the automatic recognition of its supremacy is so immediate. There is a plenty of acceptable literature which deals largely in approximations, but it may be likened to a fine landscape seen through the rain; the right word would dismiss the rain, then you would see it better. It doesn't rain when Howells is at work.

And where does he get the easy and effortless flow of his speech? and its cadenced and undulating rhythm? and its architectural felicities of construction, its graces of expression, its pemmican quality of compression, and all that? Born to him, no doubt. All in shining good order in the beginning, all extraordinary; and all just as shining, just as extraordinary to-day, after forty years of diligent wear and tear and use. He passed his fortieth year long and long ago; but I think his English of today—his perfect English, I wish to say—can throw down the glove before his English of that antique time and not be afraid.

I will go back to the paper on Machiavelli now, and ask the reader to examine this passage from it which I append. I do not mean examine it in a bird's-eye way; I mean search it, study it. And, of course, read it aloud. I may be wrong, still it is my conviction that one cannot get out of finely wrought literature all that is in it by reading it mutely:

Mr. Dyer is rather of the opinion, first luminously suggested by Macaulay, that Machiavelli was in earnest, but must not be judged as a political moralist of our time and race would be judged. He thinks that Machiavelli was in earnest, as none but an idealist can be, and he is the first to imagine him an idealist immersed in realities, who involuntarily transmutes the events under his eye into something like the visionary issues of reverie. The Machiavelli whom he depicts does not cease to be politically a republican and socially a just man because he holds up an atrocious despot like Cesare Borgia as a mirror for rulers. What Machiavelli beheld round him in Italy was a civic disorder in which there was oppression without statecraft, and revolt without patriotism. When a miscreant like Borgia appeared upon the scene and reduced both tyrants and rebels to an apparent quiescence, he might very well seem to such a dreamer the savior of society whom a certain sort of dreamers are always looking for. Machiavelli was no less honest when he honored the diabolical force of Cesare Borgia than Carlyle was when at different times he extolled the strong man who destroys liberty in creating order. But Carlyle has only just ceased to be mistaken for a reformer, while it is still Machiavelli's hard fate to be so trammeled in his material that his name stands for whatever is most malevolent and perfidious in human nature.

You see how easy and flowing it is; how unvexed by ruggednesses, clumsinesses, broken meters; how simple and—so far as you or I can make out—unstudied; how clear, how limpid, how understandable, how unconfused by cross-currents, eddies, undertows; how seemingly unadorned, yet is all adornment, like the lily-of-the-valley; and how compressed, how compact, without a complacency-signal hung out anywhere to call attention to it.

There are twenty-three lines in the quoted passage. After reading it several times aloud, one perceives that a good deal of matter is crowded into that small space. I think it is a model of compactness. When I take its materials apart and work them over and put them together in my way, I find I cannot crowd the result back into the same hole, there not being room enough. I find it a case of a woman packing a man's trunk: he can get the things out, but he can't ever get them back again.

The proffered paragraph is a just and fair sample; the rest of the article is as compact as it is; there are no waste words. The sample is just in other ways: limpid, fluent, graceful, and rhythmical as it is, it holds no superiority in these respects over the rest of the essay. Also, the choice phrasing noticeable in the sample is not lonely; there is a plenty of its kin distributed through the other paragraphs. This is claiming much when that kin must face the challenge of a phrase like the one in the middle sentence: "an idealist immersed in realities who involuntarily transmutes the events under his eye into something like the visionary issues of reverie." With a hundred words to do it with, the literary artisan could catch that airy thought and tie it down and reduce it to a concrete condition, visible, substantial, understandable and all right, like a cabbage; but the artist does it with twenty, and the result is a flower.

The quoted phrase, like a thousand others that have come from the same source, has the quality of certain scraps of verse which take hold of us and stay in our memories, we do not understand why, at first: all the words being the right words, none of them is conspicuous, and so they all seem inconspicuous, therefore we wonder what it is about them that makes their message take hold.

> The mossy marbles rest
> On the lips that he has prest
>   In their bloom,
> And the names he loved to hear
> Have been carved for many a year
>   On the tomb.

It is like a dreamy strain of moving music, with no sharp notes in it. The words are all "right" words, and all the same size. We do not notice it at first. We get the effect, it goes straight home to us, but we do not know why. It is when the right words are conspicuous that they thunder:

> The glory that was Greece and the grandeur that was Rome!

When I go back from Howells old to Howells young I find him arranging and clustering English words well, but not any better than now. He is not more felicitous in concreting abstractions now than he was in translating, then, the visions of the eyes of flesh into words that reproduced their forms and colors:

> In Venetian streets they give the fallen snow no rest. It is at once shoveled into the canals by hundreds of half-naked *facchini;* and now in St. Mark's Place the music of innumerable shovels smote upon my ear; and I saw the shivering legion of poverty as it engaged the elements in a struggle for the possession of the Piazza. But the snow continued to

fall, and through the twilight of the descending flakes all this toil and encounter looked like that weary kind of effort in dreams, when the most determined industry seems only to renew the task. The lofty crest of the bell-tower was hidden in the folds of falling snow, and I could no longer see the golden angel upon its summit. But looked at across the Piazza, the beautiful outline of St. Mark's Church was perfectly penciled in the air, and the shifting threads of the snowfall were woven into a spell of novel enchantment around the structure that always seemed to me too exquisite in its fantastic loveliness to be anything but the creation of magic. The tender snow had compassionated the beautiful edifice for all the wrongs of time, and so hid the stains and ugliness of decay that it looked as if just from the hand of the builder—or, better said, just from the brain of the architect. There was marvelous freshness in the colors of the mosaics in the great arches of the facade, and all that gracious harmony into which the temple rises, of marble scrolls and leafy exuberance airily supporting the statues of the saints, was a hundred times etherealized by the purity and whiteness of the drifting flakes. The snow lay lightly on the golden globes that tremble like peacock-crests above the vast domes, and plumed them with softest white; it robed the saints in ermine; and it danced over all its work, as if exulting in its beauty—beauty which filled me with subtle, selfish yearning to keep such evanescent loveliness for the little-while-longer of my whole life, and with despair to think that even the poor lifeless shadow of it could never be fairly reflected in picture or poem.

Through the wavering snowfall, the Saint Theodore upon one of the granite pillars of the Piazzetta did not show so grim as his wont is, and the winged lion on the other might have been a winged lamb, so gentle and mild he looked by the tender light of the storm. The towers of the island churches loomed faint and far away in the dimness; the sailors in the rigging of the ships that lay in the Basin wrought like phantoms among the shrouds; the gondolas stole in and out of the opaque distance more noiselessly and dreamily than ever; and a silence, almost palpable, lay upon the mutest city in the world.

The spirit of Venice is there: of a city where Age and Decay, fagged with distributing damage and repulsiveness among the other cities of the planet in accordance with the policy and business of their profession, come for rest and play between seasons, and treat themselves to the luxury and relaxation of sinking the shop and inventing and squandering charms all about, instead of abolishing such as they find, as is their habit when not on vacation.

In the working season they do business in Boston sometimes, and a character in *The Undiscovered Country* takes accurate note of pathetic effects wrought by them upon the aspects of a street of once dignified and elegant homes whose occupants have moved away and left them a prey to neglect and gradual ruin and progressive degradation; a descent which reaches bottom at last, when the street becomes a roost for humble professionals of the faith-cure and fortune-telling sort.

> What a queer, melancholy house, what a queer, melancholy street! I don't think I was ever in a street before where quite so many professional ladies, with English surnames, preferred Madam to Mrs. on their door-plates. And the poor old place has such a desperately conscious air of going to the deuce. Every house seems to wince as you go by, and button itself up to the chin for fear you should find out it had no shirt on—so to speak. I don't know what's the reason, but these material tokens of a social decay afflict me terribly: a tipsy woman isn't dreadfuler than a haggard old house, that's once been a home, in a street like this.

Mr. Howells's pictures are not mere stiff, hard, accurate photographs; they are photographs with feeling in them, and sentiment, photographs taken in a dream, one might say.

As concerns his humor, I will not try to say anything, yet I would try, if I had the words that might approximately reach up to its high place. I do not think any one else can play with humorous fancies so gracefully and delicately and deliciously as he does, nor has so many to play with, nor can come so near making them look as if they were doing the playing themselves and he was not aware that they were at it. For they are unobtrusive, and quiet in their ways, and well conducted. His is a humor which flows softly all around about and over and through the mesh of the page, persuasive, refreshing, healthgiving, and makes no more show and no more noise than does the circulation of the blood.

There is another thing which is contentingly noticeable in Mr. Howells's books. That is his "stage directions"—those artifices which authors employ to throw a kind of human naturalness around a scene and a conversation, and help the reader to see the one and get at meanings in the other which might not be perceived if intrusted unexplained to the bare words of the talk. Some authors overdo the stage directions, they elaborate them quite beyond necessity; they spend so much time and take up so much room in telling us how a person said a thing and how he looked and acted when he said it that we get tired and vexed and wish he hadn't said it at all. Other authors' directions are brief enough, but it is seldom that the brevity contains either wit or information. Writers of this school go in rags, in the matter of stage directions; the majority of them have nothing in stock but a cigar, a laugh, a blush, and a bursting into tears. In their poverty they work these sorry things to the bone. They say:

"... replied Alfred, flipping the ash from his cigar." (This explains nothing; it only wastes space.)

"... responded Richard, with a laugh." (There was nothing to laugh about; there never is. The writer puts it in from habit—automatically; he is paying no attention to his work, or he would see that there is nothing to laugh at; often, when a remark is unusually and poignantly flat and silly, he tries to deceive the reader by enlarging the stage direction and making Richard break into "frenzies of uncontrollable laughter." This makes the reader sad.)

"... murmured Gladys, blushing." (This poor old shop-worn blush is a tiresome thing. We get so we would rather Gladys would fall out of the book and break her neck than do it again. She is always doing it, and usually irrelevantly. Whenever it is her turn to murmur she hangs out her blush; it is the only thing she's got. In a little while we hate her, just as we do Richard.)

"... repeated Evelyn, bursting into tears." (This kind keep a book damp all the time. They can't say a thing without crying. They cry so much about nothing that by and by when they have something to cry *about* they have gone dry; they sob, and fetch nothing; we are not moved. We are only glad.)

They gravel me, these stale and overworked stage directions, these carbon films that got burnt out long ago and cannot now carry any faintest thread of light. It would be well if they could be relieved from duty and flung out in the literary back yard to rot and disappear along with the discarded and forgotten "steeds" and "halidomes" and similar stage-properties once so dear to our grandfathers. But I am friendly to Mr. Howells's stage directions; more friendly to them than to any one else's, I think. They are done with a competent and discriminating art, and are faithful to the requirements of a stage direction's proper and lawful office, which is to inform. Sometimes they convey a scene and its conditions so well that I believe I could see the scene and get the spirit and meaning of the accompanying dialogue if some one would read merely the stage directions to me and leave out the talk. For instance, a scene like this, from *The Undiscovered Country:*

"...and she laid her arms with a beseeching gesture on her father's shoulder."

"...she answered, following his gesture with a glance."

"...she said, laughing nervously."

"...she asked, turning swiftly upon him that strange, searching glance."

"...she answered, vaguely."

"...she reluctantly admitted."

"...but her voice died wearily away, and she stood looking into his face with puzzled entreaty."

Mr. Howells does not repeat his forms, and does not need to; he can invent fresh ones without limit. It is mainly the repetition over and over again, by the third-rates, of worn and commonplace and juiceless forms that makes their novels such a weariness and vexation to us, I think. We do not mind one or two deliveries of their wares, but as we turn the pages over and keep on meeting them we presently get tired of them and wish they would do other things for a change:

"... replied Alfred, flipping the ash from his cigar."

"... responded Richard, with a laugh.' '

"... murmured Gladys, blushing."

"... repeated Evelyn, bursting into tears."

"... replied the Earl, flipping the ash from his cigar."

"... responded the undertaker, with a laugh."

"... murmured the chambermaid, blushing."

"... repeated the burglar, bursting into tears."

"... replied the conductor, flipping the ash from his cigar."

"... responded Arkwright, with a laugh."

"... murmured the chief of police, blushing."

"... repeated the house-cat, bursting into tears."

And so on and so on; till at last it ceases to excite.

I always notice stage directions, because they fret me and keep me trying to get out of their way, just as the automobiles do. At first; then by and by they become monotonous and I get run over.

Mr. Howells has done much work, and the spirit of it is as beautiful as the make of it. I have held him in admiration and affection so many years that I know by the number of those years that he is old now; but his heart isn't, nor his pen; and years do not count. Let him have plenty of them: there is profit in them for us.

1912

Comparison of this essay done in the high Jamesian style with James's essay of 1886 reveals how far both James and Howells had traveled in thirty years. This essay and the previous one in this collection show the distance between Henry James and Mark Twain in their literary practices and in their responses to Howells. Somehow, Howells was able to maintain the friendship and respect of both. The occasion for this letter was Howells' seventy-fifth birthday. By this time, both Howells and James could feel that a new generation of writers and critics was leaving them behind. As James prophesied, the "really beautiful time" of both was yet to come.

HENRY JAMES

A Letter to Mr. Howells

IT IS made known to me that they are soon to feast in New York the newest and freshest of the splendid birthdays to which you keep treating us, and that your many friends will meet round you to rejoice in it and reaffirm their allegiance. I shall not be there, to my sorrow; and, though this is inevitable, I yet want to be missed, peculiarly and monstrously missed, so that these words shall be a public apology for my absence: read by you, if you like and can stand it, but, better still, read *to* you and, in fact, straight *at* you by whoever will be so kind and so loud and so distinct. For I doubt, you see, whether any of your toasters and acclaimers have anything like my ground and title for being with you at such an hour. There can scarce be one, I think, to-day who has known you from so far

---

From the *North American Review,* CXCV (April, 1912), 558-62. Reprinted with the permission of Charles Scribner's Sons and of Paul R. Reynolds & Son from *The Letters of Henry James,* II (ed. Percy Lubbock).

back, who has kept so close to you for so long, and who has such fine old reasons—so old, yet so well preserved—to feel your virtue and sound your praise. My debt to you began well-nigh half a century ago in the most personal way possible, and then kept growing and growing with your own admirable growth—but always rooted in the early intimate benefit. This benefit was that you held out your open editorial hand to me at the time I began to write—and I allude especially to the summer of 1866—with a frankness and sweetness of hospitality that was really the making of me, the making of the confidence that required help and sympathy and that I should otherwise, I think, have strayed and stumbled about a long time without acquiring. You showed me the way and opened me the door; you wrote to me and confessed yourself struck with me—I have never forgotten the beautiful thrill of *that.* You published me at once—and paid me, above all, with a dazzling promptitude; magnificently, I felt, and so that nothing since has ever quite come up to it. More than this even, you cheered me on with a sympathy that was in itself an inspiration. I mean that you talked to me and listened to me—ever so patiently and genially and suggestively conversed and consorted with me. This won me to you irresistibly and made you the most interesting person I knew—lost as I was in the charming sense that my best friend was an editor, and an almost insatiable editor, and that such a delicious being as that was a kind of property of my own. Yet how didn't that interest still quicken and spread when I became aware that—with such attention as you could spare from us, for I recognized my fellow-beneficiaries—you had started to cultivate *your* great garden as well; the tract of virgin soil that, beginning as a cluster of bright, fresh, sunny, and savory patches close about the house, as it were, was to become that vast goodly pleasaunce of art and observation, of appreciation and creation, in which you have labored, without a break or a lapse, to this day, and in which you have grown so grand a show of—well, really of everything. Your liberal visits to *my* plot and your free-handed purchases there were still greater events when I began to see you handle, yourself, with such ease the key to our rich and inexhaustible mystery. Then the question of what you would make of your own powers began to be even more interesting than the question of what you would make of mine —all the more, I confess, as you had ended by settling this one so happily. My confidence in myself, which you had so helped me to, gave way to a fascinated impression of your own spread and growth, for you broke out so insistently and variously that it was a charm to watch and an excitement to follow you. The only drawback that I remember suffering from was that *I*, your original debtor, couldn't print or publish or pay you—which would have been a sort of ideal of *re*payment and of enhanced credit; you could take care of yourself so beautifully, and I could (unless by some occasional happy chance or rare favor) scarce so much as glance at your proofs or have a glimpse of your "endings." I could only read you, full-blown and finished, always so beautifully finished—and see, with the rest of the world, how you were doing it again and again.

That, then, was what I had with time to settle down to—the common attitude of seeing you do it again and again; keep on doing it, with your heroic consistency and your noble, genial abundance, during all the years that have seen so many apparitions come and go, so many vain flourishes attempted and achieved, so many little fortunes made and unmade, so many weaker inspirations betrayed and spent. Having myself to practise meaner economies, I have admired from period to period your so ample and liberal flow; wondered at your secret for doing positively a little—what do I say, a little? I mean a magnificent deal!—of Everything. I seem to myself to have faltered and languished, to have missed more occasions than I have grasped, while you have piled up your monument just by remaining at your post. For you have had the advantage, after all, of breathing an air that has suited and nourished you; of sitting up to your neck, as I may say—or at least up to your waist—amid the sources of your inspiration. There and so you were at your post; there and so the spell could ever work for you, there and so your relation to all your material grow closer and stronger, your perception penetrate, your authority accumulate. They make a great array, a literature in themselves, your studies of American life so acute, so direct, so disinterested, so preoccupied but with the fine truth of the case; and the more attaching to me always for their referring themselves to a time and an order when we knew together what American life *was*—or thought we did, deluded though we may have been! I don't pretend to measure the effect or to sound the depths, if they be not the shallows, of the huge wholesale importations and so-called assimilations of this later time; I only feel and speak for those conditions in which, as "quiet observers," as careful painters, as sincere artists, we could still in our native, our human and social element, know more or less where we were and feel more or less what we had hold of. You knew and felt these things better than I; you had learned them earlier and more intimately, and it was impossible, I think, to be in more instinctive and more informed possession of the general truth of your subject than you happily found yourself. The *real* affair of the American case and character, as it met your view and brushed your sensibility, that was what inspired and attached you, and, heedless of foolish flurries from other quarters, of all wild or weak slashings of the air and wavings in the void, you gave yourself to it with an incorruptible faith. You saw your field with a rare lucidity: you saw all it had to give in the way of the romance of the real and the interest and the thrill and the charm of the common, as one may put it; the character and the comedy, the point, the pathos, the tragedy, the particular homegrown humanity under your eyes and your hand and with which the life all about you was closely interknitted. Your hand reached out to these things with a fondness that was in itself a literary gift and played with them as the artist only and always can play: freely, quaintly, incalculably, with all the assurance of his fancy and his irony, and yet with that fine taste for the truth and the pity and the meaning of the matter which keeps the temper of observation both sharp and sweet. To observe by such an instinct and by such reflection is to find work to one's hands and a challenge in every bush; and as the familiar American scene thus bristled about you, so year by year your vision more and more justly responded and swarmed. You put forth *A Modern Instance,* and *The Rise of Silas Lapham,* and *A Hazard of New Fortunes,* and *The Landlord at Lion's Head,* and *The Kentons* (that perfectly classic illustration of your spirit and your form) after having put forth in perhaps lighter-fingered prelude *A Foregone Conclusion,* and *The Undiscovered Country,* and *The Lady of the Aroostook,* and *The Minister's Charge* —to make of a long list too short a one; with the effect again and again of a feeling for the human relation, as the social climate of our country qualifies, intensifies, generally conditions and colors it, which, married in perfect felicity to the expression you found for its service, constituted the originality that we want to fasten upon you as with silver nails to-night. Stroke by stroke and book by book your work was to become for this exquisite notation of our whole democratic light and shade and give and take in the highest degree *documentary,* so that none other, through all your fine long season, could approach it in value and amplitude. None, let me say, too, was to approach it in essential distinction; for you had grown master, by insidious practices best known to yourself, of a method so easy and so natural, so marked with the personal element of your humor and the play, not less personal, of your sympathy, that the critic kept coming on its secret connection with the grace of letters much as Fenimore Cooper's Leatherstocking—so knowing to be able to do it!—comes in the forest on the subtle tracks of Indian braves. However, these things take us far, and what I wished mainly to put on record is my sense of that unfailing, testifying truth in you which will keep you from ever being neglected. The critical intelligence—if any such fitful and discredited light may still be conceived as within our sphere—has not at all begun to render you its tribute. The more inquiringly and perceivingly it shall still be projected upon the American life we used to know, the more it shall be moved by the analytic and historic spirit, the more indispensable, the more a vessel of light, will you be found. It's a great thing to have used one's genius and done one's work with such quiet and robust consistency that they fall by their own weight into that happy service. You may remember perhaps, and I like to recall, how the great and admirable Taine, in one of the fine excursions of his French curiosity, greeted you as a precious painter and a sovereign witness. But his appreciation, I want you to believe with me, will yet be carried much further, and then—though you may have argued yourself happy, in your generous way and with your incurable optimism, even while noting yourself not understood—your really beautiful time will come. Nothing so much as feeling that he may himself perhaps help a little to bring it on can give pleasure to yours all faithfully,

HENRY JAMES

1917

Howells recognized in the last years of his life that the literary movement he had helped start was no longer friendly to him. "I am a comparatively dead cult with my statues cut down and the grass growing over them in the pale moonlight," he wrote to Henry James. His eminence as dean of American letters was as much a call to ridicule as to respect. Sharp as is H. L. Mencken's attack on Howells, it is also one of the most readable essays ever written about him. It appeared originally in the Smart Set *for January, 1917, two months before the celebration of Howells' eightieth birthday.*

H. L. MENCKEN

The Dean

AMERICANS, obsessed by the problem of conduct, usually judge their authors, not as artists, but as citizens, Christians, men. Edgar Allan Poe, I daresay, will never live down the fact that he was a periodical drunkard, and died in an alcoholic ward. Mark Twain, the incomparable artist, will probably never shake off Mark Twain, the after-dinner comedian, the flaunter of white dress clothes, the public character, the national wag. As for William Dean Howells, he gains rather than loses by this confusion of values, for, like the late Joseph H. Choate, he is almost the national ideal: an urbane and highly respectable old gentleman, a sitter on committees, an intimate of professors and the prophets of movements, a worthy vouched for by both the *Atlantic Monthly* and Alexander Harvey, a placid conformist. The result is his general acceptance as a member of the literary peerage, and of the rank of earl at least. For twenty years

From *Prejudices, First Series* (New York, 1919), pp. 52-58. By permission of Alfred A. Knopf, Inc.

past his successive books have not been criticized, nor even adequately reviewed; they have been merely fawned over; the lady critics of the newspapers would no more question them than they would question Lincoln's Gettysburg speech, or Paul Elmer More, or their own virginity. The dean of American letters in point of years, and in point of published quantity, and in point of public prominence and influence, he has been gradually enveloped in a web of superstitious reverence, and it grates harshly to hear his actual achievement discussed in cold blood.

Nevertheless, all this merited respect for an industrious and inoffensive man is bound, soon or late, to yield to a critical examination of the artist within, and that examination, I fear, will have its bitter moments for those who naively accept the Howells legend. It will show, without doubt, a first-rate journeyman, a contriver of pretty things, a clever stylist—but it will also show a long row of uninspired and hollow books, with no more ideas in them than so many volumes of the *Ladies' Home Journal,* and no more deep and contagious feeling than so many reports of autopsies, and no more glow and gusto than so many tables of bond prices. The profound dread and agony of life, the surge of passion and aspiration, the grand crash and glitter of things, the tragedy that runs eternally under the surface—all this the critic of the future will seek in vain in Dr. Howells' elegant and shallow volumes. And seeking it in vain, he will probably dismiss all of them together with fewer words than he gives to "Huckleberry Finn."...

Already, indeed, the Howells legend tends to become a mere legend, and empty of all genuine significance. Who actually reads the Howells novels? Who even remembers their names? "The Minister's Charge," "An Imperative Duty," "The Unexpected Guests," "Out of the Question," "No Love Lost"—these titles are already as meaningless as a roll of Sumerian kings. Perhaps "The Rise of Silas Lapham" survives—but go read it if you would tumble downstairs. The truth about Howells is that he really has nothing to say, for all the charm he gets into saying it. His psychology is superficial, amateurish, often nonsensical; his irony is scarcely more than a polite facetiousness; his characters simply refuse to live. No figure even remotely comparable to Norris' McTeague or Dreiser's Frank Cowperwood is to be encountered in his novels. He is quite unequal to any such evocation of the race-spirit, of the essential conflict of forces among us, of the peculiar drift and color of American life. The world he moves in is suburban, caged, flabby. He could no more have written the last chapters of "Lord Jim" than he could have written the Book of Mark.

The vacuity of his method is well revealed by one of the books of his old age, "The Leatherwood God." Its composition, we are told, spread over many years; its genesis was in the days of his full maturity. An examination of it shows nothing but a suave piling up of words, a vast accumulation of nothings. The central character, one Dylks, is a backwoods evangelist who acquires a belief in his own buncombe, and ends by announcing that he is God. The job before the author was obviously that of tracing the psychological steps whereby this mountebank proceeds to that conclusion; the fact, indeed, is recognized in the canned review, which says that the book is a "study of American religious psychology." But an inspection of the text shows that no such study is really in it. Dr. Howells does not *show* how Dylks came to believe himself God; he merely *says* that he did so. The whole discussion of the process, indeed, is confined to two pages—172 and 173—and is quite infantile in its inadequacy. Nor do we get anything approaching a revealing look into the heads of the other converts—the saleratus-sodden, hell-crazy, half-witted Methodists and Baptists of a remote Ohio settlement of seventy or eighty years ago. All we have is the casual statement that they are converted, and begin to offer Dylks their howls of devotion. And when, in the end, they go back to their original bosh, dethroning Dylks overnight and restoring the gaseous vertebrate of Calvin and Wesley—when this contrary process is recorded, it is accompanied by no more illumination. In brief, the story is not a "study" at all, whether psychological or otherwise, but simply an anecdote, and without either point or interest. Its virtues are all negative ones; it is short, it keeps on the track, it deals with a religious maniac and yet contrives to offer no offense to other religious maniacs. But on the positive side it merely skims the skin.

So in all of the other Howells novels that I know. Somehow, he seems blissfully ignorant that life is a serious business, and full of mystery; it is a sort of college town *Weltanschauung* that one finds in him; he is an Agnes Repplier in pantaloons. In one of the later stories, "New Leaf Mills," he makes a faltering gesture of recognition. Here, so to speak, one gets at least a sniff of the universal mystery; Howells seems about to grow profound at last. But the sniff is only a sniff. The tragedy, at the end, peters out. Compare the story to E. W. Howe's "The Story of a Country Town," which Howells himself has intelligently praised, and you will get some measure of his own failure. Howe sets much the same stage and deals with much the same people. His story is full of technical defects—for one thing, it is overladen with melodrama and sentimentality. But nevertheless it achieves the prime purpose of a work of the imagination: it grips and stirs the emotions, it implants a sense of something experienced. Such a book leaves scars; one is not quite the same after reading it. But it would be difficult to point to a Howells book that produces any such effect. If he actually tries, like Conrad, "to make you hear, to make you feel—before all, to make you *see*," then he fails almost completely. One often suspects, indeed, that he doesn't really feel or see himself. . . .

As a critic he belongs to a higher level, if only because of his eager curiosity, his gusto in novelty. His praise of Howe I have mentioned. He dealt valiant licks for other debutantes: Frank Norris, Edith Wharton and William Vaughn Moody among them. He brought forward the Russians diligently and persuasively, albeit they left no mark upon his own manner. In his ingratiating way, back in the seventies and eighties, he made war upon the prevailing sentimentalities. But his history as a critic is full of errors and omissions. One finds him loosing a fanfare for W. B. Trites, the

Philadelphia Zola, and praising Frank A. Munsey—and one finds him leaving the discovery of all the Shaws, George Moores, Dreisers, Synges, Galsworthys, Phillipses and George Ades to the Pollards, Meltzers and Hunekers. Busy in the sideshows, he didn't see the elephants go by.... Here temperamental defects handicapped him. Turn to his "My Mark Twain" and you will see what I mean. The Mark that is exhibited in this book is a Mark whose Himalayan outlines are discerned but hazily through a pink fog of Howells. There is a moral note in the tale—an obvious effort to palliate, to touch up, to excuse. The poor fellow, of course, was charming, and there was talent in him, but what a weakness he had for thinking aloud—and such shocking thoughts! What oaths in his speech! What awful cigars he smoked! How barbarous his contempt for the strict sonata form! It seems incredible, indeed, that two men so unlike should have found common denominators for a friendship lasting forty-four years. The one derived from Rabelais, Chaucer, the Elizabethans and Benvenuto—buccaneers of the literary high seas, loud laughers, law-breakers, giants of a lordlier day; the other came down from Jane Austen, Washington Irving and Hannah More. The one wrote English as Michelangelo hacked marble, broadly, brutally, magnificently; the other was a maker of pretty waxen groups. The one was utterly unconscious of the way he achieved his staggering effects; the other was the most toilsome, fastidious and self-conscious of craftsmen....

What remains of Howells is his style. He invented a new harmony of "the old, old words." He destroyed the stately periods of the Poe tradition, and erected upon the ruins a complex and savory carelessness, full of naïvetés that were sophisticated to the last degree. He loosened the tightness of English, and let a blast of Elizabethan air into it. He achieved, for all his triviality, for all his narrowness of vision, a pungent and admirable style.

Part II

Critical Studies Since 1920

I. The Howells Revival

IT SHOULD *not be said that Howells, at his death in 1920, was completely forgotten except as an object of scorn. D. G. Cooke's critical study appeared in 1922, and O. W. Firkins' excellent* William Dean Howells *in 1924. Yet the tributes at his death and after came from members of the older generation, from long-time acquaintances, or from younger authors Howells had befriended. The rising generation of writers—Fitzgerald, Hemingway, Dos Passos—had scarcely heard of him. Academic critics kept his reputation alive during the twenties, but they stimulated few people to read Howells' books.*

In 1930, Sinclair Lewis retouched the portrait Mencken had left, saying, in his Nobel Prize speech, "Mr. Howells was one of the gentlest, sweetest, and most honest of men, but he had the code of a pious old maid whose greatest delight was to have tea at the vicarage." C. Hartley Grattan's essay of the same year reached much the same conclusion, but it showed a more careful and thorough reading of Howells' works than either Mencken or Lewis had troubled himself with. The essay is included here (as first published, though there are some minor mistakes in titles and names) because it raises questions about the essential weaknesses in Howells' fiction which are still difficult to answer. Mr. Grattan is not an academic man, but a practicing man of letters. He published his first essay (on James Russell Lowell) in Mencken's American Mercury *just after the magazine was founded. His chief literary work is* The Three Jameses: A Family of Minds *(1932).*

From 1930 on, most of the critical articles about Howells call attention to his virtues or, accepting his worth as established, closely pursue topics of special interest to literary scholars. The author of the second article in this section, Herbert Edwards, was an assistant professor at Ohio State University when the piece was published. It appeared in the scholarly journal, American Literature, *then in its third year. Both facts emphasize the importance of universities and formal academic studies in the revival of interest in Howells' work.*

The third of these essays, also by an academic scholar and critic, appeared in the New Republic *in 1937. By this time it was possible to see that the deprecation of Howells in the twenties was not to be the final verdict. Without inflating Howells' achievements, Mr. Arvin pointed out what has now become a commonplace, that "Howells is one of the decisive figures in the development of our literary culture." At the time this essay was written, Mr. Arvin was teaching at Smith where he has been a faculty member from 1922 to the present. He has published biographies of Hawthorne, Whitman, and Melville, in addition to much critical writing for various periodicals.*

The final essay is by Edwin Cady, now on the faculty at Indiana University. Since this essay was published, Professor Cady has amplified and modified his views in his two-volume biography of Howells, The Road to Realism *and* The Realist at War, *completed in 1958. In drawing attention to Howells' neuroticism, Professor Cady's article probably made Howells a more interesting literary figure to modern critics sensitive to the relationship between art and neuroses.*

C. HARTLEY GRATTAN

Howells: Ten Years After

WILLIAM DEAN HOWELLS placed himself accurately in relation to his predecessors in American literature when he said at his seventy-fifth birthday dinner in 1912: "I knew Hawthorne and Emerson and Walt Whitman; I knew Longfellow and Holmes and Whittier and Lowell; I knew Bryant and Bancroft and Motley; I knew Harriet Beecher Stowe and Julia Ward Howe; I knew Artemus Ward and Stockton and Mark Twain; I knew Parkman and Fiske." Four years later he could have spoken of his intimate friend, Henry James, in the past tense also. If we add that he was born (in 1837) before the deaths of Poe, Irving, and Cooper it will be seen that his lifetime touched all of the important American writers. His own first book appeared in 1860 and his last posthumously in 1920. In 1916 he recorded, in commenting bitterly on a rejection, that he could look back on "fifty years of inevitable acceptance." His constant friendliness enabled him to meet the young men of his last days. He was friendly, for example, with Hamlin Garland, Booth Tarkington and Brand Whitlock. He was kind to Stephen Crane. He was interviewed by Van Wyck Brooks. Thus his lifetime spanned almost the whole course of American literature, while he was active himself for sixty years. There is no other American literary career of anything approaching the same length.

He originated in frontier Ohio, and, attaching himself to New England, became the heir and assign of the Boston tradition and the first "foreign" editor of the *Atlantic Monthly.* He was typical of the early frontier writer in that he took color from the dominant culture of the community in which he aspired to make a place. It

From the *American Mercury,* XX (May, 1930), 42-50. By permission.

was as necessary for a writer from the frontier to do that as it was for a frontier social aspirant to adopt his manners to the urban amenities. Howells' position is further defined when it is noted that he was the first American writer to undertake realistic fiction. There were plenty of earlier writers of fiction, but they were either not theoretical realists or not pure fictionists. Lastly, as a critic he was among the earliest to make contemporary foreign literatures common intellectual currency in this country, especially the literatures of Russia, Spain, and Italy, and he wielded an incalculable influence in giving a realistic (as he understood it) color to American reading. In the last analysis it may turn out that he was more important to the history of American taste than to the history of American literature.

In fact, his extrinsic literary importance is so great that it is easy to forget his intrinsic unimportance. If that seems paradoxical it is because the truth about the man was always paradoxical. As a fiction writer he brought out more than forty volumes, and it was as a novelist that he chiefly sought recognition. He professed to be a realist deriving his doctrines from Europe, somewhat from Zola but more especially from the Spanish writers. He had a high admiration for the Russian novelists, especially Turgenev, for long his *beau ideal,* Tolstoi, his final admiration, and Dostoievsky. Sir Edmund Gosse accurately defined his true relation to European realism in the phrase, "he was shaken by the wind of Zola's doctrine." But when it reached Howells it was little more than a breeze.

A novel to him was not a matter of plot, nor was it an interpretation of life, nor a temperamental reaction to life, but a transcription with a minimum of interference by the personality of the transcriber. Detachment was the theoretical essence of his method. A novel was a piece of life, neatly rounded off and put into a book. In actuality, his work is simply a reflection of his own temperamental limitations and of the literary prejudices of his environment. That is proved when we consider this definition of what he did not do, made by one of his most ardent admirers:

In these forty volumes, adultery is never pictured; seduction never; divorce once and sparingly; marriage discordant to the point of cleavage, only once and in the same novel with divorce; crime only once with any fulness; politics never; religion passingly and superficially; science only in crepuscular psychology; mechanics, athletics, bodily exploits or collisions, very rarely.

II

Howells was born and brought up in a community which was but little less of a frontier settlement than the community which nourished Mark Twain. Yet no one ever thinks of calling him a frontier writer. If we recall, however, that Henry James fled in despair from what he regarded as the hopeless crudities of Cambridge and went to England, and that to Howells these same crudities represented an equal advance in civilization over his homeland, the nature of his early environment is more obvious.

When he got to Boston he thought himself in Valhalla. He never tried to escape America, yet when he abandoned the frontier he cut himself off from the most fundamental sources of his possible literary strength. For while it may profit an artist to remove himself from his environment temporarily for perspective, it profits him nothing to abandon his environment altogether for another which he considers "better." The fundamental environment returns to haunt him as it did Henry James, and as it did Edgar Lee Masters' Archibald Higbie.

In 1895 Howells confessed that "my own youth seems to me rather more alien than that of any other person"; yet he was able to record in the completest detail his early literary experiences, or, as he for some reason or other called them, passions. But if reading was his passion and his life, it gave him no identification with his environment and no standing in it. The last career to be justified in a frontier community is the literary career, and it takes a strong personality to make literature a lifework in the face of environmental hostility.

Howells did not have a robust personality; so he sought the company of women who were most sympathetic to literary interests, and escaped the situation altogether as soon as he could. "I have a feeling," he wrote, "of something like treason to the men I knew at that time, when I own that I preferred the society of women to theirs." He thus increased his deflection from actuality by reading what women would, in those days, read, and by building up an attitude which later ruled him completely: he was a life-long slave to the young girl bugaboo in literature. In his later days his wife was his censor. "She became with her unerring artistic taste and conscience my constant impulse toward reality and sincerity in my work." He began to believe in the end that no books should be written and no classics republished which would "offend the modesty of a pure woman."

When he settled in Boston he was thoroughly prepared to accept the traditional culture of that exhausted community. In spite of the fact that he came from the frontier and was theoretically a barbarian, his whole mental set was alien to the iconoclasm which would have led him to perceive the limitations of his new environment. Because he was so thoroughly detached from the frontier he failed to see that the only real vitality in America was in the region from which he had come. While the drive of American society was westward, he was retreating to the East, and even to Boston, which was more of a backwater than, say, New York City. Thus he left a christening to attend a funeral. His attempt to make a place for himself in what was still the chief cultural center of America would not have been so unfortunate had he taken a realistic attitude toward the matter. But instead of trying to infuse some new vitality into a moribund society, he accepted it as it stood. How thoroughly he fell in with Boston may be judged by the fact that at the Whittier birthday dinner in 1877 it was he who was most severely shocked by Mark Twain's celebrated speech.

Like any convert, he became more Bostonian than the Bostonians. His deferential and uncritical attitude was clearly betrayed in "Literary Friends and Acquaintances." He accepted Boston as the be-all and end-all of civilization, and Boston judgments became his judgments. He never perceived that the Boston attitudes and manners, like any other, were but temporary congelations of human adaptations. That he never penetrated the surface of the town is clearly shown by his books, which judge all problems, trivial and profound, in terms of the Boston *mores*. The emphasis is always on Boston alone; the rest of the Yankees, who were equally decadent with the Bostonians, appear but fleetingly in his fiction, and always in the background. He saw that these Yankees were decadent, as one may determine from the opening pages of "Mrs. Farrell"; but he never essayed the inadequacies of Boston.

Howells was a victim of circumstances. The frontier community failed to give satisfactory approval to the literary type that he represented, and he was to discover that in Boston he was a "foreigner" socially. For however he may have been accepted among the writers, he never got into society. In "The Quality of Mercy" he makes it clear that writers were not countenanced socially *qua* writers and that when they did get in it was because of non-literary circumstances. Having no standing among men of action and no standing socially, a writer could justify himself only by a firm literary creed. Howells, however, was always afraid of himself; even so early as 1880, Moncure Conway, in a review of "Poems by Two Friends" (Howells and Piatt), printed in the *Dial,* noted as his chief weakness "a certain fear of himself." He was haunted by a feeling of victimization, and once wrote:

> My reading gave me no standing among the boys, and I did not expect it to rank me with boys who were more valiant in fight or in play; and I have since found that literature gives one no more certain station in the world of men's activities, either idle or useful. We literary folk try to believe that it does, but that is all nonsense. At every period of life, among boys or men, we are accepted when they are at leisure, and want to be amused, and at best we are tolerated rather than accepted.

Since he was "tolerated rather than accepted" it was natural that he should do nothing to offend the prejudices of his audience. He therefore avoided all subjects on which it was touchy. He wrote nothing about sexual maladjustment or adventure (although he confessed archly in "Indian Summer" that "after eighteen hundred years, the man is still imperfectly monogamous"), or on religion, and his attitude toward business we shall shortly examine. Not only did he avoid sex in his own novels, but he wanted all others to avoid it too. As late as 1916 he proclaimed himself "Victorian in my preference for decency."

The truth is that, while he was "as much of a realist as I could be," he had a paralyzing distaste for anything which offended him personally, and he denied all such matters a place in his fiction. Thus, by temperamental limitations, he was debarred from penetrating below the superficial manners of society, and by environmental deflections was carried still further from reality. He commented plaintively on the situation, but expressed his revolt only in his garden-party Socialism. He had no penetrative understanding of American society, and so his Socialism is more an expression of finical dislike than anything else. As D. G. Cooke puts it: "Those who in his novels wage war on Dryfooses (business men) and gimcrackeries do so for the most part in the Utopian manner."

It tells one little to know that he read and studied foreign writers, particularly, at the last, Tolstoi, for in some curious fashion he was able to dissociate reading from practice. He was in the position of a professor of historical sociology in "The Vacation of the Kelwyns": "He was a very well-read and careful scholar in his department of historical sociology—with no thought of applying his science to his own life and conduct." While Howells wanted the Russians read in this country he did not want American society portrayed in their fiercely veridic fashion. As an academic critic concludes in disgust: "In our country [according to Howells] we write for young ladies. Is not that a pretty box in which to shut our budding Tolstoi! Grown-up Americans may have their Flaubert and Zola, because the books can be locked up; but let our writers continue to write realism for young ladies!"

Yet Howells sought his chief justification as realist in the novels of European writers: in those of Turgenev "who was of that great race which has more than any other fully and freely uttered human nature, without either false pride or false shame in its nakedness"; in Palacio Valdes, whose "Marta y Maria" he considered "one of the most truthful and profound fictions I have read"; and in, to conclude briefly, Verga's "I Malavaglia," "a story of infinite beauty, tenderness, and truth." Of Tolstoi he confessed to Van Wyck Brooks, "As a writer I have not been influenced by him—my work has no trace of his influence." Elsewhere he wrote that Tolstoi "has given many of his readers a bad conscience, and a bad conscience is the best thing a man can have." From Tolstoi, then, Howells got a bad conscience; but what a singular reason for reading him! Not only is there a contradiction between Howells' reading and his practice, but there is as sharp a contradiction between the books he recommended and his own view of life. His view was singularly passionless, not to say tepid. In "The World of Chance" he wrote: "Our common notion of tragedy is that it alters the nature of those involved, as if it were some spiritual chemistry combining the elements of character anew. But it is merely an incident in our being, and, for all we can perceive, is of no more vital effect than many storms in the material world." Is not that view of life contradicted by, to mention no others, "Marta y Maria" and "I Malavaglia"?

Howells felt strongly that he was merely tolerated by his social "superiors" yet he hastened to endorse their view of society. His Socialism amounts to nothing in the last analysis. His recorded views clearly indicate his failure to see the real America of his day. Because he could or would not see tragedy and brutality in American life, (as the *bourgeoisie* also could not see it) he concluded that it was not there. It is altogether probable that he could not readily find such things in Boston, but that was certainly untrue of America at large. Even he, indeed, discovered corruption in Boston business ("The Quality of Mercy").

This novel pertinently illustrates his limitations as a social novelist: he deals at length with the moral corruption of the peculator, but not at all with his business life. One never knows what his mills make. In spite of the fact that Howells knew that Northwick's "gentlemanly decorum and grave repose of manner masked a complete ignorance of the things that interest cultivated people, and that he was merely and purely a business man, a figment of commercial civilization, with only the crudest tastes and ambitions outside the narrow circle of money-making," he was willing to accept the tolerance of the class he represented. Of America he wrote in 1891:

It is one of the reflections suggested by Dostoievsky's novel, "Crime and the Punishment," that whoever struck a note so profoundly tragic in American fiction would do a false and mistaken thing—as false and as mistaken in its way as dealing in American fiction with certain nudities which the Latin peoples seem to find edifying. Whatever their deserts, very few American novelists have been led out to be shot, or exiled to the rigors of a Winter at Duluth; and in a land where journeymen carpenters and plumbers strike for four dollars a day the sum of hunger and cold is comparatively small, and the wrong from class to class has been almost inappreciable, though all this is changing for the worse. Our novelists, therefore, concern themselves with the most smiling aspects of life, which are the more American, and seek the universal in the individual rather than the social interests.

It is worth-while even at the risk of being called commonplace, to be true to our well-to-do actualities; the very passions themselves seem to be softened and modified by conditions which formerly at least could not be said to wrong any one, to cramp endeavor, or to cross lawful desire. Sin and suffering and sham there must always be in the world, I suppose, but I believe that in this new world of ours it is still mainly from one to another one, and oftener still from one to one's self. We have death too in America, and a great deal of disagreeable and painful disease, which the multiplicity of our patent medicines does not seem to cure; but this is tragedy that comes in the very nature of things, and is not peculiarly American, as the large, cheerful average of health and happy life is. It will not do to boast, but it is well to be true to the facts, and to see that, apart from these purely mortal troubles, the race here has enjoyed conditions in which most of the ills that have darkened its annals might be averted by honest work and unselfish behavior.

The America that Howells is talking about is the America between the close of the Civil War and the date of the quotation. During those years labor and capital organizations struck their roots into American life. It was a period of decided and often tragic social maladjustment. Not to go outside fiction for evidence, one may refer to Frank Harris' tragedy of social revolt, "The Bomb"; White's "Book of Daniel Drew," and to the novels of Henry B. Fuller and Theodore Dreiser. All these writers derived their material from this period and discovered in it tragedy, passion, and dramatic struggle. Even Fuller, whose talent was slight, perceived in the welter of commercial Chicago a tragedy of the artistic personality and called it "On the Stairs," and a tragedy of social pushing and called it "The Cliff-Dwellers." What prevented Howells from seeing literary material in the hurly-burly of American industrial and commercial life — the fundamental life of the day—was simply his complete deflection from reality. The result is that his view of America is scarcely distinguishable from Andrew Carnegie's, whose attitude was that of the triumphant *bourgeoisie.* Howells was their novelist.

III

It should not be supposed that his limitations were not perceived by his contemporaries. As far back as 1880 W. C. Brownell permitted himself some caustic reflections in the *Nation.* He noted a certain lack of virility in the Howells' men; he pointed out that "cuteness" was the dominant characteristic of his women; and that there was "a certain slenderness at the pith" of the novels. Brownell proposed *roman de société* as the proper designation for the Howells novel. And Barrett Wendell, who was certainly not given to deprecation of New Englanders, real or adopted, noted his "timidity." Frank Norris, as a literary rebel, characterized him as being as "respectable as a church and proper as a deacon." Nevertheless the prevailing attitude was one of deference. The deference paid him was indeed colossal.

What he did as a novelist is our chief concern here. Though he wrote forty, I believe that he may be adequately measured by seven novels: "A Modern Instance" (1881), "The Rise of Silas Lapham" (1885), "Indian Summer" (1886), "A Hazard of New Fortunes" (1890), "The Landlord at Lion's Head" (1889), "The Kentons" (1902), and "The Son of Royal Langbrith" (1904). These are not all successes, even of the Howells method, but they are representative. In them it is possible to discover his range and power as a writer of fiction.

In "A Modern Instance" he made, as Professor Firkins puts it, his single venture at portraying "divorce . . . sparingly . . . and marriage discordant to the point of cleavage." An unsophisticated country girl marries a young go-getter just out of college. They settle in Boston, and Bartley Hubbard exhibits in journalism his alleged lack of moral stamina. His penchant is toward yellow journalism. In addition, he takes up beer drinking and puts on some soggy fat. On one occasion he actually gets drunk. By thus offending his wife's stiff Yankee morality he makes his marriage "discordant to the point of cleavage."

To complicate matters, Ben Halleck, a college friend of Hubbard's, loves Mrs. Hubbard and deplores her situation. Halleck is a Boston aristocrat. Hubbard cleaves the marriage by running away. After months of debate Mrs. Hubbard determines to find her husband and divorce him. Her final determination is precipitated after she discovers that he has himself instituted proceedings. Mrs. Hubbard is a typical Howells woman. Her long delay is occasioned by her absurd loyalty to her husband as a husband. She is also "unworldly" (a merit in the Howells view of women) as to be blind to his caddishness. For Hubbard is not really, as Howells tries to make out, a moral degenerate. The evidence for that is too feeble: beer drinking, getting fat and a penchant for yellow journalism. He is simply a bounder. Once divorce is determined upon it is pushed through with the assistance of Ben Halleck.

The questions of the novel are two, and both of them could only be problems in an extremely special, limited, and narrow social situation. The first is whether divorce is ever justified, which is decided in the affirmative, though a divorced woman, it is indicated, must reconcile herself to losing social caste. The second is whether a man should marry a woman he has loved before her divorce, while she was another man's wife—loved unavowedly and at a distance. This is decided in the negative.

I have summarized this novel at length because it is as fundamental in its human basis as any effort of Howells', and because it is so obvious that the counters in his thinking were the conventions of bourgeois society. In "A Modern Instance" there is no probing of human life and character, but only a measuring of both by social prejudices and conventions. Once those prejudices and conventions shift in nature or emphasis, the novel loses heavily in significance. It illustrates accurately the fallacy of the Howells method, which sacrificed the penetrating analysis of mankind to accuracy in the rendition of externals. In seeking to look closely at the "insipid face" of real life, Howells captured the temporary insipidities and missed the fundamental realities.

It has been remarked that in "The Quality of Mercy" there is no emphasis on business; all the emphasis is personal. That is strictly in line with Howells' principle that an American novelist must "seek the universal in the individual." In "The Rise of Silas Lapham" there is the same personal emphasis, and the same avoidance of business. Though the fundamental aspect of Lapham's career is his rise from poverty to comparative business success, it is definitely and decidedly subordinated to a problem in hothouse social conduct. This problem is, in O. W. Firkin's summary, "whether a girl may decently marry the man she loves if the joint anticipations of two families have previously bestowed him on a consenting sister." The same use of business as a subordinate background occurs in "The Son of Royal Langbrith." The son reveres his father as a saint, though the father cheated the father of the girl the son loves out of thousands of dollars and drove him to opium, and for years kept a mistress. The problem of the story is whether or not the son should be saved from his parental adulation by a revelation of the truth. The revelation is made accidentally by a cynical uncle, but the Howells verdict seems to be that all concerned should have kept still.

Equally trivial problems, occasioned by the confusion of the transient with the permanent, may be discovered in the other novels. "A Hazard of New Fortunes" has a little more bulk and beam. Though it illustrates, along with "The Story of a Play" and "The World of Chance," the abominable triviality of Howells' conception of the novel, it also contains his best pictures of industrial conflict. In no other story does he show so clearly his social sympathy with the workers. Further, in his portrait of the vulgar, newly rich Dryfooses he well displays the foolish intolerance and emptiness of the self-made business man. But here as elsewhere the lack of any fundamental conception of social revolt—either its expression or its genesis—is apparent. The reverse side of Howells' social radicalism is shown in his anaemic, ladylike Utopian romances, "A Traveller from Altruria" and "Through the Eye of the Needle." His attitude toward ameliorative activities comes out in "Annie Kilburne"; it is noncommittal.

Since it was his conviction that the American novelist should "seek the universal in the individual," we may reasonably look for an outstanding portrait of an individual in his work. The novel which comes nearest to supplying it is "The Landlord at Lion's Head," where the protagonist is Jeff Durgin. In spite of the fact that qualifications must be made, Jeff Durgin is the best character in Howells. He originates in a degenerate New England country family which, under the direction of an energetic mother, transfers its attention from farming to summer hotel-keeping. Young Durgin is destined for Harvard, the law, and respectability. Because of supposedly fundamental defects of personality he achieves none of these except the Harvard degree, and that only when pressed to it.

His defects are predatory cupidity, selfishness, boorishness, and caddishness. Obviously, predatory cupidity characterizes the more gross sort of American business man. It is an important characteristic of Dreiser's Frank Cowperwood. Howells, however, does not portray Durgin in business; he was unable to do so, as we have seen. His conception of the man must be derived more from his comment than it is from the man's actions.

That fact marks the outstanding weakness of his character drawing, here and elsewhere. For the actions he instances as evidence of a character's goodness or badness never seem to warrant either evaluation. Durgin is put down as selfish because he places his own comfort of mind above loyalty to the uninformed ideas of his mother; that is, because he fails to fall in with the mother-worship convention of American society. He is boorish because he does not make a fraternity at Harvard and is awkward in Boston Society. He is a cad because he gets the brother drunk and makes amiable love to the sister with no serious intent; he is amusing himself. His cupidity is exampled by the fact that he places the attaining of his ends above the accidents of the means of their attainment.

Predatory cupidity seems to me to be the central strength of Durgin's character, and the axis on which his life turns; it gives him substance and reality; but Howells equally emphasizes his other faults, which are more the product of lack of social education than of anything else. When he attempts to prove that Durgin is not quite all he should be by instancing his frequent attendance at the Boston theatres, and by revealing that he spent a night in jail under the false accusation of breaking a street light, one is moved to laugh. The trouble here, as always, is that to Howells it was as much a moral error of the first order to use the wrong fork at dinner as to run off with a million dollars. He was beset by a middle-class horror of doing the wrong thing, no matter on what level. This horror vitiated his whole understanding of character, and so he was more successful at setting forth the "peculiarities" of people than at revealing their fundamental traits.

If Durgin is the best character of Howells, nothing need be said of the rest. The same inadequacy characterizes them all. Though he drew many women, he rarely gave anything but a superficial view of them. Every chance flash of insight is quickly hidden in a covering barrage of exculpations: witness the drawing of Mrs. Farrell. He seems to have regarded women as being admirable in proportion as they were unaware of the actualities of the world. Nevertheless, he saw them as the keepers of men's consciences; they gave, in his view, a high moral tone to American culture. Yet at the same time they were ignorant and trivial and petty-minded. Howells' women were compounded from the elements of the American myth about women. His attitude, as is that myth, was at once adulatory and insulting. It is summed up in his references to the "heavenly whiteness" of Mrs. Clemens.

Subtract every attempt at depth of character-analysis and all sociological intent, and the remainder is "Indian Summer" and "The Kentons." The latter, in 1912, was hailed by Henry James as "that perfectly classic illustration of your spirit and your form." It is precisely what Mr. Brownell called a *roman de société.* The story carries an Ohio family to New York City and then to Europe and back. The drive behind it is supplied by the love affairs of the eldest daughter. The pilgrimage begins with her socially unfortunate infatuation with Bitterage, a vulgar, facetious newspaper man. The family seeks to escape him. They go to New York, and he pursues. They go to Europe, and on the way over the daughter's love is somehow transferred to a facetious minister.

Once it is settled that she may love a second time and not commit a breach of the moral law of the universe, all is happy. The book is enlivened by a portrait of Boyne Kenton, who forecasts Tarkington's "Seventeen," and by the social contrasts incident to the pilgrimage. This light, fluffy novel shows Howells at his trivial best.

Of the same quality and significance is "Indian Summer." Once one convinces oneself that the portrait of Colville is not a libel on the intelligence of newspaper editors, all is well. The action is laid in Florence and tells the story of the drawing-room love affair of a middle-aged man (Colville) and a middle-aged woman, temporarily interrupted by the man's affair with a young, sentimental girl. In the handling of this situation Howells exhibits all of his ability to deal skilfully with the trials and tribulations of the drawing-room and to somehow convince himself that life is a placid, even tepid affair. His error is, of course, to assume that the tea-table situations rule the world at large—that whether a man has his tie on straight and his shoes shined is just as significant, say, as his adjustment to the universe, as the clash of men in finance and industry, or as the relation of the sexes. No novelist ever more completely lacked a sense of relative values.

One of Howells' chief assets was his amazingly supple style. The ease and grace and comprehensive finality of that style are very deceptive. Apparently nothing is beyond his power of definition. Yet this seemingly unlimited scope of utterance reveals how circumscribed his vision and feeling really were, for it is only a man who sees and feels little who can find precise utterance. But it must be admitted, none the less, that his style represents a very considerable achievement. Its most constant devices are repetition and internal comparison. It is a perfect vehicle for faint emotions and "notions" (in contrast to convictions). It is linear and not organic. It is thin and not robust. It is alacritous, rapid, superficial. It is the style of a consummate craftsman rather than of a true artist. A competent craftsman Howells certainly was.

IV

His influence, by and large, was baleful. His greatest service was to taste: he turned American fiction toward realism. But this service was largely vitiated by his reservations both in precept and practice. The school of local color, largely a product of his cultivation, failed because it placed the accurate recording of environmental peculiarities above fundamental studies of man. It is impossible to name a single figure upon whom he had any influence that was otherwise than unfortunate, or to name a single successor in fiction who, following his tradition, became one of the first-rate writers of the day. The authors who openly revolted against him are among the greatest—for example, Norris, Crane, and Dreiser.

Howells' whole life shaped him for eventual failure, no matter how great his temporary success. That failure was rooted in his particular inability to absorb his frontier environment—in the deflection from reality which the literature he was reading gave him. It is quite probable that if he had started with Tolstoi his case would have been different, but Tolstoi came too late to modify profoundly either his life or his fiction. His deflection threw him into the society of women, which destroyed the masculinity of his point of view. He accepted the New England environment at Boston's evaluation and took Boston's judgments as his own. Consequently, he came to represent no more than a narrow class response to a disturbing society.

Though he was vaguely disquieted both by his personal position and by social conditions, he never clearly analyzed either. He accepted the tolerance of a society he could not, in his more thoughtful moments, respect, and won success by conformance to its attitudes and prejudices. He never cut through the surface and became a true portrayer of human life as it appeared in the United States. In the end he can only stand forth as the perfect exponent of the late Nineteenth Century bourgeois spirit in American literature.

1931

HERBERT EDWARDS

Howells and the Controversy Over Realism in American Fiction

WHEN William Dean Howells took charge of the "Editor's Study" of *Harper's Magazine* in 1885, he began more vigorously than ever to champion the cause of realism in American fiction. There can be little doubt that at this time Howells occupied a most influential position in American letters. For nine years, from 1872 to 1881, he had been editor-in-chief of *The Atlantic Monthly.* He had just published *The Rise of Silas Lapham;* he was already the author of ten books, and among them were *A Foregone Conclusion* and *A Modern Instance,* two of the most popular novels he ever wrote. It must not be supposed, however, that the respect with which he was regarded by the American critics and public ever partook of the nature of reverence or veneration. *The Nation* had not hesitated to state in regard to his work: "One feels the lack of something that is indispensable in the equipment of a novelist of the highest order—a lack of romantic imagination,"[1] and *The Critic* had declared in a review of *The Rise of Silas Lapham,* "It is a book which has been enjoyed, but not one that will be remembered."[2]

Howells never tried to conciliate a critic who wanted "a romantic imagination" in fiction. Indeed, he seemed entirely indifferent to the regard of critics and public. In June, 1887, in the "Editor's Study," he severely arraigned American critics for bad manners, bad principles, and ignorance.[3] His vigorous and ironical manner is illustrated in his comment upon the popular romantic novelist of the day:

The kind of novels he likes, and likes to write, are intended to take his reader's mind, or what that reader would probably call his mind, off

From *American Literature,* III (November, 1931), 237-48. By permission.

himself; they make one forget life and all its cares and duties; they are not in the least like the novels which make you think of these, and shame you into at least wishing to be a helpfuler and wholesomer creature than you are. No sordid details of verity here, if you please; no wretched being humbly and weakly struggling to do right and to be true, suffering for his follies and his sins, tasting joy only through the mortification of self, and in the help of others; nothing of all this, but instead a great, whirling splendor of peril and achievement, a wild scene of heroic adventure . . . with a stage "picture" at the fall of the curtain, and all the good characters in a row, their left hands pressed upon their hearts, and kissing their right hands to the audience in the good old way that has always charmed and always will, Heaven bless it![4]

He criticized fiction which merely amuses, in the following manner:

Once more we say these amusements have their place, as the circus has, and the burlesque, and negro minstrelsy, and the ballet, and prestidigitation. No one of these is to be despised in its place; but we had better understand that it is not the highest place, and that it is hardly an intellectual delight.[5]

It was inevitable that such criticism should provoke rejoinders in an America which, to a large extent, still preferred the ideal to the real in fiction, which "loved and worshipped sweetness, but not light." Agnes Repplier replied in *The Atlantic Monthly* by quoting Rochefoucauld to the effect that "he who lives without folly is hardly so wise as he thinks." She said: "We read the *Bostonians* and *The Rise of Silas Lapham* with a due appreciation of their minute perfections, but we go to bed quite cheerfully at our usual hour, and are content to wait an interval of leisure to resume them."[6] It was perhaps natural that a sharper note in the criticism of Howells's work should begin to be distinguished. When *April Hopes* appeared in 1887, it was criticized by *The Dial* for lack of human interest of any attractive sort, and for characters "distinguished above their earlier prototypes for vulgarity both of thought and expression."[7] *The Nation* said of the same novel:

April Hopes is, in a conventional moral sense, above reproach; but its tendency to blight germs of spirituality is hardly less harmful to character than is the corrupting influence of novels which describe the base or vicious sides of life. No one is the better for its trivial worldly wisdom, while the young and impressionable are apt to be the worse.[8]

In the "Editor's Study" for July, 1888, Howells spoke for democracy in literature, for the exaltation of the common, the average: "Such beauty and such grandeur as we have is common beauty, common grandeur.... The talent which is robust enough to front the everyday world and catch the charm of its work-worn, care-worn, brave, kindly face, need not fear the encounter, though it seems terrible to the sort nurtured in the superstition of the romantic, the bizarre, the heroic, the distinguished, as the thing alone worthy of painting or carving or writing."[9] Howells also declared that the true artist found nothing in life insignificant, that everything was important for destiny and character, that nothing God had made was contemptible, and so the true artist could not look upon human life and declare this or that thing unworthy of notice, any more than the scientist could declare a fact of the material world beneath the dignity of his inquiry. James Lane Allen, chief among the Southern romantic novelists of the day, attempted to reduce Howells's contentions to the absurd in an article, "Caterpillar Critics," in *The Forum:* "If Mr. Howells is measured for a coat, which proves a misfit, does he still enjoy wearing it, as an expression of actuality in the tailor's thought and feeling? Does he calmly eat a badly-cooked breakfast as one of the works of nature—the cook's nature—God having made the cook?"[10] A literary critic of the time, Maurice Thompson, maintained that Howells had said that "mediocrity is all of human life that is interesting—that a mild sort of vulgarity is the one living truth in the character of men and women." Thompson then proceeded to condemn all realists; they dealt only with the faults of human character, "instead of attempting to imagine noble instances of human self-sacrifice, of lofty aspiration and of soul-stirring passion." He further declared that "All this worship of the vulgar, the commonplace and the insignificant... is the last stage of vulgarity, hopelessness and decadence."[11]

The appearance of *Annie Kilburn* (1888) was the occasion of much unfavorable criticism of Howells. *The Nation* found it "unprofitable,"[12] *The Critic* "wearisome,"[13] and *The Literary World* said: "Howells's new books we find ourselves opening less and less with a feeling of zest, and more and more from a sense of duty.... We are beginning to find him tiresome. The market is falling, and *Annie Kilburn* does not arrest the decline."[14] But if *The Critic* found Howells's novel "wearisome," it could unhesitatingly recommend *Greifenstein,* by F. Marion Crawford, as "a very vigorous and poetic protest against the Howells school of novelists.... This is realism of a very poetic sort, such as one likes better than the Laphams."[15] Crawford's unreal melodrama was considered superior to the work of both Howells and James by this periodical. It is not unlikely that Howells had in mind just such shallow judgments when he wrote in *Harper's Magazine* for November, 1889:

> When you have portrayed "passion" instead of feeling, and used "power" instead of common sense, and shown yourself a "genius" instead of an artist, the applause is so prompt and the glory so cheap that really anything else seems wickedly wasteful of one's time. One may not make the reader enjoy or suffer nobly, but one may give him the kind of pleasure that arises from conjuring, or from a puppet show, or a modern stage play, and leave him, if he is an old fool, in the sort of stupor that comes from hitting the pipe; or if he is a young fool, half-crazed with the spectacle of qualities and impulses like his own in an apotheosis of achievement and fruition far beyond earthly experience.[16]

Each month in the years between 1885 and 1892 the "Editor's Study" of *Harper's Magazine* was certain to contain exposition and defense of realism. In July, 1890, Howells explained that "the realistic novel depended for its effect upon the faithful, almost photographic delineation of actual life, with its motives, impulses, springs of action laid bare to the eye, but with no unnatural straining after the intenser and coarser emotions of blood and fire, no intentional effort to drag in murder, crime, or fierce interludes of passion without adequate reason." He satirized the American imitators of English romanticism in fiction:

> We have in America our imitators of that romance and that criticism: poor provincials who actually object to meeting certain people in literature because they do not meet such people in society! It is mostly these Little Peddlingtonians, trying so hard to be little Londoners, who do the crying out for the "ideal" among us: for the thing that they think ought to be, rather than the thing that is, as if they, peradventure, knew what ought to be better than God who made what is![17]

In September of the same year he ridiculed the reader who "must have the problem of a novel solved for him by a marriage or a murder, who must be spoon-victualled with a moral minced small and then thinned with milk and water, and familiarly flavored with sentimentality or religiosity."[18]

II

In 1892 Howells published his volume of essays entitled *Criticism and Fiction,* in which he reiterated the critical doctrine he had been advocating in the pages of *Harper's Magazine* for the last few years. But he extended his criticism to include many of the "classics," and this portion of the book drew down upon his head the renewed ire of the critics. He stated, in part:

> What is unpretentious and what is true is always beautiful and good, and nothing else is so; no author is an authority except in those moments when he holds his ear close to Nature's lips and catches her very accent; these moments were not continuous with any authors in the past, and they are rare with all; therefore the so-called greatest classics are sometimes not at all great, and we can profit by them only when we hold them, like our meanest contemporaries, to a strict accounting, and verify their work by the standard of the arts we all have in our power—the simple, the natural, and the honest.

The Nation had said of the ideas set forth in the volume:

The excitement, such as it was, of seeing an author of position jeering at his predecessors, pitying Scott, depreciating Thackeray, and in general working himself up into a state of mind whenever the poor "classics" on their comfortable upper shelves came into his thoughts, was amusing for a while, but now it is an old story. There are two leading ideas in the work: first, that the critics are sorry fellows; second, that the art of fiction is finer than it ever was before—that is, provided it is practiced in Mr. Howells's way.[19]

The *Literary World* condemned the book for egotism, whimsicality, and lofty patronage of great authors whose places had long been secure in literature. It denied Howells's contention that "the whole belief in genius . . . if not mischievous always . . . is still a superstition." It quoted a bit of ridicule by James M. Barrie, in which an American realistic novelist speaks as follows: "I have written three volumes about a lady and a gentleman who met on a car. . . . Nothing happened. That is the point of the story. . . . To us it is hard work to put all we have to say about a lady and gentleman who agree not to become engaged in three volumes." The parting shot of the periodical in regard to Howells was: "Many of his dicta are as entertaining and instructive as the judgments of a Pawnee brave in the galleries of the Louvre would be."[20] Not all of the criticism which the book aroused was as intemperate as this, however. *The Atlantic Monthly,* after criticizing Howells for his depreciation of the past, and his "intemperate zeal" in the advocacy of his theory, said: "We are more disposed to think that what is technically known as realism is a phase of literature which corresponds with much that is contemporary in science and religion, but that so far from being the final word in literature, it will simply make its contribution to art and give place to purer idealism."[21] *The Dial* was equally moderate.[22]

A defense of Howells appeared in *The New England Magazine* for December, 1893; Celia Parker Wooley was the defender. She declared:

This criticism [of Howells] is often honest, and to a degree intelligent, but much of it is undiscerning, flippant, and coarse. Its source lies in the suspicion and dislike of those principles of realism in art, felt by the average critic of the day, and of which Mr. Howells is the leading exponent in this country.

He had been criticized, said Miss Wooley, by moralists and romanticists who said that his writings had no worthy motive, that they were essentially superficial and commonplace, that there was nothing heroic or startling in them. These romanticists complained that nothing ever happened in his novels. "But," said Miss Wooley, "what ever happens in the lives of the majority of the men and women we see around us? We no longer live in the days of tournaments and knightly emprise; but life was never of such intense human interest as it is today." And Howells has sympathy and humanitarian purpose: "His sympathy with all kinds and classes of people is as broad, if not as fervent, as that of the author of *Adam Bede.* Through all the sadness and suffering, the human spirit shows and triumphs over all." But Miss Wooley was an exception among the critics; by far the greater number of them held to the romantic, idealistic point of view which characterized the period.

The reading public's fondness for romance was reflected in a communication from a reader which appeared in *The Atlantic Monthly* about this time. The reader expressed dislike of the melancholy of modern realistic novels and entered a plea for a more cheerful note, frankly as an anodyne against life. He said:

As another example of this school of fiction writing whose aim is to depict life as it is, take *The House by the Medlar Tree.* It is too unhappily true to life to be tolerable reading for anyone past youth who knows what trouble is, who does not need and does not wish to have the woe of life thrust upon his notice and pressed down into his soul more than it already and inevitably is. For my own part, I think that a preface by Mr. Howells, recommending a book for its realism, will hereafter be enough to guard me against it. Some may agree with him and prize such novels as masterpieces of modern art, but is the depression they produce a wholesome effect to receive from a work of art? To read such books is gratuitously to weaken one's vitality, which the mere fact of living does for most of us in such measure that what we need is tonic treatment, and views of life that tend to hopefulness, not gloom.[23]

One of the prominent novelists and critics of the day, Amelia E. Barr, deprecated the type of "heroine" that was found in the realistic novel:

She is not a nice girl. She talks too much, and talks in a slangy, jerky way that is odiously vulgar. She is frank, too frank, on every subject and occasion. She is contemptuous of authority, even of parental authority, and behaves in a high-handed way about her love affairs. She is alas! something of a freethinker. She rides a bicycle, and plays tennis, and rows a boat. She laughs loudly, and dresses in manly fashion, and acts altogether in accord with an epoch that travels its sixty miles an hour. She is very smart and clever, but in her better moments she makes us sigh for the girls who thought their parents infallible and who were reverent churchwomen—the girls who were so shrinkingly modest, and yet so brave in emergencies—the girls who were so fully accomplished, and so beautiful, and who yet had no higher ambition than to be the dearly-loved wife of a noble-hearted man and the good house-mother of happy children.[24]

What the American people liked to read in 1893 was revealed by Hamilton W. Mabie in an article entitled "The Most Popular Novels in America," which was published in *The Forum* for December, 1893. *David Copperfield, Ivanhoe, The Scarlet Letter, Uncle Tom's Cabin,* and *Ben Hur* headed the list, while *The Rise of Silas Lapham* trailed near the end. General Lew Wallace's grandiose, rococo romance, *The Prince of India,* had just appeared and was being received with a popular enthusiasm almost equal to that which *Ben Hur* had aroused. *The Literary World* commented upon the popularity of the novel as follows:

His works seem to suit the average American temper; they are full of movement and are written in a smooth, harmonious style, while their themes are concerned with religion and ecclesiastical history. Perhaps there is a vague survival of the Puritan spirit in the modern citizens of the United States which likes to have its pleasures rendered serious by the conveying of useful information and by the baptism of a pious purpose.[25]

Protests against the realistic novel had continually appeared in most of the leading periodicals for the past ten years. In 1883 Charles Dudley Warner had declared in *The Atlantic Monthly* that the aim of the novel should be "to lighten the burdens of life by taking us for a time out of our humdrum and perhaps sordid conditions, so that we can see familiar life somewhat idealized," and had criticized realism because it did not give "hope and cheer."[26] *The Dial* and *The Critic* had declared that the world was bored with realism, and the latter had defended "happy endings" as "healthful and sane" and had declared that "a taste for disappointing conclusions is an artificial one, acquired at the expense of much that is necessary to perfect moral sanity . . . people who marry and live happily ever after are the very salt of the earth, and it is good to know them; it is good to find them at the close of a fiction. They are real people."[27] When George Du Maurier's *Trilby* ushered in a "revival of romanticism" in 1894, it was almost joyfully received by most of the leading critics and periodicals. *The Atlantic Monthly* said: "That the grace, the bonhomie, of the book will appeal to another generation depends, we think, on how far another generation will be as tired as ours is of fiction which wrestles with all the problems of life."[28] *The Literary World* stated that "the world is tired of Kodak pictures of the dreary commonplaces of life,"[29] and *The Dial* eagerly welcomed "a man who has viewed life with tenderness and a sane outlook."[30]

III

William Dean Howells resolutely opposed all such opinions. Henry James, Hamlin Garland, Stephen Crane, and Frank Norris he defended vigorously, together with many minor realists long since forgotten, such as Mrs. Lillie C. Wyman and Harold Frederic. Of

Mrs. Wyman's *Poverty Grass* he said, after commending its truth of life: "It is surely not a book for those who would like fiction to make out that life is a pretty play or an amusing game, and would have all sorrows end well, that their sensibilities may be tickled and pampered."[31] In the "Editor's Study" for October, 1890, Howells declared what a pity it was that people preferred Rider Haggard and Kipling when "such important and artistic books" as Frederic's were within their reach.[32] Not only such distinctly minor realists as Frederic did Howells aid, but such men as Henry James he found himself under the necessity of defending from the attacks of the critics. In the October, 1888, number of *Harper's Magazine,* he said of James: "It will certainly amaze a future day that such things as his could be done in ours and meet only a feeble and conditional acceptance from the "best" criticism, with something little short of ribald insult from the common cry of literary paragraphers."[33] James was condemned by most of the critics for lack of "pathos and power,"[34] lack of "passion and emotion,"[35] for "immorality,"[36] "lack of interest,"[37] for "subtlety and circumlocution."[38]

In Hamlin Garland's recent book *Roadside Meetings* (1930), he describes the inspiration he, as a young and struggling author, received from Howells. In 1890 he published a defense of Howells in which the realism of the master was praised as "as much the product of the times as the electric car."[39] Immediately upon the appearance of Garland's *Main Travelled Roads* in 1891, Howells wrote in the pages of the "Editor's Study":

> The type caught in Mr. Garland's book is not pretty; it is ugly and often ridiculous; but it is heart-breaking in its rude despair . . . he has the fine courage to leave a fact with the reader ungarnished and unvarnished, which is almost the rarest trait in an Anglo-Saxon writer, so infantile and feeble is the custom of our art.

The volume was received by the critics with mingled praise and blame, Howells anticipating the tenor of the latter when he said of Garland: "He has a certain harshness and bluntness, an indifference to the more delicate charms of style, and he has still to learn that though the thistle is full of an unrecognized poetry, the rose has a poetry, too, that even over-praise cannot spoil." If these kindly words are compared with the much harsher criticism of such a magazine as *The Atlantic Monthly,* it can be readily perceived how really encouraging Howells must have been to the struggling and sensitive young author. *The Atlantic Monthly* said of *Main Travelled Roads:* "It is partly his lack of training, partly his scorn of refinements, which make the sturdy, homespun style, generally so effective, always rough, and often perversely incorrect. The same reasons may serve to account for the sometimes unnecessarily frank, sometimes even brutal realism."[40]

The active interest Howells took in Stephen Crane was typical of his efforts in behalf of most of the young realistic writers of the day. Crane was an obscure young journalist when Garland discovered him and introduced him to Howells. Howells took the young author under his wing, and in turn introduced him to literary friends likely to encourage his aspirations.[41] At this time Crane had written his first novel, *Maggie, a Girl of the Streets,* but unable to find a publisher, had printed 1100 paperbacked copies at his own expense. In a year's time he had disposed of exactly one hundred of these (including gift copies). None of the book shops, except Brentano's, would take any of the books for sale, and Brentano's returned ten of the twelve copies it had taken. Howells now endeavored to find a publisher for the book, wrote a laudatory introduction for it, and went from publisher to publisher, but none of them had the courage to allow his name to appear upon the title page. It was not until after the success of *The Red Badge of Courage* in 1896 that a publisher was found. Late in life, in 1913, Howells said of his experiences in trying to secure a publisher for *Maggie:* "To this hour I cannot understand the attitude of the publishers. I saw several of them personally and tried to interest Mr. Brentano.... I shall never understand what was found offensive in the little tragedy."[42]

When Crane departed from what Howells believed a sincere

endeavor to portray the facts of life, Howells was as quick to condemn as he had been to praise. *The Red Badge of Courage* was a great popular success, and was highly praised by the critics for its "power," "color," and "rich profusion of metaphor and simile,"[43] but William Dean Howells was disappointed. He called it a failure in spite of its popular success, and declared that the author had "lost himself in a whirl of wild guesses at the facts, from the ground of insufficient witness."[44] In his criticism Howells always exalted principle above personal friendship and an inherent kindliness.

Another young realistic novelist whom Howells befriended was Frank Norris. Howells was among the first who found a "new thrill" in *McTeague,* and was probably the first to say so in print. Howells was largely instrumental in bringing Norris into public notice, although he never had an opportunity of meeting him personally. It was Howells's favorable notice of Norris which had brought the young author to the attention of McClure, the publisher, and which thus paved the way for Norris's later fame. When Norris died suddenly in 1902, Howells wrote the first essay of appreciation which appeared after his death. In this essay Howells declared that Norris had not been sufficiently appreciated in America, and he referred bitterly to the rococo romances to which the public had given precedence.[45] But Howells was shortly to see a realistic novel attain popularity, both with the critics and the reading public. Norris's *The Pit* enjoyed a posthumous popularity. In March, 1903, it stood first in the list of best sellers in the United States; and as late as May, 1904, there were more library calls for it than for any other work of recent fiction.

Thus the venerable champion of realism saw at least a measure of success crown his efforts of the last two decades—at last a realistic novel was popular in America. Certainly it can be safely said that the appetite for actualities which has been the most distinctive characteristic of the American reading public in the twentieth century, was to a certain extent, at least, the result of the long battle waged for realism in American fiction by William Dean Howells.

1. *The Nation,* XXXI, 50 (July, 1880).
2. *The Critic,* VII, 122 (September 12, 1885).
3. *Harper's Magazine,* LXXV, 155-158 (June, 1887).
4. *Harper's Magazine,* LXXV, 318 (July, 1887).
5. *Harper's Magazine,* LXXV, 638 (September, 1887).
6. *The Atlantic Monthly,* LX, 75 (July, 1887).
7. *The Dial,* VIII, 267-268 (March, 1888).
8. *The Nation,* XLVI, 142 (February 16, 1888).
9. *Harper's Magazine,* LXXVII, 317-318 (July, 1888).
10. *The Forum,* IV, 332-341 (November, 1887).
11. Published in *The Chicago Sunday Times;* quoted by *The Literary World,* XVIII, 281 (September 3, 1887).
12. *The Nation,* XLVIII, 165-166 (February 21, 1889).
13. *The Critic,* XI, 63 (February 9, 1889).
14. *The Literary World,* XX, 35 (February 2, 1889).
15. *The Critic,* XII, 213 (November 2, 1889).
16. *Harper's Magazine,* LXXIX, 965 (November, 1889).
17. *Harper's Magazine,* LXXXI, 317 (July, 1890).
18. *Harper's Magazine,* LXXXI, 639-640 (September, 1890).
19. *The Nation,* LIII, 73 (July 23, 1891).
20. *The Literary World,* XXII, 208 (June 20, 1891).
21. *The Atlantic Monthly,* LXVIII, 566-569 (October, 1891).
22. *The Dial,* XII, 144 (September, 1891).
23. *The Atlantic Monthly,* LXIX, 716-717 (May, 1892).
24. *The North American Review.* CLIX, 592 (November, 1894).
25. *The Literary World,* XXIV, 283 (September 9, 1893).
26. *The Atlantic Monthly,* LI, 464-474 (April, 1883).
27. *The Dial,* VI, 121 (September, 1885). *The Critic,* VI, 21 (July 10, 1886).
28. *The Atlantic Monthly,* LXXV, 269-270 (February, 1895).
29. *The Literary World,* XXV, 299 (September 22, 1894).
30. *The Dial,* XVII, 264 (November 1, 1894).
31. *Harper's Magazine,* LXXIV, 483 (February, 1887).
32. *Harper's Magazine,* LXXXI, 801 (October, 1890).
33. *Harper's Magazine,* LXXVII, 800 (October, 1888).
34. *The Literary World,* XXI, 232 (July 19, 1890).
35. *The Nation,* LVII, 417 (November 30, 1893).
36. *The Literary World,* XXVIII, 454 (December 11, 1897).
37. *The Dial,* XXII, 311 (May 16, 1897).
38. *The Nation,* LXXV, 330 (October 23, 1902).
39. *The New England Magazine,* II, 243 (May, 1890).
40. *The Atlantic Monthly,* LXXVI, 840 (December, 1895).
41. *The Bookman,* I, 229-230 (May, 1895), contains an interesting account of the discovery of Crane.
42. Quoted by Beer in his life of Stephen Crane, p. 96.
43. See *The Critic,* XXIV, 363 (November 30, 1895); *The Dial,* XX, 80, (February 1, 1896); *The Literary World,* XXVII, 120 (April 1, 1896); *The Bookman,* V, 436 (July, 1897).
44. *The North American Review,* CLXXV, 770 (October, 1902).
45. *The North American Review,* CLXXV, 769 (October, 1902).

1937

NEWTON ARVIN

The Usableness of Howells

IT LOOKS very much as if William Dean Howells were lucky in the timing of his centenary—luckier than some other writers whose names have cropped up for the same reason in the last half-dozen years, and certainly luckier than Howells himself was in rounding out his long career during those ten or fifteen years that preceded 1920. The whole disposition of criticism at the moment is immeasurably warmer and friendlier toward him than it was when, a year or so after the outbreak of the war in Europe, Howells himself could write to Henry James, with what painful feelings we can well imagine: "I am comparatively a dead cult with my statues cut down and the grass growing over them in the pale moonlight." There was almost no exaggeration in this melancholy remark, as anyone knows who can remember the distinguished obscurity in which he spent his last few years, or as anyone can now learn for himself by reading, for example, the essay which Mencken, with characteristic amenity and characteristic moderation, devoted to Howells and his work a year or two before his death. According to Mencken's view, the older man of letters was "an Agnes Repplier in pantaloons," "a contriver of pretty things," the author of "a long row of uninspired and hollow books, with no more ideas in them than so many volumes of The Ladies' Home Journal and no more deep and contagious feeling than so many reports of autopsies."

Judgments such as these, of course, have now taken their place among the curiosities of literary history, and the essay can be recommended only to those who want to be entertained by the spectacle of H. L. Mencken taxing Howells with "triviality" and "narrowness of

---

From the *New Republic,* XCI (June 30, 1937), 227-28. By permission.

vision." There is a Howells legend, however, a legend that was set in motion by Mencken's generation, and it has by no means even now been wholly discredited: the legend that represents him as merely a servile idolater at the shrine of Bostonian self-complacency; as a pander to the shallowest pruderies of the Brown Decades; as, at the best, a writer whose vision of human life was limited to the suburban horse-car, the summer colony and the front piazza. No one, I think, will now be tempted, in rejecting this caricature, to swing over to the opposite extreme and attribute to the author of "New Fortunes" the stature of a Stendhal or a Turgenev. But it is clear enough to the critical sense of this decade that, with all his deficiencies, Howells is one of the decisive figures in the development of our literary culture. The meaning of his career it is no longer possible to neglect or to belittle: he was the first of our important imaginative writers thoughtfully to consider and intelligently to comprehend what was happening to the form and quality of American life as it moved away from the simplicity, the social fluidity, the relative freedoms, of the mid-century toward the ugly disharmonies of monopolism and empire. He was the author of the first realistic novels of permanent interest in which the effects of that development are represented dramatically with any fullness or clarity.

Nothing could be less critical than to judge Howells simply in comparison with the severest and most powerful of his successors: his true achievement comes into focus not only when he is seen beside Dreiser or Dos Passos but when his work is set against that of his predecessors and contemporaries. What he left for Frank Norris and Jack London to do is no more important than what he did that Hawthorne and Melville, Simms and Cooke and Cable had left undone. Dreiser, in a later generation, was the creator of Cowperwood, true; but his portrait of that titanic financier was made possible partly because the creator of old Dryfoos had already, in his zeal for the cultivation of a sound realism among us, cast out the old Jacksonian and romantic illusions and faced all the implications of the fact that "business," as he said, "is the national ideal, and the successful business man is the American type." In the growing realization of this—for it had once been hoped, of course, that the farmer or the professional man would dominate the life of the republic—Howells had made a scrupulous study of the old-fashioned business man at his best in his portrait of Silas Lapham. But even in that novel, in the figures of Lapham's competitors, he had more than hinted that the pace was no longer being set by men like the old paint-manufacturer; and in later novels he proceeded to call into being a series of more typical money-makers—the coarsely avaricious and boorish Dryfoos of "A Hazard of New Fortunes," the tight-fisted, pettily tyrannical Gerrish of "Annie Kilburn," the thievish and cowardly Northwick of "The Quality of Mercy," and the unpitying sensualist Langbrith of "The Son of Royal Langbrith." With these personae in mind, can we believe that Howells was expressing no private emotion when he allowed his old Socialist, Lindau, to rage against "this oligarchy of traders and tricksters, this aristocracy of railroad wreckers and stock gamblers and ... mill-serf owners"?

It is too much to suppose so, though in his own person he habitually spoke more mildly. He believed as profoundly as any American writer has ever believed in the principle of equality, and he discerned as plainly as any later writer—as Upton Sinclair, let us say—that the sure effect of the business man's economy was "to establish insuperable inequalities" among us. No other native writer of his time was so constantly preoccupied with the question of class, and no other watched so responsibly or so anxiously the sharpening of class lines and the stiffening of class barriers in the world about him. In his earlier work, in such books as "A Chance Acquaintance" and "The Lady of the Aroostook," he had made the contrasts between social groups, in an ostensibly democratic order, the object of a lightly ironic or genially comic treatment, though even in such books one can sometimes detect the rumbling of more tragic undertones. The rumbling becomes easily audible in "A Woman's Reason," of the early eighties—with its treatment of a young woman's descent, temporary though it is, from her own leisure class to that of the wage-earners—and in "The Minister's Charge" and "Annie Kilburn," which belong to the year of the Haymarket trials, that gloomy sound has drowned out most other noises. The "apprenticeship," in the first of these, that the country boy Lemuel Barker undergoes is a course of sorts in the drawing of class lines with the hardness and the finality with which city people, as he discovers, know how to draw them. Howells' picture, in "Annie Kilburn," of life in a small New England mill town that is also a summer resort of the well-to-do, may be touched with some of the gentler ironies; but the grave theme of the book—the harshness of class distinctions in such a community and the hopelessness of extending any true good will or fellow feeling above them—was broached in it for the first time by a major American realist.

In his love of genuine equality, Howells, like his friend Mark Twain, simply preserved and expressed the finest social feelings of the old Middle Western life of the forties and fifties: his father before him had been a courageous champion of equal rights and political freedom. Unlike Mark Twain, however, Howells came to see that there was a real clash between freedom as Americans had largely conceived it—freedom to pile up money and to sweat other men—and the equality he so passionately desired; and he came also to see that a merely political equality is a tricky and superficial thing. Such insights make an essential difference in all the fiction he wrote after "Silas Lapham," but they are of course most explicitly given out in his two Utopian novels and in some of those fugitive essays on social matters which it would now seem to be high time for someone to collect and reprint in a volume. "Freedom," he wrote in one of them, "is only occasionally a political affair, a civic affair: it is constantly a social affair, a pecuniary affair, an economic affair. Liberty and poverty are incompatible, and, if the poverty is extreme, liberty is impossible to it." He was no less realistic, no less free from the older delusions, in his view of equality. "Economic equality," he said in a different essay, "is the mother of all other equalities."

These propositions may be commonplaces today; they were anything but commonplaces to old-fashioned Americans in Howells' time, and they were not embodied in painstaking narratives by other writers until he had shown the way. For of course it is not simply a question of Howells' having arrived intellectually at certain political convictions as a result of fusing his inherited social values with the results of his observation and reading. It is a question of imaginative understanding, of fresh ethical and social perceptions; and on that ground Howells did much to make possible a new orientation for American fiction in its sober rendering of American life. If such later writers as Dos Passos have based a series of novels on their sense that the world about them is a planless and wasteful chaos, they were worthily anticipated by the man who made Basil March, one of his most transparent fictional spokesmen, denounce "this economic chance-world in which we live"; who made another character speak of "the squalid struggle which is the plutocratic conception of life"; and who, in "The World of Chance," gave over a whole novel to the deliberate representation of a way of life dominated not by purpose and control but by accident, hazard and whim. The "formlessness" for which Howells has often been reproached, and which this book exemplifies, is as little a defect as the formlessness, so-called, of "1919." He had the astuteness to see that a disordered world cannot be shadowed forth in the well made fictions that may do justice to a small and harmonious scene.

He cared for order, for fraternity, for union, as deeply as he cared for equality, and he cared at least as much for a genuine individualism. But he saw that a rich personal development not only is not fostered but is actively and tragically frustrated by the egotism and the self-interest that are the ruling motives in an individualistic society. It was Howells' Altrurian, and not some later critic, who, describing in "Through the Eye of the Needle" the Americans of the turn of the century, uttered that phrase about "their warped and stunted and perverted lives," and certainly few writers have ever realized so keenly what happened to the old dogmas of self-help and self-cultivation by the time the triumph of industry had taken its toll of them. Again, it was a young New England farmer in "A Traveler from Altruria," not one of Anderson's characters, who was perhaps the first to say plainly: "If you want to see American individuality, the real, simon-pure article, you ought to go down to one of our big factory towns, and look at the mill-hands coming home in droves after a day's work, young girls and old women, boys and men, all fluffed over with cotton, and so dead-tired that they can hardly walk. They come shambling along with all the individuality of a flock of sheep." Of course it was in the nature of the case that Howells made relatively little, in fiction, of the terrible sacrifice of personal wholeness among the industrial workers; but who can fail to discern, in so many of his middle-class characters, restless or ill occupied or discontented or self-seeking men and women that they are, his implicit criticism of an egocentric culture?

It is true that his criticism remained within certain limits that later writers have fortunately overleapt; it did so, too, partly because of that fastidiousness of which so much has been made, and which in fact was almost as heavy a handicap, for a serious realist, as some critics have taken it to be. Even more fundamental, though less damaging in practice, was the fact that he never broke entirely with the Swedenborgian mysticism on which he had been brought up or with the foggy idealism of the Transcendentalist epigoni he lived among: the remark by one of his characters that our prejudice against crime and injustice comes "from somewhere outside of what we call Nature" points straight at the philosophically shaky basis of his realism. It was the basis, however, on which Howells was bound to write, given the circumstances; and if it qualifies, it does not at all undermine the extraordinary interest of his work for us, or keep it from being "usable" in a sense in which the work of no one of his contemporaries quite is. Its vitality is more evident, at the moment of his centenary, than it has ever been before.

1946

EDWIN H. CADY

The Neuroticism of William Dean Howells

SINCE THE DEATH of William Dean Howells in 1920 it has become a commonplace of criticism to remark that he failed to carry his theories of realism into an artistic practice adequate to all of the central facts in American life. He did not treat what William James called "the slaughter-houses and indecencies without end on which our life is founded"[1] and which formed much of the content of the novels of such Howells proteges as Crane, Garland, and Norris. There can hardly be room to challenge this. Howells never truly faced the violent and sordid facets of reality. Mention and object to them as evil he could; leave the abstract and deal with them intimately, personally, objectively, or even imaginatively he could not. I should like here to suggest that the primary source of that inability was simply that life-long psychological difficulties left Howells with a neurotic condition which literally made it impossible for him to know and understand as realities the portions of pain and filth and terror in human living with which a major writer must be at least vicariously intimate. How much the production of the mass of autobiographical material which he produced during the latter decades of his life might represent an attempt to purge himself of the neurotic influences which seem to have haunted his mind throughout the peak years of his fecund artistic career I am not competent to say. But it seems clear that he shrank neurotically from the imaginative absorption of painful reality which truly searching American novels would have necessitated.

From *Publications of the Modern Language Association,* LXI (March, 1946), 229-38. By permission.

This is not to say that Howells could or should have written like Theodore Dreiser or Upton Sinclair or any of the host of muckraking and naturalistic novelists whose right to be heard he fought to establish. His naturally gentle mind, the code of the traditionally reticent and modest society in which he lived, his responsibilities as an editor and immensely influential public spokesman, and the commercial requirements of Victorian publishing would all have restrained any such impulses within him. Nevertheless, I cannot help feeling that Howells, with his fine gifts and talents, should have been a very great writer: and among all his often very good books almost no one seems to find a really great one. Without seeking to blame or damn Howells for what he was not, I think it evident that his failure to realize his potentialities was initially and basically the fault of an adolescent psychological breakdown and its hangover, into adulthood, of neuroticism. It would seem useful, therefore, as a step preliminary to understanding his mind and his books to investigate, as objectively as possible, the roots and the nature of that neuroticism.

An intensely sensitive child whose earliest memory was of the transcendent beauty of a back-yard peach tree in bloom,[2] Howells seems to have been morbid almost from infancy for reasons which are difficult to name. Never does he suggest any parental relationship or family conflict which would account for his difficulties. On the contrary, every mention of his parents is full of affection and respect; and his letters to them, as to both brothers and sisters, convey the same impression. Yet he remembered in old age that fear was for him "the prevailing mood of childhood,"[3] that "the dreams of childhood are oftenest evil,"[4] and that "his home was cheerful and most happy, but he peopled all its nooks and corners with shapes of doom and horror."[5] *My Year in a Log Cabin* relates how his first boyish visit to an aunt and uncle who lived a very few miles away was ruined by a homesickness so acute that it nauseated him, prostrated him with crying spells, and forced his uncle to take him home out of pity before the visit had fairly begun.[6] He tortured himself with all sorts of morbid nonsense and superstitions, some of them so vivid that he could remember them in detail sixty and seventy years after.[7] Especially acute was his fear of ghosts[8] and all this in a quiet, liberal, mildly Swedenborgian home!

The seemingly innate Howells affinity for literature began to assert itself very early, and the result was that he came to lead a "kind of double life."[9] The books so eagerly read "filled his soul with their witchery, and often held him aloof with their charm in the midst of the plays from which they could not lure him wholly away."[10] He withdrew "more and more" from the objective, external world of work in his father's print-shop and play with his brothers and friends until at length "he saw much of the outer world through a veil of fancies quivering like an autumn haze between him and its realities, softening their harsh outlines, and giving them a fairy coloring."[11] Living "in a world of dreamery" compounded of books and of imaginative recreation of bookish experience, he yet contrived to make terms socially with the outside by concealing his "riot of emotions behind the child's shy silence."[12] Psychologically he would seem to have been on very unstable footing as he entered upon adolescence.

Where some children escape into action or at least socialized activity upon entering adolescence, Howells simply intensified his earlier tendencies inward. The years of his adolescence made him a literary creature rather than a normal personality. His self-imposed daily schedule of work "without method and without stint"[13] would have cracked the vitality of an athlete; and, as his tintypes show, young Howells was slender and wan.[14] Now "the love of literature, and the hope of doing something in it, had become my life to the exclusion of all other interests," he wrote, "or it was at least the great reality, and all other things were as shadows."[15] His shyness grew until he became "intolerably conscious"; he remained "morbidly sensitive"[16] and fed his morbidity on such authors as De Quincey[17] and Ossian.[18] But the thing which broke him at the last was the unsupportable labor he expended in studying and writing after the completion of a normal day's work as a printer. Six days a week he began to set type by hand in his father's shop at seven in the morning, thawing out his frosty case over the roaring, wood-burning stove on wintry dawns. The swift but painstaking work which made the Howells-owned *Ashtabula Sentinel* a well-printed paper lasted for young Will until two in the afternoon when he paced down the gravel walks of little Jefferson, Ohio, gulped down his lunch, and plunged into the big closet under the stairs which was his study. There he taught himself to read Spanish, German, some Latin and French, a little Greek and Italian, paging through volume after volume in all the literature he could read and obtain. At six in the evening he emerged, heavy-eyed and hazy of mind, to sit abstracted through supper until he could return to read until ten or twelve, isolated from normal life like nothing so much as a thought-proud scholar in a romance of Hawthorne.[19] But his strength broke at last, and his "nerves gave way in all manner of hypochondriacal fears. These finally resolved themselves," he continued, "into one, incessant, inexorable."[20]

More than sixty years later Howells struggled between reticence and either honesty or the desire to be understood when he wrote, "I have hesitated to make any record of this episode, but I think it essential to the study of my very morbid boyhood."[21] From childhood one of his familiar terrors had been of hydrophobia[22]—of which, of course, in those years before Pasteur nothing really scientific was known. Bitten by a dog just when his exhaustion was approaching its peak, he was thrust over the brink of self-possession by a brutally ignorant remark. As Howells tells the story:

> By some chance there was talk with our village doctor about hydrophobia, and the capricious way the poison of a dog's bite may work. 'Works round in your system,' he said, 'for seven years or more, and then it breaks out and kills you.' The words he let heedlessly fall fell into a mind prepared by ill-health for their deadly potency, and when summer heat came I was helpless under it. Somehow I knew what the symptoms of the malady were, and I began to force it upon myself by watching for

them. The splash of water anywhere was a sound I had to set my teeth against, lest the dreaded spasms should seize me; my fancy turned the scent of the forest fires burning round the village into the subjective odor of smoke which stifles the victim. I had no release from my obsession, except in the dreamless sleep which I fell into exhausted at night, or that little instant of waking in the morning, when I had not yet had time to gather my terrors about me, or to begin the frenzied stress of my effort to experience the thing I dreaded.[23]

Only his wise and gentle father's sound pragmatism in seeking and finding fairly effective means of therapy, it would seem, saved him from genuine psychopathy.

So deep-rooted a malady could by such amateur methods be combatted but, not, however, eradicated. Constantly sympathetic and alert, the senior Howells stood by his son to assure him that he could and would recover and that he really suffered not from the hidden disease or even directly from the fear of its striking but from "the fear of the fear,"[24] from "the exaggeration of an apprehension without ground in reality."[25] Young Howells learned at length "to deal with my own state of mind as another would deal with it, and to combat my fears as if they were alien."[26] A time of "a sort of crisis" came and passed without the long-expected convulsion, and he began "imperceptibly to get the better of my demon."[27] The nature love which Howells's father had taught him from earliest years provided escape into a "shining solitude" which had always seemed to "liberate" him from fear.[28] Taking a gun by way of excuse, he tramped "day after day through the deep-primeval woods" to return poetically elevated in spirit and possessed of a "wholesome" fatigue.[29] As might be expected, literature came to his aid too. The sudden discovery of Tennyson provided him with a new and powerful literary passion.[30] And in an obscure romance he found a significant and liberating image. Following the hero of Theodore Mügge's *Afraja,* he came upon

a supreme moment when he was sailing through the fiords, and finding himself apparently locked in by their mountain walls without sign or

> hope of escape, but always escaping by some unimagined channel, and keeping on. The lesson for him was one of trust and courage; and I, who seemed then to be shut in upon a mountain-walled fiord without inlet or outlet, took the lesson home and promised myself not to lose heart again. It seems a little odd that this passage of a book, by no means of the greatest, should have had such an effect with me... but it is true that I have never since found myself in circumstances where there seemed to be no getting forward or going back without a vision of that fiord scenery, and then a rise of faith, that if I kept on I should, somehow, come out of my prisoning environment.[31]

Whether the hit-or-miss therapy or merely the passage of time did the healing, he continued to improve to the point where he was able to become effectively active again. But he seems more to have buried and suppressed his trouble than to have wiped it out. "The effect went deeper than I could say without accusing myself of exaggeration,"[32] Howells wrote of it sixty years later. It seems to have left him with a permanent failure of nerve.

In 1856 Howells was given his first chance to enter the great outer world which he had yearned to conquer. Given a post as secretary to the Ohio legislature as a political reward, his father went to Columbus and took his brilliant son along partly for education and emotional release, no doubt, and partly to help him prepare letters to influential papers in Cleveland and Cincinnati reporting legislative events. Howells blossomed in the comparatively cosmopolitan air of the state capitol. He made literary and journalistic friends, enjoyed himself pretty thoroughly, and seemed to be well on the way toward complete recovery. A great opportunity came to him at the end of the legislative session. The editor of the Cincinnati *Gazette,* who had become a family friend, offered to take him on as city editor at the then fabulous salary of a thousand dollars a year. Howells was to go and take his time learning the business; he was even to room with the editor. Everyone, including himself, was overjoyed. But the moment he was separated from his father and the sympathetic sister who had kept house for them in Columbus, the full truth about the devastation of morale which his breakdown had left behind it became clear. He flunked out completely.

From the moment he arrived in Cincinnati to begin work he was "tormented by my old malady of homesickness."[33] But the thing which ruined him was the sudden appearance of a state which was to afflict him for the rest of his life: he discovered a "necessity of my morbid nerves to save themselves from abhorrent contacts."[34] An exaggerated sexual prudery seems to have been one source of difficulty. Eating in restaurants for the first time, he was shocked by his suspicions of the shop-girls who dared to appear alone in public places. And a single night as a police reporter finished him. Having sketched the state of mind he was in at the time, Howells asks, "how could I intelligently endure the ravings of the drunken woman which I heard one night in the police station whither my abhorred duties took me for the detestable news of the place?" The experience "clinched my resolve to have no more to do with the money-chance offered me in journalism" he said. In a desperate attempt to give him time, one supposes, his friend sent him to report on a sermon—which gave him "a sense of cleansing from the squalor of the station-house"—and on the graduation ceremonies of a "young ladies' seminary." These he enjoyed; but he knew they were not the real work of the paper, and after a fortnight of suffering and failure he gave up and was trundled back across the state to his sympathetic but disappointed family. He had discovered what was to remain true: he dared not, for the health of his own mind, step beyond the bounds of "the cleanly respectabilities" in life.[35]

Shock, disappointment, and subsequent illness set him back seriously. The next fall, his father's post having expired, he went down alone to Columbus to take up his legislative correspondence again. But now he was afflicted by vertigo. One morning he "woke to find the room going round me like a wheel... everywhere, the sure and firm-set earth waved and billowed under my feet."[36] Failing finally to fight it off, he was forced to relinquish his post to the rising young Whitelaw Reid and crawl back once more to heart-burning and despair at home. Another course of rest and nature-walks and, he says, "I got the better of my malady, which gradually left me for no more reason apparently than it came upon me. But I was still far from well, and I was in despair of my future."[37] Adolescently melodramatic and literary though his letter of October 27, 1857, to his sister Victoria is, it does express his frustration and depression. "Alas for me!" he cried:

I am proud, vain, and poor. I want to make money, and be rich and grand. But I don't know that I shall live an hour—a minute! I am wretched. I want to be out in the world, though I know I am not formed to battle with life. I want to succeed, yet I am of too indolent a nature to begin... I know myself, and I speak by the card, when I pronounce myself a mistake.[38]

Shortly, however, he was rescued by an offer from the *Ohio State Journal* of a post, still at half his Cincinnati salary, where his duties would be of the congenial literary and abstractly political sort. He left Jefferson and his parents' home never again really to live there.

In Columbus Howells, now twenty-one, gained poise and maturity swiftly. He succeeded professionally and was accepted socially into the "best circles" of Columbus. James Russell Lowell published two of his poems in the *Atlantic Monthly* and began to take a fatherly interest in the young Westerner which ripened into decided favor and friendship when Howells visited him and the whole Boston and Concord literary galaxy in the summer of 1860. Yet his neuroticism subsided but slowly and none too surely. He was "sometimes almost intolerably homesick" and "still sometimes haunted" by his "hypochondria."[39] On August 14, 1859, he wrote his mother:

I feel particularly light-hearted today. For two months, my familiar devil, Hypochondria, had tormented me, so that I sometimes thought that death would be a relief. Yesterday, I could bear it no longer, and went to Dr. Smith, telling him my trouble, and receiving for answer that there was nothing the matter with me.—You may mention this to father.[40]

After his campaign biography of Lincoln won him the United States consulship at Venice, however, the years of residence abroad seemed to do him good. In January of 1862 he wrote announcing his dread of the coming hot weather which "always makes me hypochondriacal."[41] But he overcame both weather and the old homesickness to write in April of the same year, "My health is perfectly restored, and though I am often lonesome, I'm not homesick, nor low-spirited ... with a new access of earnestness, I have won new self-respect. . . . "[42] And a year later, just after his marriage in Paris to a Vermont girl whom he had met in Columbus, he wrote to his mother: "I was never better, nor so well in my life, and have almost forgotten that I was ever unwell or downhearted."[43]

Though he never broke down again, he never quite forgot that fear had once overwhelmed him. The word "hydrophobia" itself frightened him for years after. "I shut the book or threw from me the paper where I found it in print," he wrote in 1917; "and even now, after sixty years, I cannot bring myself to write it or speak it without some such shutting of the heart as I knew at the sight or sound of it in that dreadful time."[44]

Free as he had learned to become in Venice, he wrote to his father at the instant of return to America that he hesitated to come home. Beneath all the happiness of marriage, success, and new personal confidence he still held "my old morbid horror of going back to live in a place where I have been so wretched. If you did not live in J. [Jefferson] . . . I never should enter the town again. It cannot change so much but I shall always hate it," he wrote.[45] He could bury all this by plunging himself into the "cleanly respectabilities" of editing and writing and living in Cambridge, but in all his life to come he never dared to take a serious risk of shock, pain, or fear lest somehow it rise to grip him again.

Repeatedly one senses either the stirring of the old fear deep in Howells's mind or the adoption of techniques to avoid stimulating it. Somehow it becomes significant that he wrote Henry James in 1869 admiring a walk near Cambridge which led down "a lonely road, full of that safe wildness which pleases me."[46] Safety was imperative. He continued to react violently against unchastity and brutal fact. To Charles Eliot Norton he wrote in 1878, "What I can't abide is the matter between Helen and Casanova. I no longer wish to be put in pain about a woman's virtue, or to ask that suffering from others."[47] And he implored Mark Twain to suppress parts of his brother Orion Clemens's autobiography. He wrote:

... the writer's soul is laid *too* bare; it is shocking. I can't risk the paper in the *Atlantic;* and if you print it anywhere, I hope you won't let your love of the naked truth prevent you from striking out some of the most intimate pages. *Don't* let any one else even *see* those passages about the autopsy.[48]

Even after his allegiance to realism had become complete in the late 1870's and after he had been converted to Tolstoyan idealism after 1885, he could bear to glance only obliquely and hurriedly at the sordid truths which as a realist and socialist he was bound to admit and to try to ameliorate. Partly out of a sense of duty and partly, as certain similarities of situation would suggest, to gather materials for the early misadventures of Lemuel Barker in *The Minister's Charge* (1887), he made two visits to a Boston police court, probably in 1886, though they are reported in *Impressions and Experiences* (1896). He managed to sit them out, fortified by his new philosophy; but they horrified him,[49] and in *The Minister's Charge* he utilized one of the least serious and squalid instances, to which he had applied a prophylactic coat of sweetness and light. Even then one may guess from a speech in *Through the Eye of the Needle* (1907) that police courts still upset him; for the herione writes to her friends, explaining the superiority of Altrurian criminology to American:

Did you ever see the inside of one of our police-stations at night? Or smell it? I did, once, when I went to give bail for a wretched girl who had been my servant, and had gone wrong... I assure you that the sight and the smell woke me in the night for a month afterwards, and I have never quite ceased to dream about it.[50]

This was the sort of queasy, neurotic reaction to painful realities which made the Howells who had written his novels, articles, and Utopian romances to condemn and then to reform materialistic society[51] fail utterly to deal with its sordid, squalid evils authoritatively as young realists like Garland, Crane, and Norris, whom he encouraged and aided, and such successors of theirs as Sinclair and Lewis.

Battle as he might on abstract, intellectual planes, Howells always drew back from the consideration of disturbing facts. In political and social thought, for all his talking, he was forced at last into the damning, do-nothing compromise. He agreed with Mark Twain that "we are theoretical socialists and practical aristocrats. But it is a comfort to be right theoretically and ashamed of oneself practically."[52] Shamefacedly viewing from a safe, warm cab "The Midnight Platoon" of cold and ragged men huddled in a Broadway bread line, he came again to much the same conclusion.[53] It was all very clever and comforting; but what could be more corrosive to the conscience and the artistic integrity of a socialist and realist? The same sort of neurotic cowardice contributed in part to his much-debated exclusion of sex from the novel. In *Criticism and Fiction* he trumpeted, "Let fiction cease to lie about life."[54] The realist, the only true novelist, "cannot look upon human life and declare this thing or that thing unworthy of notice, any more than the scientist can declare a fact of the material world beneath the dignity of his inquiry."[55] And in a letter of 1893, "realism excludes nothing that is true."[56] Yet Howells has become notorious for his intolerance of sex, a proverbially real and true fact of life. He found it "simply abhorrent" as subject matter even for Zola.[57] Literature which treats it directly and simply he characterized as "poisonous."[58] He even let himself be forced into a lame appeal to "taste" as the reason for excluding sex. "The virtues are so clean, the vices so repulsively dirty. . . . The iniquities make you uncomfortable,"[59] he explained! According to his light, Howells was a sincere and earnest realist and social critic; but he dared not follow his light into a direct exploration of the brutal realities of American life which he could deplore from afar but must ever shun because of "the necessity of my morbid nerves to save themselves from abhorrent contacts." There is as little need to condemn as there is to praise Howells for his neuroticism. But no proper understanding of him as an important and interesting American writer and most influential critic can be achieved which does not early read the history which he himself created of those never soundly healed adolescent wounds to his psyche.

1. *The Varieties of Religious Experience* (New York, 1902), p. 90.
2. *A Boy's Town* (New York, 1890), p. 7.
3. *Years of My Youth* (New York, 1916), p. 59.
4. *Ibid.*, p. 35.
5. *A Boy's Town*, p. 18.
6. *My Year in a Log Cabin* (New York, 1893), pp. 54-56; cp. *Years of My Youth*, p. 61.
7. *A Boy's Town*, pp. 197-204, has an extended list of these.
8. See *Years of My Youth*, pp. 19, 60, and 80; *My Literary Passions* (New York, 1910), pp. 51-52; and *My Year in a Log Cabin*, p. 38.
9. *A Boy's Town*, p. 189.
10. *Ibid.*, p. 171.
11. *Ibid.*, p. 240.
12. *Ibid.*, p. 182.
13. *My Literary Passions* (New York, 1910), p. 71.
14. *The Life and Letters of William Dean Howells*, ed. Mildred Howells (New York, 1928), has as frontispiece and as illustration facing volume I, p. 10, two very interesting and, I think, revealing pictures of Howells in youth.
15. *My Literary Passions*, p. 121; cf. p. 194 and *Years of My Youth*, p. 238.
16. *Literary Friends and Acquaintance* (New York, 1910), p. 66.
17. *My Literary Passions*, p. 131.
18. *Ibid.*, p. 53.
19. See *Years of My Youth*, *passim*, and the early chapters of *My Literary Passions*.
20. *My Literary Passions*, p. 71.
21. *Years of My Youth*, p. 91.
22. *Ibid.*, pp. 22, 91.
23. *Years of My Youth*, p. 92.
24. *Ibid.*, p. 93.
25. *Ibid.*, p. 91.
26. *Ibid.*, p. 93.
27. *Ibid.*, p. 93. Cp. *My Literary Passions*, pp. 114-115.
28. *My Year in a Log Cabin*, pp. 44-45.
29. *My Literary Passions*, p. 134.

30. *Ibid.*, pp. 177, 122.
31. *Ibid.*, pp. 135-136.
32. *Years of My Youth,* p. 93.
33. *My Literary Passions,* pp. 124-125.
34. *Years of My Youth,* p. 141.
35. *Ibid.*, pp. 142-143.
36. *My Literary Passions,* pp. 132-133.
37. *Ibid.*, pp. 134-135.
38. *Letters,* I, 14.
39. *Years of My Youth,* p. 230.
40. *Letters,* I, 22.
41. *Ibid.*, I, 49.
42. *Letters,* I, 57.
43. *Ibid.*, I, 68.
44. *Years of My Youth,* p. 94.
45. *Letters,* I, 89.
46. *Letters,* I, 175.
47. *Ibid.*, I, 25.
48. *Ibid.*, I, 288.
49. *Impressions and Experiences* (New York, 1896), p. 90.
50. *Through the Eye of the Needle* (New York, 1907), p. 168.
51. Howells's reform writings are excellently handled in W. F. Taylor's *The Economic Novel in America* (Chapel Hill, 1942), pp. 214-243.
52. *Letters,* II, p. 1.
53. *Literature and Life* (New York, 1902), pp. 154-160.
54. *Criticism and Fiction* (New York, 1910), p. 244.
55. *Ibid.*, p. 201.
56. *Letters,* II, p. 35.
57. *My Literary Passions,* p. 246.
58. *Criticism and Fiction,* p. 238.
59. *Imaginary Interviews,* p. 165.

II. Realism and Reticence

NO SUBJECT *has aroused more controversy, and more interest, than Howells' supposed preoccupation with the smiling aspects of life and his evasion of the sexual aspects. The two are related: Howells himself referred to his fictional practice as "reticent realism." The most devoted Howells admirer has had to acknowledge his avoidance of the extremes of many varieties of passion; those who can't abide him usually begin by citing the "smiling aspects" phrase or by calling attention to his shrinking from the physical manifestations of love.*

One way of meeting these charges is to cite the support Howells gave to bolder novels than he himself wrote. Stephen Crane's Maggie, *Frank Norris's* McTeague, *and E. W. Howe's* Story of a Country Town *are among the novels he praised. The essay by James B. Stronks, a young scholar at the University of Illinois, gives a detailed account of the relationship between Howells and E. W. Howe.*

Mr. Cady's "Note on the Smiling Aspects" asks that consideration be given to the context of that remark. This "Note" helped provoke other scholars to re-examine Criticism and Fiction, *in which the phrase appears. Everett Carter, author of the next essay in this section, has an excellent discussion of the assembling of that book in his* Howells and the Age of Realism *(1954). His essay in this collection is directly concerned with Howells and the sexual conventions of his time. The final piece, "Howells' Kisses," grew out of a dissertation on Howells completed at Columbia University in 1956 by the editor of this volume. The counting of kisses leads to some conjectures about Howells' real reluctance to involve his characters in physical love.*

1958

JAMES B. STRONKS

William Dean Howells, Ed Howe, And The Story of a Country Town

WHEN Ed Howe's *Story of a Country Town* was off the press in his Atchison, Kansas, printing shop in 1883, he sent a copy to William Dean Howells, who wrote to the thirty-year-old Howe, praising his bitter, anti-idealistic novel as a valuable new kind of realism in American fiction. Howells's long-buried letter is worth bring to light, as are also Howe's hitherto unpublished letters to him. Howells's large effect upon the reception of *The Story of a Country Town* and the facts of his little-known connection with Howe deepen our knowledge of his role, public and private, as leader of the early realists.

Howells's letter to Howe was typical of his thinking and critical manner in the early eighties, and reads much like the review which he wrote soon after:

Louisburg Square
Boston, April 16, 1884

DEAR SIR:

I wish to thank you for the copy of your Story of a Country Town which you sent me, and for the very great pleasure I have had in reading it. Consciously or unconsciously, it is a very remarkable piece of realism, and, whether it makes you known now or not, it constitutes your part of the only literary movement of our times [i.e., the realistic] that seems to have vitality in it. I have never lived as far West as Kansas but I have lived in your country town, and I know it is every word true, down to the perpetual Scriptural disputes of the inhabitants. Fairview and its people are also actualities, which even if I have never seen them—and I have—your book would persuade me of. Such people in the story are excellent, all natural and sentient, except the last half of your Jo, who

From *American Literature,* XXIX (January, 1958), 473-78. By permission.

slops into sentimentality and driveling wickedness, wholly unworthy. Briggs is delightful, and all his household. John Westlock is a grim and most pathetic tragedy; his wife moves me less, but she is alive, too. I have no time to specify, and I don't know how to tell you of the impressions of simple, naked humaness *(sic)* that the book gives me. It has many faults, as any fool can show you, but be sure that you have written so good a book that it will be hard for you to write a better. I am afraid that you will never write another so sincere and frank. I wish I could see you; but upon your honest piece of work I give you my hand with my heart in it.

Yours truly,
W. D. HOWELLS.

Have you read Zola or Tourguenieff? Will you send me your fotograph?[1]

To this Howe replied three weeks later in a long personal letter in which he said "I am devouring Howells's novels," adding gratefully:

I think it is very much to your credit that you have taken an interest in my poor affair; the next time I meet a lame dog I will see if I cannot do something for him. There are so many contemptible and mean men in the world that it is a real satisfaction to meet one who is not only great, but good. I mean that very few gentlemen at the top of the ladder have heart enough to reach down, and encourage those at the bottom. I have always admired W. D. Howells and Mark Twain; I will admire them more than ever now that I know what splendid fellows they are.[2] I have about concluded that every man who becomes great by his own efforts is a good man; if I have a hope to become a great man, it is also a hope to become a good one.

The letter and the picture came to hand, and I am very proud of both. I can only hope that in the future I may prove worthy of your good opinion. I intend to try and make the new story read so smoothly that Mr. Howells and Mr. Clemens can say when it appears: "I knew there was *something* (not much, but a little) in that fellow. I am glad I wrote to him." When I get out my writing at night now, it is with a view to satisfying Howells and Clemens rather than the public.[3]

Soon thereafter Howells reviewed *The Story of a Country Town* for the *Century Magazine.* Appearing in the August, 1884, number, his signed criticism beat into print by two or three months those of almost all other Eastern reviewers. His alacrity bespoke his special interest in Howe's novel, as did the fact that he reviewed it at all, for in this year he wrote criticisms of only two other books. With an economy of effort, Howells apparently kept a copy of his letter to Howe and simply expanded it to review length, re-using many of its very phrases.

As in a good many of his criticisms of realistic novels in the eighties and nineties, Howells wished not only to praise Howe's book but also to make propaganda out of it for the still new cause of realism. In such cases, as his own critics were to protest, Howells would not judge a realist's work impartially so much as he would overlook its failings in order to preach about its realism.[4] His praise was often vague, as when he says that he especially likes *The Story of a Country Town* for its "mere open humanness."[5] Also typical is the way in which Howells softens and generalizes his criticism: Howe's *Story* "has defects enough," he blandly concedes, "which no one can read far without discovering"—but he is not specific about these defects, which were in fact substantial and interesting ones. Howells's single firm objection to *The Story of a Country Town* is, characteristically, to the "sentimental excess and unbalance" of the homicidal protagonist Jo Erring, which he says "comes near spoiling the strong, hard-headed, clear-conscienced story."

Brushing aside Howe's obvious mistakes, Howells chooses to emphasize instead the fact that the new Kansas realist "perceives and states" the "conditions" of life with frankness and sincerity, and that he tells the distasteful truth as he sees it. What Howells most admires in Howe's "honest piece of work" is "the apparently unconscious fearlessness with which all the facts of the case, good, bad, and indifferent are recognized." Other reviewers, too, were to call the novel "realistic," but it was Howells, realism's chief authority, who most strongly praised Howe's "grim truth." Even the hostile H. L. Mencken of the 1920's, when he was severely attacking Howells's values, looked back admiringly at the critic's "bold partisanship" for Ed Howe's pessimistic, unlovely book in 1884.[6] Indeed, Howells's respect for such harsh, depressing material as Howe's, or that of other Midwestern realists of the eighties, suggests what an open mind he had toward ugly and painful truth in fiction; and it challenges the shallow latter-day notion that he had a stomach only for what he termed the "smiling aspects of life."

What Mencken called Howells's "bold partisanship" for *The Story of a Country Town* appears sharply when it is contrasted with Horace Scudder's judicious review in the *Atlantic,* which spoke for a large, respected, and conservative faction of polite letters. Where Howells warmly praises the "realism" in general terms, Scudder coolly criticizes the bad writing in specific ones—citing the novel's thematic and structural weakness, its trite plot, its morbidity and lack of common sense.[7] Yet Howells was at this time writing *The Rise of Silas Lapham* and was soon to begin *Indian Summer,* novels as shapely and well wrought as any which the generation was to produce; he was, that is, as sensitive to the artistic niceties, or to their abuse, as were any of the critics of *The Story of a Country Town.* His review of Ed Howe's book would have been more just, and more informative for *Century* readers, if it had specified the Kansan's shortcomings; but the point is that Howells considered Howe's literary unskilfulness to be less important than his honesty and nerve in putting squarely before the reader some unpalatable truths about human nature and the Western village. In the evolution of Howells's critical values, his enthusiasm in 1884 for Howe's inexpert novel marked a stage at which his aesthetic criteria had begun to defer to his new ethical and humanitarian ones. Truth to real life was becoming for him more important than mere technical skill. The fact was fortunate not only for the novice Ed Howe, but also for other Midwestern realists whom Howells championed in the eighties; Joseph Kirkland and Hamlin Garland, too, were to be short on literary finesse but long on honesty and accuracy.

When Howells's criticism of *The Story of a Country Town* appeared, Howe wrote to him at once. "I want to thank you for the review in the *Century,*" he said, among other things. "I cannot tell you how grateful I am, or how much I appreciate your former generous words."[8] But besides boosting Howe's book publicly and Howe's confidence privately, Howells urged his own publisher, James R. Osgood of Boston, to reprint *The Story of a Country Town.*[9] Seven Eastern publishers had rejected it in manuscript in 1883, but following Howells's influential review in the August, 1884, *Century* Osgood—competing with four other houses for the privilege—hurried to republish the book by September. And the editor of the *Century* now invited a story from the promising Westerner. Happily reporting all this to Howells, and impressed by his large debt to the critic, Howe gratefully wrote, "I sometimes regret your great fame, fearing that I can never repay you for your kindness to me."[10]

Shortly thereafter, according to Howe's assistant at the time, the first Eastern printing of *The Story of a Country Town* "went like wildfire and was exhausted the first week. The *Century* review by Howells had much to do with the early sale of the book. The second edition disappeared . . . almost as rapidly."[11] Widely publicized by Howe's publisher and by literary columnists, Howells's letter to Howe and his review of *The Story* were respectfully quoted by a whole shoal of lesser critics in 1884 and 1885. Indeed, the review was reprinted as late as 1917 as an introduction to one of the later editions of the novel, and both the review and the letter were still being exploited to the novel's prestige and profit as late as the 1927 edition.

Despite Howells's advice that he not hurry into print with his second book, Howe finished *The Mystery of the Locks* in the fall of 1884, asking Howells's advice on some points in the art of fiction. With a rather surprising confidence in a manuscript which he had not seen, Howells offered personally to find a publisher for it. Of this valuable proposal Howe wrote, "I shall always believe that your notice in the 'Century' sold 2,500 [i.e., extra] copies of 'The Story' [i.e., in the novel's first two months], and I need not say that

I am sincerely grateful to you, not only for the offer, but for many other kindnesses. . . ."[12] And in closing, Howe reflected once more on his relationship to Howells: "Whether the new story is a success or not, I shall always think of you as the chief gentleman of my acquaintance; I often wonder whether I would do as much to help a new man as you have done for me, providing I were in your position."

But Howells's help to Howe was about at an end. The new story—the one which Howe had said he was writing to please Howells rather than the public—was a poor job. In the years following it, the overworked Kansan, writing at night after getting out his Atchison *Globe* each day, ground out several more novels, but they were not worth much. The autobiographical *Story of a Country Town* had been charged with personal anger and disappointment, but Howe's contrived later fictions fell far short of its veracity and force. In "The Editor's Study" of *Harper's Monthly,* Howells was now more eager than ever to publicize good—sometimes less than good—realistic work, yet he was silent about all of Howe's later novels. Gradually it became clear that his original instinct about the Kansan had been right: upon first reading *The Story of a Country Town* he had shrewdly suspected that Howe would never again write so good a novel. This proved to be true, but meanwhile Howells had powerfully promoted the career and reputation of that remarkable American book—and had incidentally made good use of it in his own campaign for the new realism.

1. The only known extant letter among several from Howells to Howe, this is reprinted from the *Kansas City Star Magazine,* March 1, 1925, pp. 9, 17. Howells's copy of the Atchison edition of *The Story of a Country Town,* in the Howells Collection at Harvard, bears Howe's signature on the front fly-leaf, his spelling corrections at many points, and penciled crosses—presumably Howells's reading marks—throughout the text.

2. Twain, too, had written to Howe. See "Mark Twain's Criticism of *The Story of a Country Town,*" *American Literature,* XXVII, 109-112 (March, 1955).

3. Unpublished 850-word letter of May 7, 1884, in the Howells Collection, Harvard. It is quoted, as are all of Howe's letters in this paper, with the kind permission of Mr. James P. Howe.

4. See Horace Scudder, "Mr. Howells's Literary Creed," *Atlantic Monthly,* LXVIII, 567 (Oct., 1891).

5. "Two Notable Novels," *Century Magazine,* XXVIII, 633 (Aug., 1884).
6. "An American Novel," *Smart Set,* LXIV, 140 (Jan. 1921).
7. *Atlantic Monthly,* LV, 125-127 (Jan., 1885).
8. Unpublished 350-word letter of July 28, 1884, in the Howells Collection, Harvard.
9. Joseph R. Kathrens, "The Story of a Story," *Kansas City Star Magazine,* March 1, 1925, p. 9.
10. Letter of July 28, 1884.
11. Kathrens, p. 9.
12. Unpublished 425-word letter of Nov. 27, 1884, in the Howells Collection, Harvard.

1945

EDWIN HARRISON CADY

A Note on Howells and "The Smiling Aspects of Life"

A FASHION has arisen in criticism of William Dean Howells of explaining the reticence of his realism, its failure to include lust, terror, and squalor, by suggesting that he failed to face these elements in American life because he was an unconscionable Victorian optimist. Much of this opinion has centered upon a phrase lifted from its context in *Criticism and Fiction* (1891): "the more smiling aspects of life, which are the more American."[1] Yet the bulk of Howells's own work concerns itself far more with quiet disillusion than with optimism; the smiles in his books are often wry; and some of the best of his books cry to the world for social reform. In the light of this seeming conflict, a re-reading of "the smiling aspects" phrase, in its context, seems indicated. Such a reading will show, I think, that hasty treatment, fortified by the antagonism natural to younger men in revolt against "the Dean of American Letters," has led to a tradition unfair to Howells and to a popular misunderstanding of his mind.

Jejune to exponents of hard-boiled naturalism though Howells's writings may seem, there is little in his best books which could be called cheerily optimistic. His poetry, the most intimately personal portion of his work, is soaked in melancholy. Even the early, summery novels such as *A Chance Acquaintance, A Foregone Conclusion,* or *The Lady of the Aroostook* are hardly gay or Rotarian in mood. Still less so is *A Modern Instance.* It is their trademark, almost, that in them happiness is never purely bright but always overcast by social complexities and incompatibility. The later, greater novels are

From *American Literature,* XVII (May, 1945), 175-78.

full of quiet heartbreak. In *The Rise of Silas Lapham* the wreckage of lives litters the hero's path to moral melioration, and the tragic note deepens steadily throughout *Annie Kilburn, A Hazard of New Fortunes, The Quality of Mercy,* and *The World of Chance.* If *The Landlord at Lion's Head* and *The Son of Royal Langbrith,* which follow, had less of crisis and catastrophe, their pessimism is deeper; for Howells's mood, as he assayed the effects upon human personality of living in the contemporary world, approached futility. That is not to say that Howells had the outlook of a major tragedian or that all the works of his artistic maturity were sober in tone. Yet his important novels were mainly pessimistic and critical in tone and intent. They point toward the conclusion which Basil March drew from his adventures in *A Hazard of New Fortunes,* published in 1890, only a year before *Criticism and Fiction.* Ruthless materialism, March felt, was swallowing up American democracy until life became a matter for all men of "pushing and pulling, climbing and crawling, thrusting aside and trampling underfoot, lying, cheating, stealing... covered with blood and dirt and sin and shame... to a palace of our own, or to the poor-house, which is about the only possession we can claim in common with our brother-men."[2] This is not optimism.

Is there, then, a fundamental contradiction between Howells's practical pessimism and the intent of the passage which contains the "smiling aspects" phrase? A careful reading of the context will, I think, show that no such contradiction really exists. Throughout *Criticism and Fiction* Howells fought for the right of modern realism to be heard in England and America, alternating pleas with attacks upon "romanticistic" literature. At the point in question, he had begun to examine the various types of Continental realism with a view toward determining their utility as models for the writer in English. Was it possible, he asked, to write the Russian novel in America? The answer was negative:

It is one of the reflections suggested by Dostoïevsky's novel, *The Crime and the Punishment* [*sic*], that whoever struck a note so profoundly tragic in American fiction would do a false and mistaken thing. ... Whatever their deserts, very few American novelists have been led out to be shot, or finally exiled to the rigors of a winter at Duluth; and in a land where journeymen carpenters and plumbers strike for four dollars a day the sum of hunger and cold is comparatively small, and the wrong from class to class has been almost inappreciable, though all this is changing for the worse. Our novelists, therefore, concern themselves with the more smiling aspects of life, which are the more American, and seek the universal in the individual rather than the social interests. It is worth while, even at the risk of being called commonplace, to be true to our well-to-do actualities.[3]

The purpose here is to compare. That the aspects of American life were not absolutely and universally smiling, Howells testified in his novels. But he felt forced to recognize that, as against conditions in Czarist Russia,[4] our well-to-do actualities did not warrant equal gloom. The whole plea of *Criticism and Fiction* was for "the truthful treatment of material."[5] For an American to adopt the Russian mood would be to succumb like any dime-novelist to "the love of the passionate and the heroic" which "is such a crude and unwholesome thing, so deaf and blind to all the most delicate and important facts of art and life, so insensible to the subtle values in either,"[6] and against which the whole of *Criticism and Fiction* was an ardent tract.

The famous passage concerning the "smiling aspects of life" was not, then, a counsel of namby-pamby optimism to novelists. It had a direct and limited meaning designed to warn American writers away from a false and artificial injection of Russian effects into their work. Howells meant it for artistic, not social criticism. As his own novels, critical articles,[7] poems, correspondence, and acts such as the defense of the Chicago Anarchists all show, he was profoundly concerned with decidedly unsmiling aspects of American life in his own time and prepared to fall into pessimistic moods about them. In justice to the man and his mind and in justice to the student who would understand him and his seminal function in the history of recent American letters, it should no longer be said or implied that he was an irresponsible, even unintelligent, optimist because he once wrote of the "more smiling aspects of life, which are the more American."

1. *Criticism and Fiction* (Library ed., New York, 1910), p. 252. Though John Macy, in *The Spirit of American Literature* (New York, 1913), saw Howells as crippled by "the hypocrisy and superficial optimism of America" (p. 282), Van Wyck Brooks seems first to have misread this phrase in support of such a view. In *The Ordeal of Mark Twain* (New York, 1920), p. 68, Brooks held that Howells's "prime dogma" was that "the more smiling aspects of life are the more American"; see also "The Literary Life in America," *Emerson and Others* (New York, 1927), p. 239. For instances of the vogue of the phrase see Carl Van Doren, *The American Novel* (New York, 1921), pp. 138-139, and the revised ed. (New York, 1940), p. 124; Vernon L. Parrington, *The Beginnings of Critical Realism* (New York, 1930), pp. 242 and 249; James D. Hart, *The Oxford Companion to American Literature* (New York, 1941), p. 342; Ernest Marchand, *Frank Norris* (Stanford University Press, 1942), p. 4; and Edward Wagenknecht, review of Booth Tarkington's *Kate Fennigate, New York Times Book Review Section,* May 23, 1943. Even Alfred Kazin, whose understanding of Howells is unusually broad and clear, seems embarrassed and apologetic in handling the "smiling aspects" phrase (*On Native Grounds,* New York, 1942, p. 20).

2. *A Hazard of New Fortunes* (Library ed., New York, 1910), p. 507. The best treatment of the development of social protest in Howells's mind is to be found in W. F. Taylor, *The Economic Novel in America* (University of North Carolina Press, 1942), pp. 214-243.

3. *Criticism and Fiction,* p. 252. Whether it shows influence or merely coinciding thought, Robert Frost's question,

"How are we to write
The Russian novel in America
As long as life goes on so unterribly?"

gives Howells a strong and penetrating ally on this point. See "New Hampshire," *Collected Poems of Robert Frost* (New York, 1942), p. 207.

4. For a vivid account of the sufferings of Dostoevski to which Howells had reference, see A. Yarmolinsky, *Dostoievsky* (New York, 1934).

5. *Criticism and Fiction,* p. 229.

6. This passage was deleted from the Library ed. of *Criticism and Fiction,* 1910, possibly because the context attacked the "thumb-fingered" British critics who had opposed the doctrine of realism but with whom Howells presumably felt reconciled after receiving his Litt. D. Oxon. in 1904, or possibly, as Professor Clarence Gohdes pertinently suggests, because Howells now hoped for large English sales of his books. The quotation may be found, however, in the first edition of *Criticism and Fiction* (New York, 1891), pp. 124-125.

7. Howells, of course, early championed such pessimistic realists and even naturalists as Stephen Crane, Frank Norris, and Hamlin Garland. See, for instance, his preface to Garland's *Main-Travelled Roads* (Chicago, 1893); "Mr. Garland's Books," *North American Review,* CXCVI, 523-528 (Oct., 1912); and "Frank Norris," *ibid.,* CLXXV, 769-778 (Dec. 1902).

1950

EVERETT S. CARTER

The Palpitating Divan

WILLIAM DEAN HOWELLS wrote a friend in 1882: "I could not have palpitating divans in my stories." Howells was proud that his books could be read by adults with profit and by adolescents without harm; but today eschewing of the sofa and ignoring of the boudoir are regarded as serious defects, and no more damning accusation has been made against him and his fellow-writers than that of prudery. Since 1892 this charge has become standard in American criticism. In that year Ambrose Bierce, commenting upon William Dean Howells's moving to the editorship of the *Cosmopolitan,* said that "his following of fibrous virgins, fat matrons, and oleaginous clergymen has probably gone with him." Gertrude Atherton, in 1904, accused American literature of being "the most timid, the most anaemic . . . the most bourgeois, that any country has ever known"; Frank Norris talked of "the teacup school" of James and Howells. These were the voices that had spoken before Mencken berated Howells in his *Prejudices* of 1919. And after him Sinclair Lewis, in his speech accepting the Nobel prize, called Howells the poet laureate of the old maid and the vicarage. With this background of sneers and deprecation it is little wonder that the general attitude we take toward many American writers of the last half of the nineteenth century is, at its most generous, one of condescension. Poor Howells: poor, poor Eggleston and Aldrich; they had no sex. And without sex — what is life, and, hence, what is literature?

It should have occurred to modern critics, however, that authors of other days may have been as outspoken as our own writers — relative, that is, to their audience's capacity to absorb such frankness.

From the *English Journal,* XXXIX (May, 1950), 237-42. By permission.

For it is demonstrable that the major American men of letters of the end of the nineteenth century were working frankly and fully within the range of the taste and the tolerance of their readers.

One need hardly press the point of the extreme reticence of the American public in the last half of the nineteenth century. It is well known that this was the age when Hawthorne disapproved of the nude statuary in Italy, when Dreiser's Mrs. Cowperwood was mortified at the sight of undraped marble forms in her redecorated mansion, when Anthony Trollope's publishers insisted that the "fat stomachs" of Barchester be changed to "deep chests," and when Oliver Wendell Holmes's Colonel, before carving a fowl, delicately asked a young lady if she would like a bit of the "under limb." But it may not be so well known that the American reading public, after the Civil War, was shocked by the attempts of realistic writers to report truthfully not only aspects of life dealing with sexual relations but many other phases of living.

For example, when Howells wrote his second novel, *A Chance Acquaintance,* in 1872, he posed the problem of conflict between the refined East and the provincial West. His hero, Arbuton, is a Boston snob who eventually falls in love with Kitty, the pert and lively Ohio girl and the first in a line of Howells' well-drawn heroines. Howells ended the book honestly — Kitty refuses marriage, knowing she can never be happy with a member of the Brahmin caste. The reviewers were intensely displeased with this conclusion. One wrote that the work was "so provoking . . . that it is impossible to come to any other conclusion but that Mr. Howells wrote his novel experimentally." A critic for another magazine admitted that the ending was truthful and that it was made inevitable by the preceding events of the story. Nevertheless the reviewer said that he (or could it have been "she"?) "could not help feeling that we are deliberately cheated out of a marriage festival and that pleasurable emotion which one feels at the sight of a bride."

Several years later, Henry James alluded to the discussion aroused by "young Arbuton's famous repudiation of the object of his refined affections." And he went on to say that an episode in Howells' most recent work, *A Foregone Conclusion,* would probably provoke as much controversy. This episode in *A Foregone Conclusion* was the climax of the one-sided romance of the beautiful American girl, Florida Vervain, and Don Ippolito, an Italian priest. The young cleric, never a sincere Catholic, falls madly in love with the girl, who treats him as a sexless friend and confidant. When the unhappy young man finally confesses his infatuation, she is at first horrified; but seeing the tragedy of his terrible position, she impulsively takes his dark head in her hands, tenderly kisses his hair, and then commands him never to see her again. James predicted that "Miss Vervain's seizing the young priest's head and caressing it" would cause much commotion; and the same month, the *Nation* reported that it already "has had the good fortune to create something like a scandal."

When Howells' *Lady of the Aroostook* appeared in 1879, *Scribner's Monthly* was shocked and disgusted. Today we find nothing but purity in this story of a young girl who finds herself the only female passenger on a transatlantic sailing, but the contemporary reviewer talked about "the error of taste," "disagreeable fullness," and "want of healthy mental attitude in a writer who habitually takes such a gloomy view of external nature." And the reaction to *A Modern Instance* (1882) is even more revealing in this survey of the extent to which an age such as ours misjudges the effects of an author upon the Victorians. The novel is the first complete treatment of a broken home in American literature. It traces the decay of Marcia Gaylord's marriage to the attractive philanderer, Bartley Hubbard. Although Howells spoiled the book with a "lady or the tiger" ending, he managed, along the way, to portray convincingly the breakdown of a union which had nothing but physical attraction as its cement. One Grace D. Pattan, of Bangor, Maine, was moved to write a letter to the editor of the *New York Tribune* about it. "The whole thing from beginning to end is revolting," the angry lady wrote. When an anonymous letter answered the irate lady from Maine, it admitted the novel's "pitiless reality," but it defended the "sordidness" of the book on the grounds of its social value. But the *Century* agreed with Miss Pattan. "Man gains a knowledge of anatomy by stepping aside into the dissection room," this reviewer declared, "but the great majority of readers could forget anatomy, especially morbid anatomy, and be the better for it." And then, a little plaintively, the critic asked whether it were not possible that Howells was giving the public entirely too little of "the sweet fragrance of blossom time."

The appearance of *The Minister's Charge* (1887) provoked a storm of protest on the grounds of vulgarity. "The cry is all against me on the count of writing of commonplace people," Howells wrote to James; one of the loudest voices in the cry was that of the *Literary World,* which indignantly protested its own liberality but claimed that Howells had gone too far. "We are ready to admit the democratic principle in fiction," its spokeman wrote. "We believe that no phase of life is too common, too rude, or too vulgar to be seriously considered by the novelist. But," he went on, "Mr. Howells, in *The Minister's Charge,* is more than democratic, he is anarchical."

It would seem, then, that the anarchical Mr. Howells was regarded as *avant-garde* by his generation. Poor Howells complained to his good friend Henry James that " 'every halfbred rogue that groomed his mother's cow' reproaches me for introducing him to low company." And James knew exactly how he felt and was completely in sympathy with the necessity of keeping in touch with the contemporary audience and its sensitivities. James was a cosmopolite, with all the traveler's easy acceptance of human failings and imperfections, and yet he carefully refrained from treating sex in his fiction, except with suitable delicacy and indirection. He realized the limitations imposed upon a writer whose stories, to be successful, must first be published in magazines of wide circulation. As the publisher of the *Cynosure,* in James's story "John Delavoy," tells the author: "You're not writing in the *Cynosure* about the relationship of the sexes. With these relations, with the question of sex in any degree, I should suppose you would already have seen that we have nothing whatever to do. If you want to know what our public won't stand, there you have it."

There is a certain bitterness about these words, of course, since they were written after an editor had turned down, as indecent, James's essay on the younger Dumas. But usually James accepted this restriction upon the range of his reporting of life and realized that it was one of the limitations which the artist must observe. When in a conversation he heard of a situation in which a young lady committed suicide because she suspected that her mother had lovers, James thought he had the "germ" of a story. "But," he said, and in so saying summarized the obligation of the artist to paint in colors which lie within the moral spectrum of his audience, "to make something out of it I must modify it essentially—as I can't, and besides, don't particularly want to, depict in an American magazine, a woman carrying on adulteries under her daughter's eyes." If he were a Frenchman and writing for a French audience untouched by the Puritan suppression of the flesh, James realized, he would not be so restricted. But he wasn't. And so when he worried an idea for a story which involved a young lord, his fiancée, and his true love, he rejected the possibility of solving the problem by arranging a *vie à trois.* That Lord Stafford should marry his fiancée and have Lady Grosvenor as a mistress was the treatment he could adopt, he said, if he were "a Frenchman or a naturalist." Being neither, he simply had to abandon the story.

In turning another story over in his mind — the story that was later to become *Wings of the Dove,* James gave an even clearer defense of the artistic necessity of adjusting one's self to one's audience. He pondered the problem of a man who was in love with one woman and who was to pretend love to another who was wealthy and dying. The relationship that should exist between these three puzzled him. "If I were writing for a French public," he wrote in his notebook, "the whole thing would be simple — the older, the 'other' woman would simply be the mistress of the young man, and it would be a question of his taking on the dying girl for a time — having a temporary liaison with her." This solution, however, he immediately realized, would not do for an English or American public. He said that "one can do so little with English adultery — it is so much less inevitable, and so much more ugly in all its hiding and lying side. It is so undermined by our immemorial tradition of original freedom of choice, and by our practically universal acceptance of divorce." When the *Wings of the Dove* appeared, it was made amply clear that the love between Millie Theale and Merton Densher was a spiritual attachment.

Thus, both the provincial Howells and the cosmopolitan James understood that they were writing for an audience with certain inhibitions and were willing to take those inhibitions into account when they wrote their fiction. And, as even further proof of the way in which distinguished writers of this era had to create with one eye on their audience, we have the career of the robust literary frontiersman—Mark Twain. Now Mark, as we all know, was not personally one to disdain the tremendous drive that bawdiness lends to humor. Part of his magnificent manipulation of the device of the anticlimax was in terms of the improper. "Human intelligence cannot estimate what we owe to woman," he would begin one of his lectures to a male audience. "She sews on our buttons; she mends our clothes, . . . she bears our children. . . ." Then his eyes would rove the audience meditatively before he added: "Ours, as a general thing." On another occasion, when Howells wrote the praise which helped to launch *Innocents Abroad,* Mark told him: "When I read that review of yours, I felt like the woman who was so glad her baby had come white." But Mark was careful of his language in mixed society, both on the frontier and in Boston, and his fiction and travel books are almost free from any reference, even the most oblique, to relations between the sexes. He asserted that even in the near-Pike County society of Hannibal, Missouri, where he spent his boyhood, "such things were not even dreamed of . . . much less spoken of and referred to as possibilities."

When it came to reproducing his experiences for magazine and book publication, Twain was even more careful than Howells that he should not offend the public. After the manuscript of Tom Sawyer came back with Howells's marginal comments, Twain wrote him, wondering how his blue pencil missed the ejaculation "comb me all to hell" and asking if he should keep it in. Bernard DeVoto, after examining Twain's notebooks and works, came to the conclusion that "he was almost lustfully hypersensitive to sex in print; he was in fact, as a writer, rather more prudish than Howells." According to DeVoto, "of thirty-nine notebooks" that Twain "kept as banks of deposit for his books, only three contain any entries at all that deal with sex, and one of these does not contemplate its use for fiction."

On the other hand, an analysis of the criticism and fiction of Twain's supposedly prudish friend, Howells, provides some surprising revelations. In his criticism, for example, Howells rarely allowed looseness, obscenity, or even scatology to interfere with his enjoyment. His idol was Cervantes and, along with him, the unknown author of *Lazarillo de Tormes.* He had the highest regard for Emile Zola and wrote of the French naturalist that his books "though often indecent, are never immoral, but always most terribly, most pitilessly moral." He greatly admired Defoe, and declared of his *Roxana:* "It is one of the best written novels in the language." He wrote to Robert Herrick: "Your women seem to me wonderfully well done—the worse, alas! the better, through those salient qualities of evil which make baddish women so palpable." He praised Hamlin Garland for the outspokenness of *Cavanaugh:* "The girl and the mother are both mightily well [sic]; and that awful flyblown hostelry; and those old beasts of men lusting around!" Four years later, he called Garland's *Forester's Daughter* "a fine courageous book" and wrote a postscript to a letter praising it in which he said: "I am glad you have the courage to recognize the man's brute instinct for the woman. It is an important book."

It is abundantly clear, then, that Howells was not pathologically or even abnormally prudish. Like James, he was aware that the writer in England and America must generally conform to certain proscriptions. And like James, he did not avoid discussions of "sex" in his novels; he simply treated the subject in terms which were in keeping with the rigid code of nineteenth-century America. Unlike the sentimental novelist who simply accepted and reflected this code, however, Howells was enough in advance of it to mildly shock the readers of his day. For the society which Howells portrayed in his novels expected passion to be fulfilled in marriage; but in his works the ring does not always follow the kiss. Kitty, in *A Chance Acquaintance,* rejected Arbuton and incensed the reviewers; Florida Vervain kissed the priest, and critics' blood pressure went up; Marcia Gaylord and Bartley Hubbard did not make a go of their marriage, and poor Miss Pattan of Bangor was prostrated with lacerated sensitivities. In *Letters Home,* Howells developed a love affair between the hero and a girl obviously beneath him in everything but sweet good will. And Howells rejected sentimental morality by marrying the boy to an educated heiress—this despite the fact that the unfulfilled love affair had developed to the stage of frequent embraces.

But the hunter of ambiguities would find much more game in *The Shadow of a Dream* (1890). Howells was deeply interested in the significance of the subconscious and was not at all reluctant to report his own dreams. He told a friend that he dreamed one night of "carrying around a human head which from time to time I wrapped up in brown paper, flattening it down to make a neat roll. This object was bestowed on me," he said, "by the wife of *two* of my good friends; she seemed not to be exactly of good repute, and I had to escape from her premises with the ignominy and virtue of Joseph." In one of Howells' short stories, Wanhope, a psychologist, suggests to a group, of which the author is one, that it conduct an investigation into dreams. "That would be rather dreadful, wouldn't it?" Howells asked. "We do dream such scandalous, such compromising things about people!" And in Howells' novel the dream which casts its shadow over the characters is a dream about infidelity. Faulkner has the recurrent nightmare that his best friend, Nevil, who lives with him, attends his (Faulkner's) funeral and marries his wife. Faulkner dies. Nevil does become engaged to Hermia. But the marriage is canceled when Hermia learns the nature of her dead husband's dream. The story is scarcely oblique enough to be called ambiguous: a best friend living with a husband and wife, the dream of unfaithfulness, the projected union of the widow and the friend —it adds up to a story of relationship between the sexes which is distinctly provocative.

Now all the foregoing is not meant to prove a thesis that, by absolute standards or even by those of our own age, Howells, James, Twain, and their colleagues were outspoken about sex. What it does demonstrate is that the range of taste within which these authors had to work was a restricted one and that they worked within it honestly and effectively. The range gradually widened, and, when it did, Howells was quick to recommend that literature should take advantage of its expanding opportunities. In reviewing the works of Robert Herrick in 1909, Howells pointed out that Herrick was extending realism to include portrayals of "the wilfulness and waywardness of women." "It is well," Howells wrote, "to inquire into the facts with unsparing fearlessness." Then he added, showing his acceptance of the changing milieu which would make necessary a changing fictional viewpoint, "It is ground through which the pioneer must break his way, but it may be that it is time the way were broken." And by 1917 Howells was sure that a newer era was upon America with regard to facing sexual relations; one of the last reviews he wrote was of William McFee's *Casuals of the Sea,* and he reiterated the necessity of a widening point of view. "It will be very shocking," he said of McFee's book, "if you look at it in the old-fashioned way; but the modern reader may ask why you need to look at it in that way."

So it would seem that Howells was a prude only if we look at him in the "new-fashioned" way. Any fair analysis of him and his contemporaries, in the light of the attitudes of the public for which they wrote, compels us to revise the conventional estimate of them as men who were afraid to face life. The life they faced was the life of their own time. To ask them to face any other is a strange requirement for an age which is living, and may die, by the principles of relativity.

1957

KENNETH EBLE

Howells' Kisses

IT IS A CURIOUS FACT about the work of William Dean Howells that with one exception *(April Hopes),* in the thirty-four novels he wrote, a certain sign that a love affair will not lead to a happy marriage is the pre-marital kiss which the suitor forces or entreats from the pursued. If the chaste heroine permits such a liberty, or for that matter, even permits the laying of a hand upon her, she must never accept the suitor, or in the one instance that she does, the marriage ends in desertion and divorce.

Such a fact is more than curious when one considers that Howells is pre-eminently the novelist of late nineteenth-century American mating and marriage, that the question of sexual prudery both in Howells and in his age is still under discussion, and that Howells is highly respected for the accuracy of his social observations.

"I doubt if I shall ever write another story in which mating and marrying play an important part," Howells wrote to Charles Eliot Norton in 1892. "I am too old for it, and it does not interest me." But Howells could not so easily shake off the habit of a lifetime, and in six of his last dozen novels, mating and marrying are still central concerns. Well over half of his novels are principally occupied with love affairs of one kind or another, and in all of them mating or marriage and sometimes both are given considerable attention. Despite such a long-sustained interest, there is little evidence of physical ardor in his novels, and when there is some indication that the courting is more than conversational, such activities as embracing and kissing, either on hand or lip, are treated with chilly disapproval. There is an excess in his attitude toward the

From the *American Quarterly,* IX (Winter, 1957), 441-47. By permission.

courting relationships of his young couples, particularly toward the common physical acts of affection, which cannot be explained away.

It has been argued that he was no different from his contemporaries in avoiding subjects and scenes shocking to the late Victorian sense of decency. Everett Carter, in *Howells and the Age of Realism,* has pointed out that some of Howells' own novels—*A Foregone Conclusion, A Modern Instance,* even *The Lady of the Aroostook*—provoked outbursts of moral indignation. Yet, granting his boldness in choosing such subjects as a love affair between an Italian priest and an American girl, an unhappy marriage involving drinking, desertion and divorce, an unchaperoned girl among two handsome young men and a drunkard on a ship bound for Europe, subjects of the above novels, one draws back from extolling his frankness. No Howells novel had to fight for publication as did *Sister Carrie,* or suffered the scathing condemnation given Kate Chopin's *The Awakening* or submitted to publication piecemeal as did *Tess of the d'Urbervilles.*[1]

The reasons are plain enough. First of all, "guilty passion" as Howells chastely called it, has no place in his fiction. The avoidance of this subject by a novelist so much concerned with mating and marriage cannot be explained simply as being characteristic of his age. Seduction and the threat of seduction, illicit love and the unwed mother were almost popular subjects of other fiction. Herbert Ross Brown has pointed out the "appalling popularity of the seduction motif" in the sentimental American novel.[2] And in more substantial fiction, one has only to recall the names of some memorable women in American and English novels from Hester Prynne and Becky Sharp to Hetty Sorrel, Tess Durbeyfield and Esther Waters to be reminded of passions exceeding the bounds of Howells' decorum. And whereas these novels, as well as continental novels, treated the facts of love with a certain circumspection as to details, there was no concealment of the basic facts of passion, oftentimes as obvious and as unequivocal as the birth of a child.

One might propose that Howells' reticence toward sex in his

work is similar to that displayed by his great contemporaries Mark Twain and Henry James. But mating and marrying play an insignificant part in Mark Twain's work, and his novels afford no real comparison with Howells' in this respect. In James's novels it is otherwise; his stories are almost as concerned as Howells' with mating and marrying. But despite the elaborate antimacassars which covered his own "palpitating divans," in novels such as *The Portrait of a Lady, The Ambassadors* and *The Golden Bowl,* there is no mistaking the presence and importance of physical passions. In only one Howells novel is there a consummated liaison. The elder Langbrith in *The Son of Royal Langbrith* (1904) has fathered a family out of wedlock, but he is already deceased when the novel opens, and his illicit affair is mentioned very briefly as part of his evils which will not descend upon his son.

Second, Howells' attitude toward the conventions of courting, particularly toward the most serious token of affection, the kiss, strengthens the impression that he displayed more than the conventional reticence. The evidence from his novels is that the kiss, however innocent in its context and consequence, was a mark of impropriety which denied the erring couple the felicity of true and lasting union.

In *A Modern Instance,* for example, Howells' first novel of consequence, Bartley Hubbard takes liberties with Marcia Gaylord in the Gaylord parlor in a manner which bodes ill for their future marriage. Marcia quite properly resists, but Bartley, blackguard that he is, kisses her goodnight just as her father comes down the stairs. The guilt with which the act brands her can be seen plainly in her reaction as she turns to face her father:

> The blood flashed up from her heart into her face like fire, and then, as suddenly, fell back again, and left her white. She let her head droop and turn, till her eyes were wholly averted from him, and she did not speak. He closed the door behind him, and she went upstairs to her own room; in her shame, she seemed to herself to crawl thither, with her father's glance burning upon her. (p. 17)

It is obvious that Bartley is a bounder when we perceive him, a few moments later, back at his hotel. He kicks off his boots, warms a mince pie over the coals, and reflects that he had had "a grand good time; but it had left him hungry." Readers of the novel know that the marriage ends in Bartley's desertion and a subsequent divorce. Bartley himself dies in Whited Sepulchre, Arizona, shot as a result of an ill-advised squib in his paper about the domestic relations of one of the town's leading citizens.

In two other novels, a kiss which a light man extorts from the heroine in the innocence of her youth remains the problem of conscience throughout the novel. In *The Coast of Bohemia,* an obnoxious drummer steals a kiss from the heroine during a brief adolescent romance in her home town of Pymantoning, Ohio. Long after, when the girl has established herself in New York to study art, the damning kiss remains as the impediment to marriage with a righteous suitor. In *The Kentons,* the novel Henry James called "that perfectly classic illustration of your spirit and your form," a boorish young journalist named Bittridge snatches the forbidden kiss. This act of violence sends Ellen Kenton into hysterics, and gets the villain an old-fashioned cowhiding from the lady's outraged brother. Later, when Ellen does meet a proper suitor, the Reverend Hugh Breckon, she must live down the shame of this act before she can think of accepting his offer of marriage.

There are numerous other examples. In *A Foregone Conclusion,* an Italian padre temperamentally unsuited for the priesthood falls in love with an American girl. At the climax of the affair, when he declares his love, he seizes the heroine's hands and "passionately kissed either palm." She flings her arms about his neck, pulls his head down upon her heart, "weeping and moaning over him as over some hapless, harmless thing that she had unpurposely bruised or killed" (p. 215). It is interesting how Howells extenuates this breach of conduct: the kiss is on the hands not the lips, his head is upon her heart not her breast, her passion is turned into maternal sorrow, and finally the priest is emasculated into some "hapless, harmless thing" before she puts her hands against his breast, thrusts him away, and runs. In *The Minister's Charge,* the rustic hero Lemuel Barker meets a factory girl in the city. A short time later, the girl accidentally stumbles against him. "He put out his arms to save her from falling," Howells writes, "and they seemed to close around her of themselves. She threw up her face, and in a moment he had kissed her. He released her and fell back from her aghast" (p. 165). When the author philosophizes the incident, he has Lemuel think back upon his upbringing and how he had imbibed from his mother "a sense of unlawfulness, of shame, in the love-making he had seen around him all his life.... Once a big girl, much older than he, came up behind him in the play-ground and kissed him; he rubbed the kiss off with his hand, and scoured the place with sand and gravel" (p. 166).

Even a kiss on the hand is dangerous, though it may not prevent marriage. When James Staniford of *The Lady of the Aroostook* presses Lydia Blood's hand to his lips, he does not quite realize the effect it will have. But the next day when he sees her, "She was pale and looked heavy-eyed. As she lifted her glance to him, she blushed; and he felt the answering red stain his face" (p. 133). Staniford, one of Howells' most typical good young men, later proves his worth and they are eventually married, though not without some uneasiness about the details of their courtship.

In addition to such mild displays of passion as these, there are three places in Howells' novels where real passion seems to burst out. None of the incidents are permitted to couples who will become man and wife. One such scene, taken out of its context in *The Shadow of a Dream,* seems not to belong to Howells at all:

> She locked her arms around his neck, and wildly kissed him again and again, with sobs such as break from the ruin of life and love; with gasps like dying, and with a fond, passionate moaning broken by the sound of those fierce, swift kisses. (p. 195)

But these fierce, swift kisses come to nought. The man is a

minister; the woman the widow of the minister's best friend. Though the story hinges on the suspicion that the two of them may have yearned subconsciously for each other while the husband was alive, they do not marry, even after his death. Whether or not they have committed an indiscretion, the minister is swiftly removed from the scene when a few pages later he is crushed by the express.

The other incidents involve Belle Farrell in the novel *Mrs. Farrell,* and Jeff Durgin and Bessie Lynde in *The Landlord at Lion's Head.* Belle Farrell is the only woman in Howells' fiction who is something of a *femme fatale,* and in her bewitching of two scrupulous young men who meet her at a summer resort, Howells permits himself more than his normal freedom in suggesting her sensuous nature. Yet descriptions and incidents stop far short of serious amour. Jeff Durgin trifles with a girl in Boston when he should be thinking of the one back home, but though he does force the Boston girl into an embrace and takes from her a kiss she seemed not too reluctant to give, he does not marry her. Further, he is dismissed by the girl back home and eventually marries a divorcee, who having married unwisely once deserves no better a second time.

It may be that gathering these incidents together makes it seem that Howells did deal with sexual ardor. Everett Carter contends that in Howells' time "the giving of the lips by the woman, the taking of the kiss by the man, seems to have been regarded as the act of reception and possession which joined the flesh as one."[3] Carter's whole discussion is perceptive, but the implication here is misleading. For if we were to accept this interpretation, we would say as Carter does that Howells' attitude toward the kiss was one of simply accepting the contemporary euphemism for physical love. Certainly there are novels of the period (Carter cites Forster's *Room with a View*) in which the embrace or the kiss alone suggests the ultimate surrender. But we have already pointed out a number of heroines from more important novels of the period in which overwhelming passions exceed the limits of youthful kissing. In addition, it must be apparent from the examples given, that the kiss as it appears in Howells' novels is not easily confused with a woman's actually yielding her most prized possession, even though Howells seems to regard it with much alarm. For Howells, it is not that the kiss is a decorous outward symbol of sexual gratification, but that any close approximation of the act of sex is not present in his fiction.

It is interesting to compare Howells' refusal to sanction the kiss with the common convention of popular fiction of the period that the kiss, as it has to some degree before and since, sealed the love of true lovers and insured them of a blissful union. In such a stock popular novel as E. P. Roe's *An Original Belle* (1885), the author's analysis of a young couple's tender emotions indicates the subtleties of this convention:

> He was eager to take her in his arms, to place the kiss of life-long loyalty on her lips; but in her very soul she felt that it would be almost sacrilege for him to touch her; since the divine impulse to yield, without which there can be no divine sanction, was absent. (pp. 56-57)

Here, of course, the man in question is an early suitor for whom the heroine is not destined, but the implication is clear that with the proper suitor, the divine impulse, the heroine's true love, would permit the divine kiss, and the divine sanction, true and lasting union, would naturally follow. Owen Wister's *The Virginian* (1902), certainly a proper enough novel, affords another example. It is true that Molly Wood has just saved her hero's life, and he may not yet be fully in command of his senses, but he does take her in his arms, and then "she clung to him; and presently he moved and let himself kiss her with fuller passion" (p. 257). Howells' scruples deny even his many couples destined for marriage the kisses of true love which sanctify their union.

To go further and compare the conventions of courting as they appear in Howells' fiction with the actual social conventions of this time is a more complex problem. It is easy enough to examine fictional conventions as well as social ones which govern sexual behavior today. One can find the sociologist Ernest Groves pointing out in a popular periodical in 1939 that "when to kiss, when to stop kissing, and when not to kiss are three of the most important... social problems today."[4] Ten years later the Kinsey studies offered convincing proof of the complexity of modern sexual relations and conventions. For example, the study points out that most college students understand that there will be good-night kisses as soon as their dating becomes regular. But, the study also concludes that among the lower educational and occupational levels, the kiss is in general eschewed, even though intercourse itself is much more frequent. It is likely that the actual conventions of sexual behavior differed as widely in Howells' time as in our own. Unfortunately, the kind of precise notation of sexual activity which comprises the Kinsey report is not to be found in the writing, either fictional or factual, of the period. One cannot prove, therefore, that Howells' attitude toward the conventions of courting were more delicately proper than those of his age, but one can still seriously question his accuracy as a social observer when that observation involved men and women in love.

Howells observed in *Criticism and Fiction* that *Madame Bovary* and *Anna Karenina,* "the two great novels which above all others have moved the world by their study of guilty love" were recognized as masterpieces. He added:

> You cannot deal with Tolstoy's and Flaubert's subjects in the absolute artistic freedom of Tolstoy and Flaubert; since De Foe, that is unknown among us; but if you deal with them in the manner of George Eliot, of Thackeray, of Dickens, of society, you may deal with them even in the magazines. (p. 79)

But despite this admission in his criticism, his fiction simply did not deal with Tolstoy's and Flaubert's subjects, or even any close approximations. He consistently championed novels which were far freer in treating of sex than his own, but his fictional practice makes it difficult to deny that he approached the bestial passion timorously.

For all that, it would be unjust criticism which placed too much stress upon this attitude. His drawing back from the realities of sexual relationships undoubtedly limited his view, but it did not dull his perceptions when he focused on other human concerns not so alarming to his temperament as the lovers' embrace.

1. It is true that a Howells story published in the *Atlantic Monthly,* 1875-76, as "Private Theatricals" did not appear in book form until 1921 as *Mrs. Farrell.* The reason for the suppression was the objection of the woman who felt she was the original of the fictional Mrs. Farrell. For information, see "'Ricus,' A Suppressed Novel of Mr. Howells," *Bookman,* XXXII (October, 1910), 201-203.

2. *The Sentimental Novel in America 1789-1860* (Duke University Press, 1940), pp. 34-44.

3. *Howells and the Age of Realism* (Philadelphia, 1954), pp. 148-149.

4. "Too Much Kissing," *American Magazine,* CXXVIII (Dec., 1939), 22-23.

III. Howells' Social and Economic Views

THE MAJOR REASON *for a revival of interest in Howells in the thirties was recognition of his activities and writing as a critic of the American economic system. Walter F. Taylor's study of Howells' economic novels, the first essay in this section, became a chapter in an important book,* The Economic Novel in America *(1942). Mr. Taylor has been a professor of literature since he received his Ph.D. degree from the University of North Carolina in 1930. He is at present Dean of Blue Mountain College, Blue Mountain, Mississippi.*

The other two articles in this section are representative of many scholarly articles devoted to Howells' social and economic views. The first addresses itself to the subject "Complicity," a term Howells used and one that defines his social philosophy better than any other single term. The second turns to Howells' ethical beliefs, which are closely connected with his social faith. The author reaches her conclusions through an intensive study of Howells' periodical writing in the late nineteenth century, a crucial time in the formulation of his social and economic views.

Both of these studies are by scholars whose interest in Howells began with a doctoral dissertation on an aspect of his work. Arnold Fox is an associate professor of English at Northern Illinois University.

Mrs. Graham Belcher Blackstock received the Ph.D. degree from the University of Michigan. She is currently an editor of the University of Texas Press.

1932

WALTER FULLER TAYLOR

William Dean Howells And the Economic Novel

I

THOUGH Howells's interest in economic reform is well known, his economic novels[1] have not hitherto been subjected to close analysis, and Howells as a critic of industrialism has been interpreted quite differently by different historians.[2] Accordingly, I have tried to determine in the present study exactly what economic philosophy Howells expressed in the novel, and how he expressed it. I have attempted, moreover, to view Howells's work not in isolation, but in its natural place in a liberal criticism of American industry which was begun during the eighteen-seventies, and which has continued to the present. Such an examination reveals that Howells adapted his technique of objective realism with considerable skill to the treatment of economic problems, and that he advanced criticisms of American economy more radical and far-reaching than had hitherto appeared in the American novel.[3]

II

When Howells entered the field of the economic novel,[4] he brought with him a mature technique and philosophy of fiction. Merely to designate him as the realist of the commonplace, though correct, is inadequate. His theory, announced in an essay on Henry James as early as 1882, called for discarding the conventional plot and substituting therefor a study of character and situation. "The novelist's main business is to possess his reader with a due conception

From *American Literature,* IV (May, 1932), 103-13. By permission.

of his characters and the situations in which they find themselves. If he does more or less than this he equally fails."[5] The story of the modern novel, he later assumes, should become a secondary matter. The characters should be first conceived, and the story should merely trace the natural interaction of these characters on one another. Hence his approval of Turgenev: "Here was a master who was apparently not trying to work out a plot, who was not even trying to work out a character, but was standing aside from the whole affair, and letting the characters work the plot out."[6] In his own novels, moreover, Howells worked with complete objectivity, never obtruding his own opinions, and rarely interrupting his narrative, as Fielding and Thackeray had done, in order to comment on characters or incidents.

To this degree of conscious objective realism, the American economic novel, prior to Howells, had not attained.[7] In its crudest form the economic novel had been merely an old-fashioned melodramatic story, roughly adapted to a modern setting, into which certain criticisms of industrialism were arbitrarily thrust.[8] Naturally, realistic discussion and romantic story fail to fuse; the incongruity between sermon and story is not overcome. Other economic novels are built, more coherently, about the victim-of-society theme or the struggles of the radical reformer. Some of these novels—like Garland's *Jason Edwards*—are powerful argumentative tracts; some of them possess artistic merit. In none, however, is economic criticism perfectly fused with fiction proper. The absolutely lifelike interplay of incident and personality, which is the triumph of the best of fiction, is sacrificed to the support of a thesis or the exposure of an evil. Nowhere, in my judgment, is the action of sufficient general interest, nowhere is the craftsmanship of the authors of sufficient excellence, to establish these works on the firm ground of intrinsic literary merit. They remain primarily tracts.

Into this pit of didacticism the cautious Howells refused to stumble. A mature novelist, equipped with a standard of objective realism and a nice artistic conscience, he never sacrificed literary merit to the needs of economic discussion. All four of his economic novels develop with the utmost naturalness from the interaction of the characters. Two of them—*Annie Kilburn* and *A Hazard of New Fortunes*—are so wholly character-studies that plot is all but absent. In the others—*The Quality of Mercy* and *The World of Chance*—though there are culminating plots with suspense and climax, the correspondence between personality and motive, between motive and event, is well-nigh perfect.[9] That Howells' realism was wholly adequate for the treatment of his subject-matter I shall not maintain. He is able to portray only the middle and upper classes; and the real victim of industrial oppression—the blacklisted miner or the immigrant laborer in the sweatshop—is never presented in his pages.[10] But this qualification should not obscure the fact that Howells, first among American novelists, achieved the difficult task of constructing the economic problem-novel according to the methods of objective realism, and with no sacrifice of artistic merit.

While Howells thus preserved so carefully the merits of true realistic fiction, how did he give voice to his criticisms of American society? His usual approach to industrial problems is through environment. In presenting the people of *A Hazard of New Fortunes,* for example, Howells portrays them partly by showing their responses to a metropolitan traction strike.[11] There is Angus Beaton, the temperamental artist who, in a fit of anger because he has to walk five blocks, proposes that eight or ten strikers be hanged. Or, in contrast, there is the radical Socialist, Lindau, who is mortally wounded in a picketing mêlée. In like manner the measure of Fulkerson, Colonel Woodburn, the elder Dryfoos, his son Conrad, and Margaret Vance is taken by their reactions to industrial warfare. In *The World of Chance* Howells set himself a profounder and more intricate problem: What results would follow if a group of intelligent people, brought up in a remote religious colony where the sense for social justice was paramount, were suddenly thrust into the hurly-burly of a competitive metropolis? How would they adjust themselves to their new environment? How would the chaotic inequalities of modern industrialism appear when viewed by their unsophisticated eyes? Like Swift in the second book of *Gulliver's Travels,* Howells proposes a criticism of inhumanities, by those who have not from long usage become calloused to inhumanities. In *The Quality of Mercy* Howells examines the effects of a crime committed against the capitalistic order—embezzlement. How will Northwick himself, his family, and his associates, respond to his crime? In the close interrelations of modern economy, how will their lives be affected by his defalcation? Just as Hawthorne sounded out with insatiable curiosity the moral consequences of the Puritan sense of sin, so Howells sounded out, through character after character, the consequences, for American personality, of the effort to live amid the conditions wrought by competitive capitalism. In the conception of nearly every important character of his economic novels, some criticism of the industrial environment is implicit.

Explicit criticism, too, may be found in these novels; for Howells possessed a positive and liberal economic philosophy, which he wished to convey to his readers. Unwilling to violate the objectivity of his art by addressing his readers in person, he created a series of chorus characters of such nature that their speeches, while thoroughly in character, should express Howells's own views. So well did Howells succeed with this device that it is impossible to tell which characters speak for their author, except by a fairly extensive comparison of his novels with expressions in his private correspondence and his Utopian romances. Such a comparison reveals that the principal expression of Howells's philosophy is to be found in the speeches of the minister, Peck, in *Annie Kilburn;* Basil March, in *A Hazard of New Fortunes;*[12] and the patriarchal Hughes in *The World of Chance.* Less important chorus characters are Matt Hilary and the reporter Maxwell in *The Quality of Mercy,* Annie Kilburn, and the lawyer, Putney, who appears both in *Annie Kilburn* and in *The Quality of Mercy.*[13]

In fine, Howells's method of handling the economic novel was a natural consequence of his previous theory and practice of realism.

Preferring the novel of character and situation to the novel of adventure, he constructed his economic fiction as a series of studies in the interaction of personality and industrial environment. Nowhere is the story wrested from its natural course by the author's ulterior purpose. The opinions of the author are not delivered in person, as *obiter dicta,* but are unobtrusively expressed by chorus characters. This skilled craftsmanship contrasts sharply with the crudity of the economic novels preceding Howells's, and, in my judgment, justifies the critical estimate that Howells was the first American novelist to combine industrial criticism and high artistic excellence.

III

In liberalism of thought, no less than in skilled craftsmanship, the economic novels of Howells go beyond their American predecessors and contemporaries. The other novels appear to have been written primarily from the viewpoint of the independent bourgeois, out of the old doctrine of economic individualism.[14] They disclose a vigorous response to the evils of post-Civil War industry; they expose and denounce the corruption of government by Big Business, the supposed dangers of the labor union, the buccaneering tactics of railway companies, and the folly of get-rich-quick, speculative enterprise. They disclose a humanitarian sympathy for the urban poor of the tenement districts and a sincere conviction that the problem of the poor must in some way be met. But these novels never attack competitive capitalism. Moreover, they leave virtually unconsidered the profounder causes of economic unrest—such, for example, as the deflation of the currency, technological unemployment, and the closing of the frontier. They deal on the whole with superficies rather than fundamentals, effects rather than causes. First among American novelists, Howells touched certain fundamental causes of economic unrest and called in question the individualistic basis of American economy.

Howells's attack on the established system of economy is in part satirical. In *Annie Kilburn* the store-keeper Gerrish is courteously, ever so courteously, ridiculed because of his satisfaction in being a self-made man, a Success. Yet, Howells implies, in spite of the fact that Gerrish has attained to the American business ideal, what a petty thing he is! How limited in his stock of ideas, and how conceited! Because he is operating a village mercantile store, he feels quite competent to settle the American labor problem. Only the absolute rule of the employer will satisfy Gerrish. "You've got to put your foot down, as Mr. Lincoln said."[15] What, after all, is the chief factor in creating the Success which the American people worship? As if in answer to this question Howells relates, in *The World of Chance,* how the attempt of Shelley Ray to bring out his first novel is governed at every step by mere chance. Purely by chance the publisher Brandreth becomes interested in Ray's book, the title reminding him of some private theatricals he has played in. Finally Brandreth's company, on the verge of bankruptcy, brings out the novel as a desperate venture. When all their plans for advertising have failed to sell the book, an accidentally lucky review brings it to life, and the sales run over forty thousand.[16] And this doctrine of Chance Howells applies not to the publishing business alone, but to all business. "You have to trust to luck . . . in every business," Brandreth tells the young novelist. The whole business structure is as uncertain as a wager. According to the testimony of a character whose business has just failed, "It's all a game, and you don't know any more how it's comin' out—you can't bet on it with any more certainty—than you can on a trottin' match."[17]

But to Howells the implications of this doctrine of chance are more often tragic than amusing. Individual enterprise, controlled in a crowded civilization by nothing better than chance, degenerates into a mere struggle for survival in no way superior to the law of the jungle.[18] Amid the stresses and accidents of this struggle no life, even the strongest, is secure; and man's innate sense of justice, brought face to face with these realities of the competitive struggle, condemns it utterly.

What I object to [says Basil March] is this economic chance-world in which we live, and which we men seem to have created. It ought to be law as inflexible in human affairs as the order of day and night in the physical world, that if a man will work he shall both rest and eat, and shall not be harassed with any question as to how his repose and his provision shall come. Nothing less ideal than this satisfies the reason. But in our state of affairs no one is sure of this. No one is sure of finding work; no one is sure of not losing it. I may have my work taken away from me at any moment by the caprice, the mood, the indigestion of a man who has not the qualification for knowing whether I do it well or ill.[19]

Of this savage struggle for survival in a chaotic world of chance, the raucous clashes and clamor of an industrial city are the fitting symbol. In the words of the patriarchal Hughes,

I am glad I came and placed myself where I could fully realize the hideousness of a competitive metropolis. All these sights and sounds, these horrible discords, that offend every sense, physically express the spiritual principle underlying the whole social framework. . . . No one can imagine the horror, the squalor, the cruel and senseless turpitude which these things typify, except in their presence.[20]

Both by humor and by serious discussion, therefore, Howells portrays the turmoil wrought by a chance-directed individualism. These conditions he finds wholly out of harmony with the equality proclaimed in American political theory. For the effect of individualistic economy has been to produce sharply defined classes of rich and poor. Economic barriers are immediately transformed into social barriers; intermingling between the rich and poor becomes impossible; and a callousness toward the poor develops which could not be more marked in a definitely aristocratic civilization.[21] If, for instance, a new invention displaces a number of workmen, neither the employer nor the state takes any care for the subsistence of these men. They are turned into the street to survive if they are able; otherwise, to starve.

Technological unemployment makes its first appearance in the American novel with the story of Denton, lithographer and inventor, in *The World of Chance.* Sensitive and compassionate, newly come from the influence of a communistic religious colony, Denton is unable to share the general callousness toward the plight of workmen displaced by machines. Therefore, when he himself devises an invention that will displace a number of workmen, he is tortured by the conflict between his family's need for money and his personal sympathy with the doomed craftsmen. Unable to choose, unable to relieve the strain of the dilemma, he goes insane. To his unsophisticated mind, one of the fundamental causes, one of the daily commonplaces of the Machine Age, is when viewed with complete understanding of the suffering it entails, too painful to bear.

The old economic individualism, Howells feels, is plainly inadequate in dealing with such problems. The intricacy of modern society, the close relationship and interdependence of all its parts, render some sort of collectivistic thinking imperative. The welfare of all, not merely of the gifted and fortunate individual, must be considered. Better than "Success" is humanitarian brotherhood. The minister, Peck, in *Annie Kilburn,* desires the poor not to rise out of their class, lest they lose sympathy with their fellows. Not charity, but justice for the poor, should be the goal of society; and justice waits on the elimination of competitive strife; or, to put it in other words, on a collective control of industry.[22]

It is Howells's newly formed habit of thinking in collective and social terms which, in my judgment, distinguishes *The Quality of Mercy* from other studies in the psychology of crime. The book discloses little positive economic philosophy, but is written out of a profound sense of the close interdependence of all the cogs of the social machine. Society itself is made quite as responsible for the embezzlement as the unfortunate teller, Northwick, who commits it;[23] and, as the effects of Northwick's crime react on character after character in an ever-widening circle, society at large comes gradually to suffer the consequences. The words of Matt Hilary, president of

Northwick's bank, interpret the story: "There's really no measuring the sinuous reach of a disaster like this. It strikes from a coil that seems to involve everything."[24]

As a cure for the ills of a competitive, technological economy, Howells advocates a socially controlled monopoly. Peck in *Annie Kilburn* approves of a combination as a remedy for competitive strife. In *The World of Chance* David Hughes designates competition as a "Devil" and looks forward to the nationalization of all industry. The solution of industrial evils lies in an "ideal monopoly."[25] In other words, Howells would have a utopian socialism substituted for the competitive struggle for survival.[26]

As the means of establishing the ideal monopoly he hopes for, Howells consistently advocates the use of the ballot. The American ideal of democratic equality and suffrage is still just and valid, but democratic suffrage must direct its attention to economic as well as to strictly political matters. Hence Howells's spokesman, March, concludes that the socialist Lindau, who has been killed in a picketing riot, has sacrificed his life in an unworthy cause. Americans need not create seditions; for, if honest, they can *vote* any form of government they want.[27] Hence another spokesman, Putney, good-naturedly berates his trade-union friends for their neglect of political action:

> " 'You fools,' said I, 'what do you want to boycott for, when you can *vote?* What do you want to break the laws for, when you can *make* 'em? You idiots, you,' said I, 'what do you want to putter around for, persecuting non-union men, that have as good a right to their bread as you, when you might make the whole United States of America a labour union?' "[28]

These expressions correspond closely with those in Howells's letters and in *A Traveller from Altruria.* In his letters he pronounces against the use of violence by labor, but expresses the wish that a labor party embodying some practical ideas might be created, to which he would give his vote.[29] In *A Traveller from Altruria* he portrays the downfall of capitalism as a process of peaceful nationalization of industry, carried on through political agencies.[30]

IV

The economic creed expressed in Howells's novels may be summed up as follows: The system of competitive capitalism, with its accompanying ideal of individual success, is no longer satisfactory. It produces only a heartless struggle for survival, governed largely by chance, in which no life is secure; in which even invention, fruit of man's ingenuity, only adds to the misery of the unemployed. It produces, contrary to the equalitarian ideals of America, insuperable class distinctions between the rich and the poor. Competitive capitalism should therefore be replaced by socialism; the machinery of government should be employed to control production in the interest of all rather than in the interest of the exploiting few. This socialism should not be the effect or agent of class conflict, but should represent the will of the majority, peaceably expressed by suffrage.

And, when Howells's work in the economic novel is compared with that of his American predecessors and contemporaries, it appears that his original contribution, his *distinctive* achievement, is threefold:—First, he handled this form of the problem novel with a high order of craftsmanship that relieves its didacticism and preserves the artistry of good fiction. Second, he presented in the novel some of the profounder problems created by the industrial revolution —such as technological unemployment and the close interdependence of all members of an industrialized society—to which other American novelists had not penetrated. Third, he presented, for the first time in the American novel, an economic criticism definitely based on collectivism instead of the older theory of competitive, individual effort.

1. These novels are *Annie Kilburn* (New York, 1888); *A Hazard of New Fortunes* (New York, 1889); *The Quality of Mercy* (New York, 1892); and *The World of Chance* (New York, 1893). I shall not discuss Howells's two Utopian studies—*A Traveller from Altruria* (New York, 1894) and *Through*

the Eye of the Needle (New York, 1907)—except as they contribute to the understanding of the novels. An excellent brief discussion of these two Utopias may be found in Vernon Louis Parrington, *The Beginnings of Critical Realism in America* (New York, 1930), pp. 246-247.

2. Fred Lewis Pattee interprets Howells as a follower of Tolstoi in ethical earnestness and interest in social problems. (*A History of American Literature since 1870,* New York, 1915, p. 211.) Parrington interprets Howells as a Marxian socialist. (*Op. cit.,* p. 244.) The variation in these judgments is due in part to the fact that Pattee is concerned chiefly with Howells's novels; Parrington, with his Utopias.

3. The originality of Howells, it should be observed, lies less in his ideas themselves than in his adaptation of these ideas to the novel. His ethical earnestness he owes in part to Tolstoi and Henry George, his opinions to Edward Bellamy and William Morris. So completely has Howells acknowledged his own indebtedness that a study of influences would in his case be of doubtful value. For such acknowledgments, see *My Literary Passions* (New York, 1895), p. 184; *A Traveller from Altruria* (New York, 1894), pp. 212 ff. in the edition of 1908; and the preface to the 1909 edition of *A Hazard of New Fortunes.*

4. The influences which led Howells to take this step I shall not discuss here, as I have considered them in a previous article, "On the Origin of Howells's Interest in Economic Reform," *American Literature,* II, 3-14 (March, 1930).

5. William Dean Howells, "Henry James, Jr.," *The Century Illustrated Monthly Magazine,* XXV, 25-29 (November, 1882).

6. William Dean Howells, *My Literary Passions* (New York, 1895), p. 170.

7. In the absence of explicit references on Howells's part, it must remain conjectural how much he knew of American economic novels of earlier date than his own. He was certainly familiar with sociological fiction in general. He knew the humanitarianism of Dickens and the socialism of Björnson. (*My Literary Passions,* pp. 75-76, 167.) For a while he was closely associated with Hamlin Garland. The novel, he had decided by 1891, is bound to take account of the humanitarian impulse. "Art, indeed, is beginning to find out that if it does not make friends with need it must perish." Characteristically, however, he protests at the sentimentality of the victim-of-society novel. (William Dean Howells, *Criticism and Fiction,* New York, 1891, pp. 280-281). The reference is to the 1895 edition of *Criticism and Fiction* and *My Literary Passions.*

8. The evidence which supports the conclusions in this paragraph I have given in full in an unpublished thesis (now in the library of the University of North Carolina), *Economic Unrest in American Fiction, 1880-1901,* pp. 32-127. [The fullest and latest development of Mr. Taylor's thought and investigation of this subject—and of Howells' part in it—is to be found in *The Economic Novel in America* (University of North Carolina Press, 1942). Ed.] A selected list of novels, illustrating the kind of writing I have reference to, is as follows:

Aldrich, Thomas Bailey, *The Stillwater Tragedy* (Boston, 1880).
Davis, Rebecca Harding, *John Andross* (New York, 1874).
Eggleston, George Cary, and Dolores Marbourg (a pseudonym for Mrs. Mary Shell Bacon), *Juggernaut, A Veiled Record* (New York, 1891).
Garland, Hamlin, *Jason Edwards, An Average Man* (New York, 1891).
———, *A Member of the Third House* (New York, 1892).
Hay, John, *The Breadwinners* (New York, published anonymously, 1884).
Keenan, Henry Francis, *The Money Makers: A Social Parable* (New York, published anonymously, 1885).
Tourgée, Albion Winegar, *Murvale Eastman, Christian Socialist* (New York, 1890).

9. In *The World of Chance* the connection between the two character-

groups may be criticized as too artificial. No *essential* tie relates the Hughes family with the young novelist Shelley Ray and the publisher Brandreth.

10. For a similar observation, see Delmar Gross Cooke, *William Dean Howells, a Critical Study* (New York, 1922), p. 228.

11. See, for a similar interpretation, Carl Van Doren, *The American Novel* (New York, 1921), p. 149.

12. Compare the similar opinion as to March in Cooke, *op. cit.*, p. 244.

13. Compare, for example, the following pronouncements about the use of votes, not violence, in securing social justice: the statement of Putney in *Annie Kilburn*, p. 94; of March in *A Hazard of New Fortunes*, II, 272; of Howells himself in a letter written to his father on June 24, 1892 *(The Life in Letters of William Dean Howells)*, edited by Mildred Howells (New York, 1928) II, 26; and of the Altrurian in *A Traveller from Altruria* (New York, 1894), pp. 270-271. This and all succeeding references to *A Traveller from Altruria* are to the original edition. Compare also the discussion of the growth of class divisions in America in *Annie Kilburn*, pp. 190-196; *A Traveller from Altruria*, p. 98; and a letter to Mark Twain dated December 29, 1889 (*The Life in Letters.* I, 429). Compare also the Altrurian's emphasis on Christian brotherhood as the basis of the Altrurian civility (pp. 160-161, 299-300, 302) with the humanitarianism of Peck in *Annie Kilburn* (pp. 232, 240 ff., 289) and Howells's own interpretation of Peck's character in a letter to Mrs. Achille Fréchette dated October 18, 1887 (*The Life in Letters*, I, 405).

14. Evidence in support of the conclusions in this paragraph I have given in full in my unpublished thesis, *Economic Unrest in American Fiction, 1880-1901* (The University of North Carolina library), pp. 127-176.

15. *Annie Kilburn*, pp. 82-83.

16. *The World of Chance*, pp. 64-65, 346 ff.

17. *Ibid.*, pp. 22, 174.

18. See the passage describing March's reflections on the industrial city (*A Hazard of New Fortunes*, I, 243-244). Compare with this Dryfoos's comment on one of his struggles with labor, "It was dog eat dog, anyway," and March's conclusion that this was an unconscious admission of the strongest possible criticism of the system Dryfoos represents. (*Ibid.*, II, 266.)

19. *Ibid.*, II, 252-253.

20. *The World of Chance*, p. 297. To identify these opinions as Howells's own, compare with *A Traveller from Altruria*, pp. 281-282.

21. See, in this connection, *Annie Kilburn*, pp. 164, 190-196. Compare this with *A Traveller from Altruria*, p. 98, where the Altrurian asks, "Am I right in supposing that the effect of your economy is to establish insuperable inequalities among you, and to forbid the hope of the brotherhood which your polity proclaims?"

22. *Annie Kilburn*, pp. 232, 240 ff.

23. *The Quality of Mercy*, pp. 157-158.

24. *Ibid.*, p. 88.

25. *The World of Chance*, pp. 118-120.

26. I should hesitate to employ the adjective Marxian in describing Howells's socialism, as has been done by Parrington and Blankenship. (*The Beginnings of Critical Realism in America*, p. 245; *American Literature*, New York, 1931, p. 487.) For Howells, usually so conscientious in giving credit to men who influenced him, never mentions Marx. Furthermore, two important Marxian doctrines either escaped Howells's notice or were rejected by him: first, the economic interpretation of history; and, second, the inevitability of class conflict. Against the Marxian idea of a proletarian revolt should be set the words of a letter of Howells to Hamlin Garland, dated January 15, 1888: "The common-

wealth must be founded in justice even to the unjust, in generosity to the unjust rather than anything less than justice." (*The Life in Letters,* I, 407-408.)

27. *A Hazard of New Fortunes,* II, 272.

28. *Annie Kilburn,* p. 94.

29. See the letters to Thomas S. Perry and William Cooper Howells. *The Life in Letters,* I, 413 and II, 26.

30. *A Traveller from Altruria,* p. 307.

1952

ARNOLD B. FOX

Howells' Doctrine of Complicity

THE PERIOD during which William Dean Howells produced his most significant work saw the rise of two great naturalistic novelists, Zola and Hardy. Howells included both of them among his literary passions, and he was a particularly avid reader of Zola.[1] But while he admired certain qualities in the Rougon-Macquart chronicles, he remained in essential disagreement with the method used. He was too much a humanist to tolerate what he considered the brutalization of man which would result from the acceptance of determinism, and there can be no question that in his own work Howells starts with the concept of a free man who must accept the responsibility for his action. However, this was merely a necessary moral premise; from the social viewpoint Howells recognized that there was more to the problem. He came to an increasing awareness of the effects of environmental forces in shaping human behavior, and out of this grew his doctrine of complicity. Without denying either man's freedom of action or his moral responsibility, Howells tried to show the share which society has in each man's sin. Only when it is seen in the light of its causative factors can human behavior become intelligible, and only then can it be properly evaluated. What is more important, a knowledge of these factors is the *sine qua non* for dealing with social evils, for individual sin is largely a product of the sins of society. As a result of his conviction that a character cannot validly be studied in a vacuum, Howells began to examine his people as the products of environmental influences. The doctrine of complicity assumed a large part in shaping his novels, and his work became increasingly modern and significant as he reached a fuller understanding of the inter-

From *Modern Language Quarterly,* XIII (March, 1952), 56-60. By permission.

action between the human being and the society in which he lives.

The first specific statement of the doctrine of complicity appears in Mr. Sewell's sermon in *The Minister's Charge.* Preaching on the text "Remember them that are in bonds as bound with them," Mr. Sewell endeavors to give his congregation a lesson in social responsibility, to clarify the underlying interrelationships which make us so dependent on each other and which make so widespread the effects of our actions. No one is actually apart from his fellows: all, regardless of position, are joined to each other in a brotherhood which stems from the fatherhood of God. No man's sin can affect himself alone as a result; it necessarily affects the whole community. Even the good are responsible for the sin which exists, for they have neither stamped it out nor endeavored to find out how they themselves have contributed to it. It is not the one evil man who is to be held culpable, but the evil of the time and place, for that is what shaped him. Every man must accept the responsibility for his brother, and he must seek it out, must accept it voluntarily, for in doing this he will come to know God.[2]

This attitude towards a broad responsibility for human behavior led Howells to take issue with George Eliot, whom he considered in all ways but one the finest ethical novelist of the time. He objected to "the undue burden she seems to throw upon the individual, and her failure to account largely enough for motive from the social environment. There her work seems to me unphilosophical."[3] A later statement indicates the likelihood that his early Swedenborgian training may have influenced him in this direction, for he maintained that "In a world pretty full of evil there isn't any purely voluntary evil among the sane."[4] To emphasize the strength of the involuntary element in human behavior became one of the aims of Howells' novels.

A glance through these books shows how large a part this idea played his mind. We see it first in *Private Theatricals.*[5] In this novel, after presenting Mrs. Farrell in a manner which makes her revolting to most readers, Howells introduces some additional facts about her life which give us a new insight into her heart and a new understanding of the influence of her early life in shaping her behavior. The purpose of *A Modern Instance* is not at all "To picture forth the degeneracy latent in a selfish nature,"[6] but rather to show the effect that accidental circumstance and the influence of other people can have in determining which potentiality in each individual will be realized. It is not by chance that Bartley Hubbard fails to assume the proportions of the conventional villain, for it is quite clear that the fault is not his alone. Had he married someone other than Marcia, he might have turned out far better than he did, even allowing for all the obvious weaknesses of his character. In *The Minister's Charge* we see the life of Lemuel Barker shaped both by sheer accident and by the thoughtless behavior of others. The thesis is presented pointedly by the horse-car conductor and by Mr. Evans (pp. 184-85 and 235-37). *The World of Chance* presents Howells' view that man is economically almost helpless in the clutches of environmental forces which seem to operate in a purely accidental fashion. Everything appears to be determined by chance, and we see this specifically in the fate of Ray's novel. The tragedy of *A Hazard of New Fortunes* proceeds largely from the general ignorance of the interrelations and the consequent mutual responsibilities of our social organization. Finally, in *The Landlord at Lion's Head,* one of Howells' finest psychological studies, we see the development of Jeff Durgin as the logical result of his contact with a world which seeks constantly to relegate him to an inferior social position. The moving accident in the story is the success of the Lion's Head House, which brings Jeff into contact with the members of a higher social caste; when they reject him, his one thought is to get back at them and somehow force his way into their circle.

But we can probably see Howells' concept most clearly by an examination of *The Quality of Mercy.*[7] This is the story of Milton Northwick, the treasurer of the Ponkwasset Mills, who embezzles a large sum of money from his firm and escapes to Canada. The novel appeared at a time when such cases were being reported in the newspapers frequently, and in view of the great public interest in crimes of this type, Howells had the material for a very exciting and successful story. He was writing for a purpose, however, and to insure the clarity of his theme he almost deliberately deprived the novel of the incidents and treatment which would have made it attractive to a large number of readers. Northwick never appears as a figure of any significance, and at no time is his personality very well defined. He is presented as a type more than as an individual, a conventional creation of the forces which ruled his little world. As Matt Hilary describes him to a visiting Englishman:

It isn't at all a remarkable instance. There is nothing peculiar about it. Northwick was well off and he wished to be better off. He had plenty of other people's money in his hands which he controlled so entirely that he felt as if it were his own. He used it and he lost it. Then he was found out, and ran away. That's all. (p. 270)

When Brice Maxwell writes up the Northwick story for his newspaper, he points out that Northwick has merely behaved according to patterns which society has taught him and is consequently a normal product of his environment (pp. 160-61). Putney maintains that Northwick himself does not matter very much; it is what happened to him that is important.

There wasn't the stuff for an example in Northwick; I don't know that he's much of a warning. He just seems to be a kind of—incident; and a pretty common kind. He was a mere creature of circumstances—like the rest of us! His environment made him rich, and his environment made him a rogue. (p. 474)

Upon these terms Northwick's individuality is of little importance; his significance lies in the fact that he is merely typical, that in the sources of his crime we can study the sources of crime in general, and that through understanding this one case we may learn to understand the criminal.

Northwick lived in a world which idolized property, and it was only natural that he should have accepted the criteria of his society. His father's material failure and consequent loss of social standing showed him what the world thought of an unsuccessful man. Early in life he determined to be what his father had never been, to be what the world admired, a financial success. His god became property, the tangible symbol of this success, and when he contemplated absconding to Canada, what grieved him most was the thought of leaving his property behind. But the ideal which he pursued was actually one which never could be attained. He became a prisoner of his blind greed, and even though he was more than comfortable financially, he began to speculate with the funds of his firm in order to increase his wealth. In this course the world offered him tacit encouragement, for the organization of commerce and business is such, Howells felt, that in the process of making money some dirt gets on everybody's hands. Society had broken down Northwick's natural morality, for he had seen that the good were not always rewarded and the evil not always punished; as a matter of fact, no discomfort came from evil unless it was found out, and for the most part it was not found out. He had been warped by the materialistic gospel which the world had taught him, and not only did it make a criminal of him, but it left him with a distorted personality. Money had so completely become his interest, and his desire for it had so wholly consumed him, that he had felt no interest in cultivating himself in any way. As a result, during the winter which he spent at Ha-Ha Bay with Bird and Père Etienne he proved quite valueless as a companion, for he knew nothing, had no interests, and could join them in none of their discussions. Even the horses and cattle and flowers on his estate in which he took such pride had never brought him any aesthetic or scientific pleasure; they were merely possessions, merely signs of wealth which the world had taught him to value and which it would accept as proof of his success.

Howells came to believe, then, that the source of crime lies in society at least as much as it does in the individual. Society is responsible for such defalcations because it supports an economic system under which the accumulation of money is the highest aim of man, and as Howells became more acutely aware of the existing economic injustices, he came to attribute a greater share of the guilt to the environment rather than to the individual. His argument is twofold: on the one hand, society must gain a new perspective in its attitude towards those people who, having learned their lesson well, strive to attain what their environment teaches them to value; on the other, society must not think that it can teach its pernicious economic doctrines with impunity, but must realize that it will have to bear the consequences in such crimes as Northwick's.

Matt Hilary's understanding of these facts enables him to view Northwick's case with objectivity. He realizes, for one thing, that it would do no good to catch the embezzler and punish him. "It wouldn't reform him, it wouldn't reform anything. Northwick isn't the disease; he's merely the symptom. You can suppress him; but that won't cure the disease. It's the whole social body that's sick..." (p. 166). So long as society continues to provide the temptations, it will do no good to punish people when you catch them. That will not deter the others who are tempted similarly. Only by controlling the environment can we eliminate the criminal.

But there is an obverse to the doctrine of complicity. Just as Northwick's behavior is largely a product of environmental forces, his own actions will become part of that body of forces, and we see in his family, his neighbors, and his community the far-reaching influence of what he has done. In the words of Matt Hilary, "there's really no measuring the sinuous reach of a disaster like this. It strikes from a coil that seems to involve everything." (p. 88). The unhappiness he brings to his daughters is most obvious; it appears for a moment that he may have made Sue's marriage impossible. His peculations result in the failure of other people who were involved financially. Above all, he has aided in undermining the morale of the community, for many people had looked up to him, and his example was necessarily a prominent one. If society is to protect itself from the repetition of such deeds, Howells felt, it must understand fully the implications of complicity; it must understand that crime is the concern of everybody, not merely of those in the immediate circle of the criminal, and it must realize its own responsibility in preventing crime. Only then may we look for some improvement in "the monotonous endeavor and failure of society to repress the monotonous evolution of the criminal in conditions that render his evolution inevitable. . . ."[8]

But as I pointed out at the beginning, Howells never seeks entirely to relieve his malefactors of the burden of guilt. The consequences of their behavior are actually irreparable and stand as a symbol of their guilt; and just as in real life no amount of understanding can nullify the damage, so Howells does not deny it in his novels. It would be useless to try to whitewash an offender, for as Squire Gaylord says, "A man does this thing or that, and the consequence follows. I couldn't forgive Bartley so that he could escape any consequence of what he's done . . . "[9] Northwick's guilt may be lessened by the share which society must assume in it, but it is not eliminated. As a novelist Howells felt a personal obligation here, for he believed that the greatest art was that in which violated moral law prevailed, as it did in the Greek drama.[10] In consequence Northwick can in no way escape his sin. However, the real issue in the story is not Northwick at all, but society. Society, too, cannot escape the sins of its past, but the implications of the doctrine of complicity can point the way to a better future.

1. *My Literary Passions* (New York, 1895), pp. 246, 248.
2. *The Minister's Charge* (Boston, 1887), pp. 457-59.
3. *My Literary Passions,* p. 185.
4. *Imaginary Interviews* (New York, 1910), p. 164.
5. Published posthumously as *Mrs. Farrell* (New York, 1921). It first appeared serially in the *Atlantic Monthly* from November, 1875, to May, 1876.
6. Delmar Gross Cooke, *William Dean Howells* (New York, 1922), p. 240.
7. *The Quality of Mercy* (New York, 1892). The doctrine of complicity in Howells has received explicit consideration in Kirk and Kirk, *William Dean Howells* (New York, 1950).
8. *Impressions and Experiences* (New York, 1896), p. 92.
9. *A Modern Instance* (Boston, 1923), p. 189.
10. "The Plays of Henry Arthur Jones," *North American Review,* CLXXXVI (February, 1908), 208.

1943

GRAHAM BELCHER BLACKSTOCK

Howells's Opinions on the Religious Conflicts Of His Age as Exhibited in Magazine Articles

THE SPIRITUAL DEPRESSION and despair which accompanied the philosophic conflicts of the later nineteenth century did not exempt William Dean Howells from their touch. Although he has been saddled for three or four decades with the reputation of being a kind of mustachioed and fatherly Pollyanna, who insisted on presenting "the smiling aspects of life," he was frequently unable to play the "glad game." There were melancholy tendencies in his nature, trends which caused him to muse darkly over the shortcomings of our American democracy, our failures in economic and political and social equality, our inadequate treatment of the problem of crime, our narrowness and bigotry in determining the status of women, our foolish and jingoistic patriotism and nationalism. This melancholy strain was evident especially in his consideration of the philosophical and religious conflicts of his age....

[A short section reviewing the neglect of Howells and the revival of interest in his work in the thirties has been omitted. The works of W. F. Taylor, J. W. Getzels, Conrad Wright, and George Arms are cited as principal studies of the development of Howells' social and economic philosophy.]

But the philosophy of Howells included much more than his ideas on strictly social problems. Underlying these opinions were attitudes on broadly philosophical matters, on cosmical questions, on the place of man in the universe. Criticism of Howells has neglected this phase of his work. No one seems to realize that he was significant in these larger aspects of thought, that he was anxiously concerned

From *American Literature,* XV (November, 1943), 262-78. By permission.

with the problems of religion and of man's relation to the cosmos. In fact, there is prevalent the opposite view that he was almost indifferent to matters of philosophy, religion, and the church.

This opinion does injustice to the scope and the seriousness of Howells's thinking, and overlooks a very significant aspect of his work as an American writer. For sixty years, from 1860 until his death in 1920, Howells was an active magazine writer, giving to the public through the pages of the *Atlantic,* the *Forum,* the *North American Review, Harper's Monthly, Harper's Weekly, Harper's Bazaar,* the *Century,* the *Cosmopolitan, Literature,* and numerous other periodicals, his views on questions which were agitating the public mind. Of major importance among these problems were those of the religion-science controversy and of the place of religion in American life....

I. "HOPE-IN-DOUBT": COSMICAL SPECULATIONS

The effort of Howells to cling to the faith of his fathers, or, later, to achieve a new faith of his own in a supernatural order, a faith harmonious with disclosures of science, brought him small security or consolation and much perturbation of spirit. He vacillated between moments of determined hope and of yielding despair. Hardly ever did he experience a glad confidence in the supernatural comforts of religion. At its best his faith was not more than a "hope-in-doubt." The nature of his attitude toward the supernatural in religion may best be understood by following its chronological changes in emphasis.

Temperamentally Howells was an optimistic intuitionalist. He was predisposed to a belief in a benevolent God, in a purposefully directed universe, in an innate God-given sense of right and wrong, in the perfectibility of man, and in the capacity of humanity to develop an increasingly better society. His powerful belief in the human spirit and in spiritual values made the idea of death abhorrent to him. He *wanted* to believe in immortality. But the experience of life played havoc with his temperamental predispositions.

This innate tendency in Howells was emphasized by his early training in the Swedenborgian faith. It is impossible to estimate just how much influence was exerted on Howells's thought by the religious environment of his home. The mysticism of Swedenborg was inculcated in the young lad by association with parents who subscribed to his teachings and by frequent readings to the family circle from the *Arcana.* A belief in the existence and supremacy of the spiritual and the divine was early engendered. The chief impression remaining with Howells from this early training was that of the importance of religion as the good life and of man's spiritual affinities. It was perhaps an emotional yearning for the security of religious faith which made it impossible for him ever to relinquish completely the hope of immortality, even in the face of what often seemed to him overwhelming evidence against it; just as it was perhaps his disinclination for scientific analysis which made it impossible for him to follow Fiske in a rational chain of thought which led the scientist to a much surer basis of hope than any ever attained by the more tender-minded thinker.

In his years as editor of the *Atlantic* Howells entertained a sort of passive faith, bolstered by nothing stronger than a half-doubting hope, as when he speaks of "those fond hopes of eternal life which most of us cherish,"[1] when he praises "the wholesome use of Miss Preston's book [*Love in the Nineteenth Century*] in all its precepts, to cast doubt upon doubt,"[2] and when he is grateful for "a touch of the sort of wisdom which we are losing sight of in these hard days of science and fact,"[3] the sort which realizes the inadequacy of reason alone. At times he felt a sort of despair in both belief and disbelief concerning immortality: "In those fond dreams of a future life which some of us still furtively indulge, despite the hard skeptic air of our science-smitten age, nothing is more dismaying than the chaos which the conditions of eternal life seem to make of all our mortal relations."[4]

While engaged in his duties on the *Atlantic* Howells became associated with John Fiske in a friendship which lasted until Fiske's death in 1901. Fiske was to influence more strongly than any other Howells's thinking on the problems concerned with the relation of science and religion. Fiske, the philosopher, became a sort of speculative mentor for Howells, the novelist and critic. He was the guide for Howells and thousands of others of his generation through the confusions of their period. Howells's gratitude to him for arriving at a faith in God through the study of science may be accepted as an expression of a widespread attitude among Americans of the time: "He evolved from the agnosticism of the whole contemporary thinking world a deistic belief, and established our civilization in the comfort of a credence unknown outside of his following."[5]

Gradually, after moving his intellectual center to New York, and after the controversy between conservative orthodox religionists and intolerant agnostics had become more bitter, Howells's hold on faith became weaker, and his despairing mood blacker. He accepted Fiske as his guide, insofar as one mind can be guided by another, in these matters. But in the late eighties through the middle nineties, even with the reassurances of Fiske, Howells vacillated between a despairing disbelief and a yearning hope. His customary attitude was the combination of a longing for reassurance of immortality, a longing so compelling that it forced belief, with a realization that such an aspiration must remain forever unsatisfied.

Although the late eighties and nineties were the period in which Howells most fully capitulated to the arguments of agnosticism, not even then were his thought and feeling completely devoid of intuitive confidence in the subjective comforts of religion. The Christmas "Study," *Harper's Monthly,* December, 1888, treats, among other things, a new type of Christmas literature, which scorns the wisdom of science, and seeks satisfaction in the mysticism of the Bible. Howells writes ironically of the adulation of science and approvingly of the spirit of the Christmas books:

Oddly enough, after a period of scientific exaltation, in which it seemed as if man might really live by the nebular hypothesis alone if he could but have a little help from the missing link, the new Christmas literature denies that there is anything of life everlasting in these things, and it reverts openly to the New Testament as the sole source of hope and comfort.[6]

But in the early nineties Howells's mood had grown darker; there was more profoundness in his feeling that doubts could have a blighting effect:

> If I lay waste and wither up with doubt
> The blessed fields where once my faith
> Possessed itself serenely safe from death;
> If I deny the things past finding out;
> Or if I orphan my own soul of One
> That seemed a Father, and make void the place
> Within me where he dwelt in power and grace,
> What do I gain, that am myself undone?[7]

By 1900 Howells was publishing articles on this controversial subject in the *Atlantic.* In "A Difficult Case"[8] he uses a method which he was to employ frequently in his "Easy Chair" in *Harper's Monthly,* the device of dramatizing in the persons of several characters various points of view on most questions concerning which Howells had not yet reached a definitive conclusion. This study is primarily an analysis of the difficulties of a young clergyman, who, in trying to convince an agnostic of the truth of immortality, loses his own faith. It is really an expression of Howells's own uncertain opinions on the subject.

Much of Howells's despair during these years was occasioned by the fact that he accepted with complete intellectual confidence the postulates and assumptions of science regarding the life of the spirit. These were distressing to a man whose nature so ardently craved assurances of spiritual verities. But when he began to follow Fiske's lead in recognizing that there was an Unknowable whose mysteries science was incapable of probing, when he saw other scientists recognizing the limitations of science and endeavoring to effect adjustments between warring philosophies of the physical and the metaphysical, then he began to find a partial surcease from his despair. But it was only an uncertain respite. Still his questions were not definitely answered. Science had only admitted that there might be answers, though unobtainable ones.

That Howells shared in the decreasing awe in which science was held is evidenced in numerous comments scattered through his magazine contributions. As early as 1866 he questioned in the *Nation* whether the recent marvelous material progress was not nullified by spritual losses.[9] And this was before the startling discoveries and advances of the second half of the century. He wrote more definitely of the limitations of science itself in the "Study" in 1890 that "one is reminded how much of science is still conjectural";[10] he remarked somewhat heretically in the "Easy Chair" during 1901 that "'The process of evolution is not always inspiring";[11] in 1904 he minimized the authority of science because of the mutability of so much of its knowledge.[12] In his criticism of Walter Maunder's *Are the Planets Inhabited?* in 1913, he approved the author's position that science is not qualified to answer the soul's questions, because it has no experience of the facts, and science is limited to experience.[13]

One of the implications of science which gave Howells most pain was that of man's diminished consequence. To Howells, who believed so firmly in man's potentialities for advance, and in his power of shaping a great destiny for himself, the mechanistic-deterministic concept of the late nineteenth century was terrifically disillusioning. He was forced to consider its postulates; yet he rebelled against accepting them, and clutched frantically at any straw that promised the weakest support of his sinking faith in Man, and God, and Religion. Such comfort he found in *Man's Place in the Universe,* a scientific argument that only the earth was habitable, by Alfred Russell Wallace, the man who formulated contemporaneously with Darwin the theory of evolution. Howells's review of this book[14] in March, 1904, is highly significant as a revelation of some of his philosophical attitudes.

More and more from the early years of the twentieth century until his death Howells was drawing closer to a position of faith. He was never firm and secure in it, being unsettled by the slightest agnostic speculations, but he relied increasingly on his intuitive faith. His loss of confidence in science as a means of determining truth in the psychical and spiritual realms made it impossible for him to share consistently the happy calm of Fiske. His optimistic faith in man's perfectibility and his control over his destiny made it impossible for him to accept the scientific naturalistic determinism. Yet he had no rational arguments for his faith, nothing with which to nullify the evidence of science.

And so at the close of his life Howells occupied a position similar in many ways to that of his early manhood. His difficulties in following the scientists and the naturalistic determinists had forced him back to the refuge of an intuitive faith in a religion which provided for the development of man's personality and for the possibility of a future life. And yet there was an important difference between Howells's first and his final positions regarding cosmology and metaphysics. The faith of the octogenarian was not the passive, trusting faith of the boy. It was not naïve. Howells had considered the postulates of science, and had accepted them where he believed them valid. But he had disbarred science in the realm where he considered its methods inadequate, even futile. The fatal contact with science had fundamentally changed, however, the nature of his faith. It had imbued it with doubts and misgivings; it had transformed it from a faith to a wish. Howells's faith at the last was only an intermittent hope. It had become sophisticated in its contact with the modern mood.

The entire history of Howells's intellectual life as reflected in his magazine writing from 1860 to 1920 indicates the same mixture of elements: temperamental tendencies to faith in an intuitive and subjective religion, struggling with a rational recognition of facts which seemingly denied the validity of such a faith; confidence in mankind's control over his destiny, in conflict with the theory of an impersonal and harshly deterministic cosmos; hope vying with despair. These constituents were ever-present in Howells's attitudes, but not in the same proportions. During his Boston sojourn his faith was rather passive, only mildly disturbed by doubts and questionings. Then followed a period of despair when he almost lost all his faith, and yet could not find happiness and peace in the scientific explanation of the universe. For a while in the years near the turn of the century he almost persuaded himself that he had the final solution in the scientists' exploration of the supernatural. But recognizing the limitations of science in this field he was driven back into his intuitive, unreasoning, and now inadequate faith. Howells was never free from hope-in-doubt.

It is evident to a reader who follows Howells in his work for periodicals that he reflected with unusual completeness and accuracy the course of American thought in this matter of the science-theology controversy. He gave expression to its various points of view and its numerous developing phases; he reviewed significant books on the subject; he himself participated in its movement to numerous shifting positions. While he was not an orginal thinker in this field, he was eagerly interested in the discoveries and conclusions of others, and was among the first to acclaim books with new and startling interpretations. Even in his swing back toward an unreasoned faith he was progressive rather than conservative, aligning himself in this way with those independent minds who were beginning to see that science could not produce all the answers.

II. "THE VITAL FORCE IN AMERICAN DEMOCRACY": LIBERAL CHRISTIANITY, A SOCIAL RELIGION

Unable, in the midst of the religious conflicts of his age, to find any comfortable assurance in metaphysical theology, Howells turned eagerly to the social aspects of religion, and sought in them values which might serve as a guide to human conduct in the bettering of the life of man in this world. There were really two creeds in Howells's religious doctrine: an emotional faith in some supernatural power for good, a faith which was a stay for man in his hours of self-distrust, and a belief in the social responsibility of religion to minister to man's present welfare, a belief which was to guide him in his human relationships. The two creeds, though seemingly far apart, were united in their emphasis on spiritual values, and in their opposition to institutionalism. They tended to become identified, the one with the other, as man approached the attainment of more and higher spiritual qualities.

One fundamental tenet of Howells's religious attitude might be considered as a link, in a negative way, between his mystical and his social faiths. This linking tenet was his vehement insistence that true religion had no concern with creeds, rituals, theologies, and sects. These were merely man-contrived barriers which interposed between man and a communion with the truly spiritual on the one hand, and were stumbling blocks in their efforts to achieve a better earthly life on the other. The church was to him at best "the most harmless escape for the spiritual vanities and ambitions of man,"[15] a sort of "Sabbath-day dress."[16] Later he became increasingly conscious of the church's error in allowing attention to inconsequential externals to lead to neglect, even perversion, of the essential meaning of Christianity. The intolerance which is sure to come with ardent espousals of creeds he deprecated always. Reviewing H. C. Lea's *History of the Inquisition in the Middle Ages* in 1888, Howells wrote: "Whenever one man hates another for his opinion, there the Inquisition is as rife as ever.... The difference between the persecuting spirit of the past and the persecuting spirit of the present is largely a difference of ideals, of ends."[17] "Gnadenhütten," an account of the Moravians which was later published as one of the sketches in *Three Villages* (1884), is permeated with a hatred of the stupidities and cruelties of religious intolerance. So too in *Italian Journeys* (1883) Howells berates the narrow bigotry of sectarianism. One of the improvements he noticed in Italian education was a larger intellectual freedom and an interpretation of religion as conduct: "Now these schools [of Naples] are free, the children are honestly and thoroughly taught, and ... they ... are ... instructed to associate religion with morality, probably for the first time in their lives."[18]

He expressed the greatest respect for the Christian religion, but an intense disapproval of the narrowing and bigoted policies and attitudes of its institutions. Like Tolstoi, he felt that the Christian Church was far removed from the true Christian religion. He considered the teachings of Christianity conducive to the highest good which he hoped for humanity; it embodied that principle of altruism which was essential to his aspirations for the race; it was a vital force in democracy.[19] Yet he did not consider a belief in a personalized God necessary to the good life. In this respect he was reflecting a common movement within the churches themselves, which as a result of the application of scientific methods of study to the Bible and the study of comparative religion had come to emphasize less and less the supernatural, and, consequent to an acceptance of the concept of evolution and its application in religion, had assumed a new view of religious authority.

Religion to Howells was not a creed; it was a life. Real religion was conduct. It meant a way of living. This concept was the basis of Howells's hostility to revivalism, of his refusal to affiliate with the Christian Socialists (who were united by a creed), of his antipathy to Puritanism. He appeared always to associate the institutions of religion with creeds, dogmas, theologies, for all of which he possessed small patience, and he did not think of churches as effective agencies for correcting the evils of society.

His hostile interpretation of revivalism was in line with a movement within the churches to humanize religion, to put the stress on the moral rather than the theological phase of religion. These were the views being popularized by some of the great contemporary liberals in the pulpit, Henry Ward Beecher, Washington Gladden, Phillips Brooks, George A. Gordon, and Joseph Cook.

Puritanism furnished the most patent target for his shafts against religiosity. Howells's reactions to Puritanism were not all antagonistic, and they have some significant implications regarding his conception of religion. Usually he was unsympathetic in his views and sharply critical. Puritanism, to him, seemed all that a religion should not be in its elaborate and narrow theology, its theocratic aristocracy, its dogmas and doctrines which restricted the free development of man's individuality. He disapproved of the religion of the New England fathers principally because of its stress on theology and because of its frantically developed conscience. The bad effects of the narrow creeds and formal dogmatism of Puritanism on character, especially through a too tender conscience, he brings out in a comparison of American and English women:

> I have often wondered what character untouched by Puritanism was like, and I have fancied that in the Hardy heroines I have seen; and if I cannot altogether approve of it, I can own its charm, as I can willingly acknowledge the ugliness and error and soul-sickness which Puritanism produced in building up our intensely personalized American conscience.[20]

In 1888 he referred to the Puritans' "impassioned belief in their pitiless and unjust God... its infernal doctrine... [and] atrocious dogma."[21] Self-sacrifice was the particular form of slavery to conscience which Howells attacked most often. Howells's attitude toward Puritanism epitomizes his belief in regard to religion as a way of living and religion as theology and creed. Throughout his writing there are countless incidental references to the strait-laced doctrine of Puritanism, frequently accompanied by some suggestion of the permanent good derived from Puritanism and remaining in the New England character. But wherever he finds the Puritan spirit emphasizing the letter of theological dogma, rather than feeding the spiritual life, he condemns it unmistakably.

With his love for humanity and his almost consistent confidence in man's potentialities, it was not only natural, but inevitable, that Howells should construct for himself a social religion. He was one of that group of thinkers who forced the churches to discover the human race,[22] although he refused to assume any leadership in the social explorations made by organized religion. This most vital phase of Howells's religion, this belief that religion is a social gospel, this emphasis on human values in religion, was a development consequent to the changing philosophical attitudes of the period. The most significant aspect of this trend in thought, the impact of science on religion, was its deflecting of human attention and aspiration away from supernatural factors to human values. The development of naturalism centered man's thought on man in all his relationships; it encouraged the scientific study of society, and speculation and experiments in social reform. Howells was especially responsive to the new intellectual trends in this particular, in the tendency to make man in his environment in the natural world, rather than the absolute beings of the supernatural world, the center of philosophy. His predisposition to interpret the natural world and man in spiritual terms made it easy for Howells to subscribe to a religion which emphasized social implications. He had supreme faith in the spiritual values which insure life on a high plane. His love for humanity was based on a trust in its goodness, its idealism, its capacities for development continuously toward a more ideal life. The spiritual values of altruism, love, morality, were real to him, and he never lost faith in them.

In 1866 he pointed out the inescapable identity of democracy and Christianity, when both were correctly interpreted, and declared that Christianity was "the vital force in American democracy."[23] Such a conception of true religion as a force which makes for better men and for better conditions of living remained the core of his religion, and furnished the basis for his later developing social theories. In the middle eighties Howells began to emphasize increasingly the altruistic, fraternal aspect of Christianity. He called attention, in 1890, to Charles Dudley Warner's *A Little Journey in the World* and Richard Ely's *Social Aspects of Christianity* because they both made the social emphasis implied in Ely's title. He endorsed wholeheartedly Ely's message to the church that "its work is primarily to make justice and peace and love at home upon the earth, and secondarily to save souls for heaven thereby."[24] The spirit rather than the form of religion is the important thing in building a better world: "The confusion in the minds of reformers comes from finding so many Christians in a pagan society, and so many society pagans in the Christian Church, and they break out into vain censure of appearances which are the inevitable expression of the very constitution of things."[25]

This Tolstoian note suggests the relationship that existed between Howells and the Russian writer. In *My Literary Passions* (1895), Howells makes confession of his indebtedness to Tostoi in literary and ethical theory: "As much as one merely human being can help another I believe that he has helped me; he has not influenced me in aesthetics only, but in ethics, too, so that I can never again see life in the way I saw it before him."[26] In numerous magazine articles Howells expressed or implied his unbounded admiration for Tolstoi and the great influence which Tolstoi's work had upon his thought. The two men held markedly similar views on religion. Both were unhappy over the injustices in the world, and looked to religion to remedy the evils of the social order. Both conceived of religion as a way of life, not a path to heaven, although Tolstoi was more established in his skepticism concerning Christian theology than was Howells. Both were distrustful of the church as an institution, Tolstoi being the more inimical of the two, but confident in the soundness of Christ's teachings. The religion of Howells and that of Tolstoi find their common ground in an ardent support of the teachings of Christ, unperverted by the later theological emphasis and ritualistic trappings of Christianity as a church and organized institution. These doctrines they accepted joyfully because they pointed toward a just social order founded in fraternity, altruism, and justice. Howells was not completely the debtor to Tolstoi in this common possession. His own heritage of temperament, family training, and American democracy had led him to a somewhat subjective, intuitional, acceptance of this religious position. But Tolstoi gave him a rational basis for his beliefs, and reasoned confidence in them. Howells himself refers to his experience in reading Tolstoi as comparable to the experience of conversion:

> The voluntary and involuntary allegiance I had been paying to the truth which is beauty and beyond art, and to an ideal of goodness and loveliness in the commonest and cheapest lives, was here reasoned and exampled in things beyond refutation or comparison. What I had instinctively known before, I now knew rationally.[27]

In 1896 appeared perhaps the most succinctly and effectively written of Howells's magazine articles dealing with the social implications of religion, "Who Are Our Brethren?" Here he tellingly arraigns society for its narrow concept of a brother as a blood relation, and for its failure to accept its responsibility for the welfare of all. He charges the church and its membership with a completely inadequate understanding of the teaching of Christ:

> We have never risen to a conception of fraternity such as Christ meant. Our only notion of fraternity is through a confused and rebellious sense of natural brotherhood, with its factitious duties imposed by society, so that when fraternity is proposed to us as the ideal state, we shrink from it in dismay at the thought of any more brothers... the supreme lesson of his [Christ's] life is voluntary brotherhood, fraternity.[28]

A social religion, from its very nature, puts a special emphasis upon its ethic. As attention and emphasis are diverted from the supernatural and from theological sanctions they are directed toward human conduct and human standards of morality. Such a religion as Howells's implied an ethic based on human nature. Religion as a way of life was essentially a code of morals. And religion which scorned theologies and was unsure of a guiding deity was forced to reliance on human moral judgments. Only to one such as Howells, confident of the moral quality of man, certain of the divine essence in every human being, could such a position be tenable. On the great ethical problem of what is to be the standard for judging morality,

Howells believed firmly in the conscience. This is the logical attitude for one who held his views of the worth of humanity.

Yet this concept of morality was not altogether sufficient for Howells. Just as he could not rest content in a religion which devoted its attention exclusively to the betterment of life on this earth and ignored the supernatural, so he could not remain satisfied with an ethic which made no provision for supernatural sanctions. To Howard Pyle in 1890 he confessed the necessity for a union of morality and religion, the inadequacy of morality as conduct merely:

> I think I should gloss your revelation in this form:
> "The kingdom of heaven is not to be regained by self-denial, *for self-denial's sake;* nor by virtue, *for virtue's sake;* no, nor by good itself, *for goodness' sake.*
> But the more I take thought of the kingdom, the farther off from it I seem to be. Sometimes I feel that I must live entirely on the earthly plane, unless I wish to be an arrogant ass, and meddle with things above me; and yet I must meddle with them, both in my own defective conduct and in the imagined lives of others.[29]

The religion which actuated Howells's own conduct, and to which he could hold rationally and consistently without qualms, apologies, or qualifications was the social gospel. But this was never quite enough. The child of a Swedenborgian household, the tender-minded intuitionalist, craved a mystic religion. He never brought himself to discard completely this secondary religion. There was a measure of truth for Howells in "all the prophets and all the religions."[30] This generous tolerance made it impossible to limit his conception of the ideal to any one credo, but his yearning for the idealistic One brought "... faith in a God who is always in His world, very near at hand, and so approachable that whenever we go wholly out of ourselves we can find Him, not only in every wretchedest fellow-being, but in the meanest thing he has made."[31] Religion as a spiritual bulwark was necessary in Howells's scheme of life, though it did not imply the existence of a God according to orthodox conception. It was a corollary to his interpretation of the meaning of life. But for him it was never a reasoned, convincing metaphysics; it was at best only a subjective faith in a benevolent spiritual force. It was only an emotional supplement to his active, vital religion. Christianity shorn of its creeds, its dogmas, its theologies, its rituals, and its superstitions; Christianity reduced to the teachings and practice of Jesus; Christianity as a way of building a better world for a nobler humanity — that was the real religion of Howells. . . .

[NOTE: The first five notes have been omitted, as they pertained to the portion of the original article which does not appear here. The remaining notes have been renumbered.—ED.]

1. *Atlantic Monthly,* XXXII, 105 (July, 1873).
2. *Ibid.,* XXXII, 376 (Sept., 1873).
3. *Ibid.,* XXXIV, 492 (Oct., 1874).
4. *Ibid.,* XXXV, 105 (Jan., 1875).
5. "Easy Chair," *Harper's Monthly,* CXL, 279 (Jan., 1920).
6. "Study," *Harper's Monthly,* LXXVIII, 158 (Dec., 1888).
7. "What Shall It Profit?" *Harper's Monthly,* LXXXII, 384 (Feb., 1891).
8. *Atlantic Monthly,* LXXXVI, 24-36, 205-217 (July, Aug., 1900).
9. "Minor Topics," *Nation,* II, 133 (Feb. 1, 1866).
10. "Study," *Harper's Monthly,* LXXXI, 966 (Nov., 1890).
11. "Easy Chair," *Harper's Monthly,* CIII, 492 (Aug., 1901).
12. "Easy Chair," *Harper's Monthly,* CIX, 481 (Aug., 1904).
13. "Easy Chair," *Harper's Monthly,* CXXVIII, 151 (Dec., 1913).
14. "Easy Chair," *Harper's Monthly,* CVIII, 640-644 (March, 1904).
15. *Atlantic Monthly,* XXIV, 763 (Dec., 1869).
16. *Ibid.*
17. "Study," *Harper's Monthly,* LXXVI, 640 (March, 1888).
18. *Italian Journeys,* pp. 126-127.
19. *Harper's Monthly,* LXXII, 154 (June, 1886).
20. *Heroines of Fiction,* II, 179-180.
21. *Harper's Monthly,* LXXVII, 477 (Aug., 1888).
22. Modification of the phrase used as the title of Chapter X in W. E. Garrison's *The March of Faith* (New York, 1933).
23. *Atlantic Monthly,* XVIII, 253 (Aug., 1866).
24. *Harper's Monthly,* LXXX, 484 (Feb., 1890).
25. *Ibid.,* p. 485.
26. *My Literary Passions,* p. 250.
27. *North American Review,* CLXXXVIII, 851 (Dec., 1908).
28. *Century,* XXIX, 932 (April, 1896).
29. *Life in Letters* (Garden City, 1928), II, 11.
30. *Harper's Monthly,* LXXX, 805 (April, 1890).
31. *Ibid.*

IV. Current Opinion

THE FINAL THREE *essays are not intended to be final words on Howells. James Woodress' essay clearly shows that Howells studies will be going on in the years ahead.*

The essay by Lloyd Morris, the social historian, is an eloquent statement of the essential greatness of Howells. It was addressed to a general intellectual audience rather than to literary scholars. As the first man to offer a formal academic course in contemporary literature (Columbia, 1923) and as author of Postscript to Yesterday *and* Not So Long Ago, *Mr. Morris was uniquely qualified to write about Howells. He died in New York City in 1954.*

Henry Steele Commager, though a historian, has helped his colleagues in literature restore Howells. In addition to articles, he edited an edition of Howells' work, Selected Writings of William Dean Howells *(1950). His review of Van Wyck Brooks's biography of Howells and his graceful and apt comparison between Howells and Brooks is a fitting conclusion to the first hundred years of Howells criticism.*

James Woodress, a member of the San Fernando State College faculty, is the author of Howells and Italy *(1952). His article serves a double purpose. It supplements my own remarks about Howells criticism since his death, and it calls the reader's attention to books and articles which I have not been able to include or mention here.*

1949

LLOYD MORRIS

Conscience in the Parlor: William Dean Howells

IN THE EIGHTEEN-EIGHTIES, as he neared his fiftieth year, William Dean Howells prepared to undertake a hazard of new fortunes. Having resigned the editorship of the *Atlantic Monthly,* he resolved to leave Boston, where he had lived happily for two decades, and make his home in New York. During that period many changes were taking place in the life of the nation, and Howells, at first, thought them good. The new industrial age opening for the United States impressed him as an age of promise. He took the hopeful view of the scientists. It was a new phase of evolutionary progress. It would advance democratic opportunity, extend prosperity to all, realize the old American vision of a society based upon equality and dedicated to noble ends.

The tone of Howells' beautiful early novels — the books which had brought him nation-wide fame at home, which had been admired by Turgenev and Tolstoy, and had won a European audience — was buoyant and optimistic. For, facing the American future with unquestioning faith, he had looked at the present with love. In the native scene, where his friend Henry James saw only social aridities, Howells saw the noble substance of the homely and familiar. He asked nothing better than "to take the slightest sort of plot, and lay the scene in the dullest kind of place, and then bring out all the possibilities." For those possibilities would not be dull. The "little everyday things" could be "told so exquisitely" that even if they faded "naturally away without any particular result," the "full meaning of everything would be brought out."

From the *American Scholar,* XVIII (Autumn, 1949), 407-16. By permission.

That this meaning was good, Howells did not doubt. His conscience and his confidence, during his earlier years in Boston, marched together. Like Mark Twain, he felt that, for any American, "the paths to fortune are innumerable and all open; there is invitation in the air and success in all his wide horizons." Others might distrust the increasing worship of business, the growing absorption of the country's energies in business and speculation, the general scramble for wealth, the gradual cheapening of standards, the insidious warping of the mind to materialistic ends — but Howells, at first, did not. Henry Adams might lament that there was no longer "means, power or hope of combined action for any unselfish end," but Howells could not agree.

He expressed his view in *The Rise of Silas Lapham,* most generous of all literary portraits of the new captains of industry. Lapham was a self-made millionaire, a producer of paint, and while others might find him vulgar, Howells showed the deep probity of his nature, his creative passion to make his paint the very finest paint possible — and showed, too, how Bromfield Corey, the Boston patrician, came to acknowledge his merit and respect his principles. And if Lapham could make paint yield honor, and even a kind of poetry, why should not others do the same with steel, and railways, and oil? The creative American genius, turning to ways of science, and applying itself to the transformation of physical environment, need not desert its "inner light."

But as time passed, and Howells looked more closely at the drift of American life, his confidence waned and his conscience grew troubled. Industrial strife spread over the land; the gulf between rich and poor was rapidly enlarging; and for every emergent Lapham there appeared to be an equivalent new area of desolation, a factory slum in which men knew no security, but instead starved and miserably perished. Somehow, the new age had betrayed its promise. The old dream of democratic equality was receding. The field of opportunity was narrowing, and for a majority of Americans the outlook no longer was bright with hope. The Haymarket riot of

1886 profoundly shocked him. The subsequent trial of the Chicago anarchists moved him to public protest, despite the personal risk in opposing a popular clamor for vengeance. "The historical perspective," he wrote when it was over, "is that this free Republic has killed five men for their opinions." He now felt that "there is no longer an American Republic, but an aristocracy-loving oligarchy in place of it." The American people, who once had taken their ideals of character and conduct from their statesmen, and then from their philosophers and men of letters, had entered a phase of material expansion and sudden towering fortunes — and there was no doubt that "the millionaire is now the American ideal" of greatness.

In past days, James Russell Lowell had wondered whether Americans, as they espoused industrial and commercial aims, would become "dispassionate and incapable of electric emotions"; whether they might not, at length, "find it too great a bore to quarrel with great public wrongs?" Howells was to show this fear groundless, in his own case, as another generation of writers were again to do much later. Meanwhile, a group of ardent social reformers was rising — among them Henry George and Edward Bellamy — and his sympathies were with their protest and their aims. He felt compelled to put his art to social use. In a series of novels very unlike his earlier ones, he began trying to portray for his fellow-citizens the gathering injustices that were blackening the American scene. In effect, his purpose was to recall them to their former state of mind, to that good will which Emerson had praised, hailing "their conviction of the great moral advantages of freedom, social equality, education and religious culture, and their determination to hold these fast."

Howells, during these years, had been reading the later works of Tolstoy, and the Christian socialism of the Russian master affected him more profoundly than Tolstoy's art. The doctrine reminded him of his father's teachings. The elder Howells had been kindled by the vision of Robert Owen, the English founder of a Utopian colony at New Harmony. He had attempted to operate a paper mill, in a forest clearing, according to cooperative principles, and the venture had failed. Nevertheless, though he lived to be a very old man, he never abandoned hope for the attainment of a "true state of things" in which Americans would transform their society into a cooperative commonweath, in this sharing the dreams of Wendell Phillips and the labor leader, Terence Powderly. William Dean Howells, remembering how the cooperative theory had been applied to family life in his childhood, had emphasized the family unity of American life, even in his earlier novels. Vaguely, he had seen the fair, fine aspects of American home life as some day extending to all social relationships. He had always cared most deeply about those aims which unite men in a family, "as private property never does." So when, at last, he declared himself a socialist, the step was less sudden than it seemed. The conditions to which his eyes had been opened, and his reading of Tolstoy, merely invoked those ideas which had been familiar to him in childhood.

Thomas Bailey Aldrich, Howells' associate and successor on the *Atlantic,* had found that in Boston "to be known as an able writer is to have the choicest society open to you." This had proved true for Howells. But, in the light of his new convictions, was it important? "Elinor and I both no longer care for the world's life," he wrote, "and would like to be settled somewhere very humbly and simply, where we could be socially identified with the principles of progress and sympathy for the struggling mass." He wondered whether the position of the artist, in modern society, was not anomalous, and perhaps even a little ridiculous: "Perhaps he will never be at home anywhere as long as there are masses whom he ought to consort with, and classes whom he cannot consort with."

This was Howells' conscience speaking, not his temperament, and it assured him that the prospect was not brilliant for any artist of his own time — "but perhaps the artist of the future will see in the flesh the accomplishment of that human equality of which the instinct has been divinely planted in the human soul." He expressed an abhorrence of "civilization." More than any of his contemporaries, he had believed that it would "come out all right in the end." He knew now that it would not. It would, indeed, come out all wrong, "unless it bases itself anew on a real equality." As for himself, an artist, he concluded that "it is very well to be confronted with ugly realities, the surviving savageries, that the smug hypocrisy of civilization denies; for till we recognize them we shall not abate them, or even try to do so."

It was conscience and conviction which made him abandon Boston for New York. The first novel that he wrote in his new environment, *A Hazard of New Fortunes,* was framed by a record of his own inward experience. "It became, to my thinking, the most vital of my fictions; through my quickened interest in the life about me, at a moment of great psychological import," he said later. A violent street-car strike broke out in New York, "and the story began to find its way to issues nobler and larger than those of the love-affairs common to fiction." The issue which Howells tried to project was that between wage-slavery—"the slavery implicated in our liberty"—and social democracy. The character of the millionaire Dryfoos showed how far along the road of social criticism he had come since writing *The Rise of Silas Lapham.* As compared with his previous work, the tone of this book was dark. The "little everyday things" no longer impressed him as being universally fair. If the surface of life showed pleasant, he would never forget that underneath there existed a black abyss of cruelty.

He was too intelligent an artist, however, not to realize that his personal experience equipped him only inadequately for the function of an American Zola, to which his conscience was impelling him. The portrayal of class conflicts on an epic scale was beyond his reach. He therefore took a hint from the work of Edward Bellamy, and the English poet, William Morris, and expressed his social criticism in two Utopian romances, *A Traveller From Altruria* and *Through the Eye of the Needle,* which exempted him from any requirements of realism.

These books masked with a deceptive and urbane irony Howells' attack on the conditions which provoked his indignation. But his purpose was deadly serious, and Howells' beautiful art proved equal to his intention. The visiting Altrurian, citizen of a socialist commonwealth, comes to investigate the "most advanced country of its time," and during his observation of it holds a series of Socratic conversations with various types of its citizenry. To them, he seems very like a bad conscience. He tests the democratic assumptions of the United States by the reality which he sees. The American democratic assumptions are identical with those of Altruria—but in Altruria, practice illustrates profession. In the United States, the Altrurian learns that it does not. The disparity of democratic principles and plutocratic practice is revealed again and again. Social injustice and ruthless exploitation are excused by teachers, clergymen, lawyers; the best minds are trapped in a moral morass of complicity. Howells attempted to forecast the course of future reform—the ultimate replacement of competition by cooperation, of rugged individualism by social altruism.

But he saw quite clearly that no merely external change of conditions can bring this about. It requires nothing less than a reorientation of the spirit of men. As he wrote to his father during an outbreak of savage industrial warfare, the troubles "must go on as long as competition goes on; they are themselves an essential part of competition." Alone among his contemporaries, Howells understood that mere "reform" is not enough—that the shape of the external world is made by the state of men's souls.

As Howells' preoccupation with social issues deepened, his concern with the state of soul of his characters increased. His earlier work had taken benevolence and benignity for granted. His later work raised questions. The social issues often did not appear directly; they were represented by problems of conscience or conduct. The "little everyday things" carried overtones of implication. In his world, the minute now stood for the large—as it had in the world of Jane Austen, for whose work he had a lifelong admiration and love.

In *The Landlord at Lion's Head,* for example, he told the story of a simple New England farm which, over the years, was transformed into an expensive, fashionable summer hotel. But, in the character of Jeff Durgin, the "landlord," he studied the moral character of the materialistically successful American. Jeff had an "earth-bound temperament," but in it was "the potentiality of all the success it aimed at." "The acceptance of the moral fact as it was, without the unconscious effort to better it, or to hold himself strictly to account for it, was the secret of the power in the man which would bring about the material results he desired; and this simplicity of the motive had its charm." Jeff's morality was fully expressed by his conviction that "you pay, or you don't pay, just as it happens." In Jeff, the old American moral sense had given way to a realistic view of affairs uncolored by any ethical preconceptions. And was not Jeff's psychology that of the eminent models of American success—the Carnegies, Hills, Schwabs, and their like?

Howells carried the problem into the next generation in *The Son of Royal Langbrith.* What would happen when the children of the "robber barons" were confronted with the true nature of the parents whom they had been taught to venerate? Howells saw two things which most social critics ignored. Many of the "robber barons" had established reputations for large-scale philanthropy. Their children, brought up remote from the arena of savage competition, were educated by the old culture and thus inoculated with traditional ideals. Royal Langbrith was a public benefactor and a private scoundrel. Shall his heir expose him, or violate conscience by nourishing the public legend which commemorates his benefactions and conceals the tragic social results of his misdeeds? Howells' solution for this problem was strictly Tolstoyan: Let God, not man, judge and punish. The book closes with the conventions upheld, lest a worse disaster occur—and with young Langbrith, from the highest ethical motives, lending himself to an hypocrisy which he despises. The second generation will continue the benefactions of the first. Its conscience will be even more guilty. Will social restitution be accomplished in full? Howells suggests no answer.

"I see a great deal of Mark Twain nowadays, and we have high good times denouncing everything," Howells wrote to his sister at the turn of the century. "We agree perfectly about the Boer war, and the Filipino war, and war generally. Then, we are old fellows, and it is pleasant to find the world so much worse than it was when we were young." It was not, really, pleasant for Howells. But he learned to live with his social disillusion, and possibly this was made easier for him because, unlike Mark Twain, he had given no personal hostages to the forces which his conscience made him indict. Then, too, believing that external change results only from a change in the state of men's souls, he could look at American life and still find areas in which the state of the soul was good. The serene and hopeful artist of his middle years survived, and co-existed with the unhappy social critic of his old age.

Because this was the case, the best work of his old age equaled in charm, and exceeded in power, that which first won him fame. When his conscience awoke to social injustice, he thought he would never again write a story "in which mating and marrying play an important part"; he was too old for the subject, and it no longer seemed a vital one. But in his later work he returned to love as a central theme with some frequency, and brought to it an insight and a perception of complexity that he had never before displayed. In some of the stories of *Questionable Shapes* and *Between the Dark and the Daylight,* in *Miss Bellard's Inspiration* and *Fennel and Rue* he recorded those darker aspects of love—its possessiveness, its cruelty, its ambivalence—which analytical psychology was later to explore.

The masterpiece of his old age was *The Kentons.* This novel reaffirmed his faith in one area of American life—the Middle Western city which, twenty years later, Sinclair Lewis was to arraign—and revived his original thesis that "wherever life is simplest and purest and kindest, that is the highest civilization." It took Howells back to the province that was peculiarly his own, the broad sphere of American middle-class existence, and studied the loyalty, affection and unity which, in his view, gave American family life its peculiar tone and special moral value. Quite rightly, Henry James called it "that perfectly classic illustration of your spirit and your form." But other critics were not so kindly. The reviewer for the *Atlantic* thought that Howells' simple Americans were the "monstrous offsprings of barbarous and illicit social relations," and protested that to pursue them intently was "like riding in pink, and with winding of horns, to a hunt of cockroaches!" This reviewer was Miss Harriet Waters Preston, herself a New England novelist, the translator of Sainte-Beuve, and a Scholarly authority in the field of Provencal poetry. At the moment, a romantic reaction had set in, and the public cared only for novels like *Janice Meredith, Monsieur Beaucaire, To Have and to Hold,* and the books of F. Marion Crawford. Howells's middle-class Americans were caustically dismissed as "commonplace people."

"I had hoped that I was helping my people to know themselves in the delicate beauty of their everyday lives, and to find cause for pride in the loveliness of an apparently homely average, but they don't want it," Howells told Brander Matthews. He confessed himself disheartened, and when Charles Eliot Norton sent him some early letters of Henry James in which James had discussed Howells' limitations as a novelist, Howells was driven to meditate the whole of his career. He found James' strictures very just, he told Norton. "He speaks of me with my style, and such mean application as I was making of it, as seeming to him like a poor man with a diamond which he does not know what to do with." Perhaps he *had* cut only rather inferior window glass with it. "But I am not sorry for having wrought in common, crude material so much that is the right American stuff; and perhaps hereafter, when my din is done, if anyone is curious to know what that noise was, it will be found to have proceeded from a small insect which was scraping about on the surface of our life and trying to get into its meaning for the sake of the other insects larger or smaller."

During his editorship of the *Atlantic Monthly,* Howells had fought to create an audience for realistic fiction. In later years he continued the battle from the "Easy Chair" of *Harper's Magazine.* There, he systematically championed the novels of a rising generation of American writers more bitterly disillusioned than himself —writers who felt the need of a realism far more drastic than his: Hamlin Garland, Stephen Crane, Frank Norris, Robert Herrick. He had been their precursor and, in a sense, their master also. He had explored the territory which was to give them their subjects. He had developed the method which they were to apply with a greater fearlessness. And this leadership brought about the withering of his own laurels. The public that he had prepared for his successors soon began to account his own work old-fashioned. A collected edition of Howells' books was launched, and presently was abandoned.

In 1915, he was writing sadly to Henry James: "I am comparatively a dead cult with my statues cut down and the grass growing over them in the pale moonlight." In his seventy-ninth year, his publishers rejected one of his stories. He did not protest, but remarked that "in fifty years the inevitable acceptance of my work everywhere had perhaps spoiled me for refusal." The passage of time transforms all literary innovators into academicians, and this was what had happened to Howells. "I am nearly eighty years old, and tired, tired," he told the novelist Henry B. Fuller. "It is a strange experience. I used only to need the chance for work; now the chance dismays me." He quietly accepted the verdict of the day, and acknowledged that "my sort of fiction is no longer desired."

But, three decades after his death, Americans, if they could be persuaded to read his books, might find that Howells still had something to say to them. In his later work, he spoke from an anxiety no less acute than their own. The problems which troubled his conscience had not been solved, and others of even graver import burdened the spirit of a generation that had forgotten him. Yet Howells, facing the troubles of his time with honest realism, had faced them also with courage and had achieved serenity. His books counseled Americans not to ignore their problems, and not to despair because of them. He suggested a ground for hope in "the fruitful fields of our common life"; a ground for faith in the energy of the American will and the vitality of the American conscience. The good fight, he intimated, might yet be won.

1959

HENRY STEELE COMMAGER

For Fifty Years a Literary Dynamo

A Review of *Howells* by Van Wyck Brooks

THE HALF CENTURY after Appomattox was the age of Mark Twain, Henry James and William Dean Howells. Critics seems to have concluded, now, that Mark Twain and James belong to the immortals, and have relegated Howells to the realm of history rather than literature.

It is interesting to recall that James couldn't abide Mark Twain —he thought him commonplace and vulgar, while Mark Twain's comment on James' novel "The Bostonians"—that he would rather be damned to John Bunyan's heaven than have to read the book— is familiar enough. But Howells loved them both and understood and welcomed them both, and both of them cherished Howells as friend and counselor. Howells was the first critic to recognize the genius of James; he published "Roderick Hudson" in The Atlantic and offered to give him "half the magazine" every issue. And Howells was Mark Twain's closest literary friend and wrote what is still the most perceptive interpretation of him in our literature.

Van Wyck Brooks here tries to re-create Howells for us, to restore him to his rightful position. It is a portrait and an interpretation rather than a full dress biography, and painted with that impressionistic technique of which Brooks is the acknowledged master. It is warm, sympathetic, penetrating; it catches what was most significant about Howells, and what was most characteristic, too. In a sense, Mr. Brooks has done for Howells what Howells himself did for Mark Twain—he has brought him to life with affection and artistry.

From the *New York Times Book Review,* October 11, 1959, pp. 1 and 16. By permission.

Howells was, indeed, as Mr. Brooks says, "the one writer who was aware of all the others." Never has there been a more perceptive literary critic, or a more catholic and sophisticated one. He opened the pages of the Atlantic to all the young writers on both sides of the water; he discovered Ed Howe; he sent Hamlin Garland back to his Wisconsin coulees; he championed Stephen Crane (and read Emily Dickinson to him); he celebrated Frank Norris and Finley Peter Dunne and Thorstein Veblen. He was the first to popularize Bjorstjerne Bjornson and Palacio Valdés; he embraced Tolstoy and Zola and Ibsen; in his old age he held out the hand of fellowship to Edwin Arlington Robinson and Vachel Lindsay and Robert Frost. He was as national as Mark Twain and as cosmopolitan as Henry James.

He was a distinguished critic, but he was far more than that. For over fifty years he dominated the American literary scene as no one had done before, and none has since. Fresh from Ohio—and Venice—he came to edit The Atlantic; when he moved to New York in the Eighties to take over Harper's, the literary center of the country moved with him. Earlier, in 1865, Howells had written on European and literary topics for The New York Times. "They paid me well and more than well," he recalled. "A personal interview with the editor in chief [Henry J. Raymond] made me feel that I had seldom met so busy a man. He praised some work of mine that he had read in his paper, but I was never recalled to his presence; and now I think he judged rightly that I should not be a lastingly good journalist."

He was pervasive; he was ubiquitous. Turn where you would, there was Howells. He wrote, it sometimes seemed, all the novels. He drew a literary portrait of Boston, and then of New York; he painted the farms and small towns of New England, and the summer resorts; he re-created the Ohio frontier.

He went traveling to Niagara or to Quebec, or abroad; he gave the surest picture not of the expatriate but of the American abroad; he added Utopian novels. But that, like the editing, was merely part of his prodigious fecundity. He was the historian and the interpreter of Italy, of Spain, above all of England; he translated all the more obscure books that Americans should know; he gave us the most extensive of literary autobiographies—an autobiography that became a history of the age; for good measure he added thirty or forty plays.

"Stroke by stroke, and book by book," Henry James wrote him, "your work was to become, for this exquisite notation of our whole democratic light and shade, and give and take, in the highest degree *documentary.*" And just the other day Lionel Trilling observed much the same thing, that Howells belonged rather to the history of culture than to literature. It is not clear that these things are exclusive; that would rule out of literature a good deal of Dickens and Balzac, of Frank Norris and Theodore Dreiser and Thomas Mann.

Certainly Howells belongs to the history of American culture; he dominated one important chapter of that history. Certainly, too, he provided documentation for much of American life; it is to Howells we turn for much of our understanding of American Victorianism. But many of Howells' novels are quite independent of history and documentation. It is for the moral problem, the analysis of character that we read "The Rise of Silas Lapham" and "A Modern Instance" and "Indian Summer" and "The Undiscovered Country," and half a dozen others. Howells was not only historian and interpreter, he was a moralist and a craftsman.

If the moral problems to which Howells addressed himself seem not so much dated as tame, that is because Howells was so faithful to his own principles of literature, because—as Henry James pointed out—"he adored the real, the natural, the colloquial, the moderate, the optimistic and the democratic," because he disliked everything that was sensational or violent. He knew that very few people are involved in the problems that confronted a Macbeth or a Faust, and he addressed himself to the problems that are commonplace and familiar.

"Ah, poor real life which I love," he said, "can I make others share the delight I find in thy foolish and insipid face?" It is charged against him, too, that he addressed himself to "the more smiling aspects of American life." He did feel that, on balance, American life was more innocent than European, and presented, perhaps, more smiling aspects; after all, most of our major writers have said this, from Crèvecoeur to Robert Frost with his wryly ironic question:

How are we to write
The Russian novel in America
As long as life goes on so unterribly?

It is proper to remember that Howells was the friend and accomplice of the rebels of his generation; that almost alone among the novelists of his time he addressed himself to the problems of labor, to the ruth of the industrial system, to the inhumanity of man to man; that he championed the victims of the Haymarket affair; that he counted himself a Socialist and provided one of the most severe of all literary indictments of American society in "A Traveler From Altruria."

"After fifty years of optimistic content with civilization and its ability to come out right in the end," wrote Howells, "I now abhor it and feel that it is coming out all wrong in the end." Abhor was a strong word for Howells; his moral sentiments were righteous rather than heroic; his books were subversive but not inflammatory, but he continued, to the end, to encourage those who were inflammatory.

In a sense, it can be said that Howells has been buried beneath the ruins of his own triumph. He vindicated realism, but few now recognize a realism so demure; he transformed literature from a New England to a national affair; he used literature as a vehicle for social protest; he familiarized Americans with the literature of modern Europe—all the things that now seem so dated.

It is eminently so appropriate that Mr. Brooks should add this study of Howells to his long row of studies of American letters, for he comes closer to occupying the position that Howells himself occupied in American criticism than does anyone else of our time. And he resembles Howells not only in the catholicity of his learning and the breadth of his sympathies and the depth of his understanding, but in this, too, that (to use Justice Holmes' phrase) for fifty years he has *been there*—a familiar and affectionate figure on the literary horizon, guide, interpreter, historian and symbol. Like Howells, too, he is suspicious of the violent and the sensational; he prefers the commonplace, the familiar, the authentic; he has an unfailing appreciation of the intricate pattern of our intellectual and cultural life.

1960

JAMES WOODRESS

The Dean's Comeback: Four Decades Of Howells Scholarship

WILLIAM DEAN HOWELLS, who died just forty years ago this spring, finally has become a major American author. Though he never dropped completely out of courses in the novel or surveys of American literature, twenty-five years ago he was distinctly an unfashionable writer. Since then on the big board of the academic exchange, Howells shares have demonstrated the steady characteristics of a growth stock. Today he is traded briskly by the most finicky critics.

In addition, the fluctuations of Howells scholarship since World War I are a sort of Dow-Jones average of larger literary trends. If the postwar Twenties was an era of rebellion, one of the things rebelled against was the long literary domination of the "Dean." If the Thirties was a period of social consciousness, Howells' novels of social protest provided a rationale for his rehabilitation. In the current era of "new criticism" Howells has been found worth reading for aesthetic considerations alone. Proof of the present high state of his reputation lies in the appearance in 1959 of four significant books: an important edition, a biography by an eminent writer, and two specialized studies from university presses. These titles plus the pair which came out in 1958 offer convincing evidence of Howells' comeback.

The noisiest of the insurgents in the rebellious Twenties, of course, was H. L. Mencken, whose attacks, while the most colorful, were nonetheless typical. His unflattering essay, "The Dean," had begun the campaign of disparagement three years before the decade began. It came out in *Smart Set* in January, 1917, two months before

From *Texas Studies in Literature and Language,* II (Spring, 1960), 115-23. By permission.

the public celebration (mostly by the old guard) of Howells' eightieth birthday.

To Mencken there were no more ideas in Howells' novels than in so many volumes of the *Ladies Home Journal,* and the list of his works was as meaningless as a roll of Sumerian kings. "The truth about Howells," he wrote, "is that he really had nothing to say... His psychology was superficial, amateurish, often nonsensical; his irony was scarcely more than a polite facetiousness; his characters simply refused to live." But one suspects that Mencken's meat-cleaver attack was based on ignorance, for of the five Howells titles he listed as forgotten novels, two are plays and a third is poetry.

Howells' reputation, however, had been declining for at least a decade when Mencken unlimbered his artillery. In 1915 Howells had written Henry James: "A change has passed upon things, we can't deny it; I could not 'serialize' a story of mine now in any American magazines... I am comparatively a dead cult with my statues cut down and the grass growing over them in the pale moonlight." Time had changed and Howells' wry note recognized that he had outlived the alarums and excursions of his middle years. The battles of the Eighties and Nineties simply had been forgotten.

During the Twenties Howells scholarship, for the most part, went underground. While writers like Hamlin Garland and Booth Tarkington wrote and spoke the "Dean's" praises, in the academies Howells was little honored. Oscar Firkins wrote the first good book on Howells *(William Dean Howells: A Study)* in 1924, but had trouble finding a publisher, and in 1928 Mildred Howells edited a two-volume collection of her father's letters *(Life in Letters of William Dean Howells).* This valuable work remains one of the primary source materials for the study of Howells. There actually had been two books on Howells prior to 1924: Alexander Harvey, *William Dean Howells: A Study of the Achievement of a Literary Artist* (New York, 1917) and D. G. Cooke, *William Dean Howells: A Critical Study* (New York, 1922). The first is worthless; the second is still useful.

The attacks continued into the Thirties with essays like C. Hartley Grattan's "Howells, Ten Year After" in the *American Mercury* for May, 1930, and Sinclair Lewis' speech accepting the Nobel Prize. Lewis declared: "Mr. Howells was one of the gentlest, sweetest, and most honest of men, but he had the code of a pious old maid whose greatest delight was to have tea at the vicarage." And Lewis further gave the knife a twist by accusing Howells of taming Mark Twain and ruining Hamlin Garland.

Simultaneous with these derogations, however, was the Depression-born attention to economics, which found academic expression in Walter Fuller Taylor's *The Economic Novel in America.* Though Taylor's book came out in 1942, his articles had appeared throughout the Thirties. He had published an article on Howells' interest in economic reform in the same year that Grattan and Lewis were demolishing Howells. Late in the Thirties *Science and Society* carried a series of articles on Howells' socialism, which helped push Howells out of the backwater and into the main stream of American experience. Finally, the third volume of Parrington's *Main Currents in American Thought: The Beginnings of Critical Realism* (1930) aided Howells' rescue.

During the past two decades the Howells revival has snowballed. In every type of activity from doctoral dissertation to book-length study Howells has been measured and analyzed by a steadily growing number of scholars. The interest in Howells, of course, does not compare with the attention Hawthorne or James receives, but it is continuing and significant.

The steady production of dissertations illustrates well this attention. Except for D. G. Cooke's dissertation at Illinois in 1917 (a real maverick) and a German study done in Berlin in 1933, no graduate student discovered Howells until George Arms wrote on Howells' social criticism in 1939. Ten dissertations followed in the next ten years, and as of May, 1959, a total of forty titles had been completed or announced. There is no sign of any slackening-off. Three of these dissertations became books, a fourth provided the nucleus for a study of the entire Howells era, and many more have been carved into very good journal articles. The Howells groundswell, which was detectable at the beginning of the Forties, became a small flood when the scholars returned from the wars. Appropriately, the inundation began with a bibliography. This initial contribution, *The Bibliography of William Dean Howells* (New York, 1948), was compiled by George Arms and William M. Gibson. It is a pioneer work that every Howells student since 1948 has been vastly indebted to. The bibliography lists Howells' books, parts of books, and periodical contributions in chronological order, and contains much useful annotation. It also includes Howells criticism in a selected list that the compilers have kept up to date through supplements in the mimeographed *Howells Sentinel* published occasionally by Clara and Rudolf Kirk of Rutgers. In addition to the Gibson-Arms bibliography, the selected bibliography in the Kirks' Howells volume in the American Writers Series is very useful. Still another important contribution to Howells bibliography is the work of John K. Reeves, who has published a descriptive finding list of Howells manuscripts (*Bulletin of the New York Public Library,* June and July, 1958). The difficult task of tracking down manuscripts has yielded nearly two hundred items, divided about equally between published and unpublished material. This detective work makes possible the future study of Howells' revisions and work methods.

New editions of Howells' works have not kept pace in variety with the study of his literary life. *The Rise of Silas Lapham* has been edited and re-edited by Rinehart, Modern Library, Oxford, Harper, and Houghton Mifflin. The last firm has also brought out *A Modern Instance. A Hazard of New Fortunes* and *Indian Summer* are in the Everyman's Library, and *A Traveler from Altruria* is on the Sagamore list. But these are the only separate titles available in inexpensive editions for classroom use. A great desideratum is an edition of Howells' fiction and nonfiction, at least a dozen titles, which have been long out of print and are now hard to obtain.

The most important new edition of Howells is the recent publication edited by Clara and Rudolf Kirk, of *Criticism and Fiction and Other Essays* (1959). *Criticism and Fiction,* first published in 1891, has been unavailable for years, despite the fact that it is one of the central documents for the study of American realism. The Kirks in addition have rescued many of Howells' fugitive pieces from the files of magazines he contributed to and placed them in context with felicitous introductions. This volume includes "European Masters" (Turgenev, Verga, Zola, Tolstoy, and others), "American Writers" (DeForest, Twain, Eggleston, James, Garland, Crane, and Norris), "Further Critical Issues" ("The Man of Letters as a Man of Business," "Professor Barrett Wendell's Notions of American Literature," "The Future of the American Novel," and so forth).

Another recent service in rescuing Howells' critical essays was performed by Gibson and Arms, aided by Frederick Marston, in *Prefaces to Contemporaries* (1957). This work gathers up thirty-four prefaces that Howells wrote for books by contemporaries between 1882 and 1920. These include James, Twain, Garland, Crane, Bellamy, E. W. Howe, Zola, and Tolstoy. There is no duplication of texts between this and the Kirks' volume, though there often is similarity in sentiment. *Prefaces to Contemporaries* reveals a sound aesthetic base for Howells' realism in his notion that the world of art is a microcosm. Howells recognized the symbolic function of art in a way that finds echoes in current criticism.

Besides the foregoing, there are two other editions of Howells that should be described. The Kirks' volume on Howells, previously mentioned, was added to the American Writers Series in 1950, shortly before the American Book Company liquidated that worthy project. This edition contains the usual competent introduction, bibliography, and notes that characterized the AWS series. Besides well-known selections from the novels and criticism, this volume includes some poetry, a bit of *Literary Friends and Acquaintance* (which ought to be reprinted), snippets from *Annie Kilburn,* and one of the farces, *The Sleeping-Car.* Random House in 1950 also brought out an edition of Howells: *Selected Writings,* edited with introduction by Henry Steele Commager. It contains, besides the easily available *Silas Lapham* and *A Modern Instance,* two very welcome titles, *A Boy's Town* and *My Mark Twain.*

The task of writing the biography of a man who lived and wrote incessantly from the age of fifteen to eighty-three was a formidable one. But Edwin H. Cady accomplished this feat very successfully in two volumes published by Syracuse University Press in 1956 and 1958. The first volume, *The Road to Realism,* carries Howells from Martin's Ferry, Ohio, where he was born on March 1, 1837, to Boston in 1885, the year he published *Silas Lapham.* It traces the development of an admirable personality, a first-rate writer, an influential editor, and a dominant literary influence. The second volume, *The Realist at War,* chronicles in a superb manner Howells' battles for realism and his growing social consciousness. Cady's discussion of the novels in both volumes is competent and illuminating.

All of the Howells scholars more or less succumb to the charm of their subject, and Cady is no exception. But his biography furnishes ample documentation to silence forever the muddle-headed, ignorant comments that used to be made about Howells two decades ago. There is no longer any excuse to equate Howells' sexual reticence in his works with a Pollyanna attitude towards all the problems of the human condition. One of the important effects of Cady's two volumes is the placing of Howells in the context of his times.

The several recent critical studies of Howells also have helped bring Howells into proper focus. The most important of these is Everett Carter's *Howells and the Age of Realism* (1954). Carter's book illuminates the entire movement towards realism, of which Howells was the leader. The contributions of DeForest, Eggleston, Twain, and others are assessed, and the relationship between Howells, Taine, and French positivism is traced. Particularly important is Carter's scrutiny of Howells' critical realism against the background of industrialism and mounting social problems in the Gilded Age. Carter deals effectively with Howells' much-misunderstood quotation: "Our novelists, therefore, concern themselves with the more smiling aspects of life, which are the more American," which Howells wrote before the Haymarket Affair and before discovering Tolstoy, two events that profoundly affected him. For two generations his detractors have quoted his "smiling aspects" out of context and have damned him.

Narrower in scope than Carter's book but the first of the recent Howells studies was James Woodress' *Howells and Italy* (1952). Its purpose was to evaluate the large impact that Howells' youthful contact with Italy had on his entire career. It gives the appearance of overstating its case by extracting from Howells' multifarious career only one of the many influences. Yet one can conclude safely that Howells' four years in Venice during the Civil War had two important effects. When he turned from poetry to prose in Venice, discovering that commonplace events furnished usable literary material, the example of Goldoni's plays gave him excellent models for using Venetian life in his own work. Then Howells' diligent study of Italian literature gave him an entree into the society of the strategically placed Italophiles in Cambridge after the War.

Two of the recent products of Howells scholarship invite comparison with each other: Olov Fryckstedt's *In Quest of America* (1958) and George Bennett's *William Dean Howells* (1959). Both have similar subtitles: "A Study of Howells' Early Development as a Novelist" and "The Development of a Novelist." At first glance one might expect both books to cover pretty much the same ground; yet in a real sense the two books complement each other. Fryckstedt's work is mainly concerned with Howells' intellectual growth with particular reference to his use of European authors, while Bennett's study devotes itself to a consideration of Howells' novels as a contribution to *belles-lettres.* Fryckstedt ends with Howells' publication of *A Modern Instance* (1882), while Bennett begins only in 1866 but carries his subject through another decade.

Fryckstedt, a Swedish scholar, has written the better of the two books. His study is densely packed with information and shows an impressive mastery of Howells bibliography. Some of the biographical data (also true of Bennett's study) is by now a thrice-told tale; but the book is full of insights, and Fryckstedt's European vantage point affords a fresh perspective. His discussion of Howells' discovery of America after returning from Europe is particularly good, and his demonstration of Howells' use of Parkman in *Their Wedding Journey* and *A Chance Acquaintance* is very illuminating. His analysis of Turgenev's impact on Howells is the best in print, and his discussion of Howells' inability to appreciate Dreiser (pp. 266-271), usually glossed over by Howells scholars, is the only adequate one this reviewer has read.

Both Fryckstedt and Bennett deal at length with Howells' friendships. Both are good on the Howells-James and Howells-Lowell relationships. While Fryckstedt puts more stress than Bennett on the differences between Howells and James and also sees Lowell as an important influence, even on Howells' early realism, these variations are differences mainly of degree. In the Howells-Twain relationship, which Fryckstedt treats only tangentially, Bennett rides his thesis too hard. He admits Twain had no obvious influence on Howells' writing career, but says that no estimate of Howells' work can be made without taking it into account. Then he argues that Twain probably was a catalyst in Howells' discovery of America—a "vital counteragent to the influence of men like Charles Eliot Norton and Henry James." This is an attractive thesis, but an impossible one to document convincingly.

Bennett's strength lies in his criticism of the novels. Though there is little that is new in his book, he is not afraid to rank the novels and discuss them as works of art without reference to their value as social documents. Whether or not he has, as the jacket blurb says, "rescued the novels from superficial treatment" (Cady's criticism is very good, for example) is certainly debatable. His essays on *A Foregone Conclusion, The Undiscovered Country,* and the major novels of the 1880-1890 decade are clear and cogent. His shrewd rejection of the tradition that Howells did not publish *Private Theatricals* in book form during his life because of a threatened law suit is very persuasive. His conclusion, based on an aesthetic approach to the novel, plus some inconclusive documentary evidence, argues that Howells simply recognized serious artistic flaws in the novel but had no time to revise it. This insight shows Bennett's critical method at its best. One wishes that he had continued his study beyond the early 1890's, for Howells wrote another dozen novels, some of which are well worth extensive discussion.

Last fall Van Wyck Brooks joined the swelling choir of Howells' admirers. His book, *Howells: His Life and World,* is good biography, for he has an amazing ability to assimilate and to draw on his wide reading. He seems to have read Howells completely, and illustrates the biographical narrative effortlessly with apt quotations from the whole corpus of Howells' work. Whether or not a reader totally unfamiliar with the subject can carry away more than a highly impressionistic portrait is a real question, but the book evokes Howells vividly for the initiate, and the usual wealth of fascinating footnotes adds depth to the picture.

One realizes as the narrative unfolds that he is reading a competent performance by an old hand at biography and literary history. In a word, Brooks creates the same sort of kaleidoscope that he already is known for through his *Makers and Finders. Howells: His Life and World* is no substitute, however, for Cady's two-volume biography, which is much fuller both in criticism and biographical narrative, but it is lively, readable, and succinct. Brooks' praise of Howells is neither too warm nor too cool. He sees Howells as significant but neglected, and as the author of "ten or a dozen novels destined to be read in a long future." Brooks has come a long way since he charged Howells with censoring and emasculating Mark Twain.

Robert L. Hough's slim little monograph, *The Quiet Rebel:*

William Dean Howells as Social Commentator, is the latest contribution to Howells scholarship. It sails a short, straight course through its narrow sea. Though the author provides no novelties for anyone who has read Cady and Carter, he does summarize well the social message in Howells' work. The heart of his study is chapters five and six, "Social Commentary" and "Howells and Reform, 1896-1920." The first gathers up ably the relevant data on Howells' socialism of the 1890's, and the latter makes clear a point not well enough known: that Howells during the last two decades of his life continued his social criticism undiminished in his magazine journalism.

Hough has done a skillful job of collecting the data, but his interpretation of the material claims too much. Howells' old-age concern with prison reform, woman suffrage, abolition of capital punishment, and world government are all treated adequately. Unfortunately, Hough goes on to argue that Howells' ideas had an impact on posterity "probably far greater than most modern historians recognize" and that the leaders of the New Deal were Howells' ideological descendants. Surely this is an overstatement that weakens the validity of the rest of the book.

The appearance of the Kirk, Fryckstedt, Bennett, and Hough books within the space of a few months shows the strength of the Howells revival in the academies; Brooks's biography suggests that now the interest in Howells may be reaching the general public. When *Howells: His Life and World* appeared last October, it was accompanied by a fanfare of front-page reviews. Whether or not publishers now will follow up with trade editions of Howells' works remains to be seen.

There is no place in a short survey to say very much about the many briefer studies of Howells that have appeared recently in journals and as parts of books. Statistically, the quantity is impressive: seventy-nine articles and thirty-four introductions or parts of books between 1950 and August, 1959. A few items will have to suffice.

An important section of Louis J. Budd's dissertation on Howells' relations with political parties appeared as "Howells, the *Atlantic Monthly,* and Republicanism" in *American Literature* in May, 1952. Paul J. Carter, Jr. has done significant work on Howells' influence on Twain (see *University of Colorado Studies, Series in Language and Literature,* No. 4, July, 1953). Harry Hayden Clark's "The Role of Science in the Thought of W. D. Howells" *(Transactions of the Wisconsin Academy of Sciences, Arts, and Letters,* XLII, 1953, 263-303) is a thorough examination of its topic, and Robert Falk's chapter, "The Rise of Realism, 1871-1891" in *Transitions in American Literary History* (1953) is well worth reading.

The most stimulating recent article on Howells was Richard Foster's "The Contemporaneity of Howells," which appeared in the *New England Quarterly* in March, 1959. Foster believes that Howells is important, perhaps almost great, because his "works have an as yet unrecognized depth and quality of insight into the predicament of... 'the modern world.'" Howells' special genius was the ability to look freshly at everyday life and "to discover in it two developing conditions that have since become major themes." These were the severance of the commercially structured present from the ways of the traditional past and the displacement of the intellectual as the traditional spokesman in public life.

Three other items that ought to be mentioned include two books containing important Howells material and another critical essay. These are James Austin's *Fields of the* Atlantic Monthly: *Letters to an Editor, 1861-1870* (1953), which prints sixteen previously unpublished letters from the Fields Collection at the Huntington Library; Virginia Harlow's *Thomas Sergeant Perry* (1950), which treats well one of Howells' most important friendships, and Lionel Trilling's discovery of Howells, "Howells and the Roots of Modern Taste," *Partisan Review* (September-October, 1951), reprinted in *The Opposing Self* (1955).

Now that Howells has been rediscovered and revaluated at length, the source studies, critical essays, biographical footnotes, and new editions will continue to appear. This is assured by important work in progress. William Gibson and Henry Nash Smith are just now bringing out an edition of the Howells-Twain correspondence. Walter Meserve has edited a collection of Howells' plays (to appear this spring),[1] which will surprise the uninitiated with the author's competent and extensive interest in the theater. Finally, Arms, Gibson, and Marston are working on an edition of Howells' letters that will supplement the few hundred published by Mildred Howells and others since 1928. They have located about ten thousand letters by and to Howells (mostly unpublished) and to date have calendared about six thousand. Completion of this large project still is several years away. By that time the claims of William Dean Howells to a prominent place in the American literary pantheon will have been established permanently.

1. Both of these have been published: *Mark Twain-Howells Letters* (Cambridge: Belknap Press of Harvard University Press, 1960), and *The Complete Plays of W. D. Howells* (New York: New York University Press, 1960).—ED.